PSYCHOLOGY SURVEY

EDITED BY
ANDREW M. COLMAN & J. GRAHAM BEAUMONT

The British
Psychological Society
and
Routledge Ltd

First published in 1989 by The British Psychological Society, St Andrews House, 48 Princess Road East,Leicester, LE1 7DR, in association with Routledge Ltd, 11 New Fetter Lane, London EC4P 4EE, and in the USA with Chapman & Hall Inc., 29 West 35th Street, New York NY 10001.

British Library Cataloguing in Publication Data

Psychology Survey
1. Psychology. Serials
I. British Psychological Society
150
ISBN 1 85433 012 8

Library of Congress Cataloging in Publication Data

Psychology Survey. no. 1–   1978–
1. Psychology — Periodicals.   I. British Psychological Society.
BF1. P853   150'.5   79-647880

Typeset by Litho Link Limited, Welshpool, Powys, Wales.
Printed and bound in Great Britain by BPCC Wheatons Ltd, Exeter.

Acknowledgements

SKILLS
Figure 1, from V.B. Brooks, *The Neural Basis of Motor Control* (1986), is reproduced by permission of the author and Oxford University Press. Figure 3, from D.B. Lee *et al.*, 'Regulation of gait in long jumping', is reproduced by permission of the authors and the American Psychological Association. Figure 4 is reproduced with the permission of the Controller of Her Majesty's Stationery Office. Figure 5, from D.E. Rumelhart and D.A. Norman, 'Simulating a skilled typist', is reprinted with the permission of the authors and the Ablex Publishing Corporation.

KNOWLEDGE REPRESENTATION
Figure 1, from J.R. Anderson, *The Architecture of Cognition* (1983), is reprinted by permission of Harvard University Press.

CRIMINOLOGICAL AND LEGAL PSYCHOLOGY
Tables 1 & 3 are reproduced with the permission of the Controller of Her Majesty's Stationery Office.

CONTENTS

PREFACE

More than a decade has elapsed since the publication of the first *Psychology Survey*. Subsequent volumes in the series have maintained its original aims of encouraging and helping students, teachers, and researchers to keep abreast of developments in rapidly evolving and newly emerging fields of basic research and applied psychology.

The series has now reached 'the magical number seven', as a famous psychologist once called it. This volume covers an even wider diversity of topics than its predecessors, from the statistical analysis of psychological data and the psychology of skills to parapsychology and psychological aspects of AIDS. With such varied subject matter, uniformity of style is, of course, an inappropriate and unattainable goal. The contributors, all of whom are acknowledged experts in their fields, were encouraged to write in simple language and at a level accessible to undergraduate readers, but they were allowed to tell their own stories in their own ways.

We wish to thank Joyce Collins and Roger Fallon of The British Psychological Society for their advice and practical help.

Andrew M. Colman
Department of Psychology
University of Leicester

J. Graham Beaumont
Department of Psychology
University College of Swansea

PSYCHOLOGICAL STATISTICS

A.W. MacRae

In his presidential address to The British Psychological Society, Levy (1981) observed that when people have what they think is a 'statistical' problem, it is almost always the result of uncertainty about what is being investigated and what bearing the numbers have on the question. If data can be interpreted, they are sure to be analysable. I agree entirely.

Analysis requires us to understand what the numbers actually signify, and for that we must understand the process by which the numbers were obtained, and need a clear concept (a 'model') of the nature of the thing measured. I see all this as part of any psychologist's task, so in my view psychological statistics is an essential part of psychology. It is not an optional extra and it cannot be wholly delegated. Thus, my first recommendation to anyone seeking fluency in psychological statistics is a book by Huck and Sandler (1979), though it does not teach any statistical methods. It invites us to consider 100 brief reports and decide if the interpretations made by the original authors are the only ones available. It sets out to train us to think about the alternative meanings that data might have, and this is the best starting-point for the study of statistics. McGuigan (1983) offers something similar, but only as part of a more orthodox book on experimental design. Another good starting-point is the miniature classic by Huff (1973), charmingly entitled *How to Lie With Statistics*. Of course, his aim is to deter you from lying with statistics and to spot lies that others perpetrate, but along the way he draws your attention to many important problems, especially in the selection of samples. Jaffe and Spirer (1987) have done something similar with new examples.

Most of the information in any body of data is utterly uninteresting. Skill in analysis consists largely in focusing on what is interesting and suppressing the rest; but the information we want cannot be extracted by applying standard rules, because the question of *what is interesting* is personal and not statistical. Different psychologists may well have different ideas about what is the interesting part of the same body of data. Thus, is it quite wrong to suppose that when you meet a 'statistical' problem all you need do is consult a statistician. In order to understand the answers you get – and even more, in order to ask the right questions – you must understand at least the basic structure and logic of statistics. This is true a thousand times over if it is a computer that you propose to turn to in your time of need. Awareness of the objectives and the problems in making use of data, and of the *sorts* of solutions provided by statistics, is absolutely necessary for any data-based psychology.

There are far too many books on psychological statistics to let me do justice even to those that I admire, so I shall just try to give a personal viewpoint on data analysis, with the aim of structuring what is far too often seen as a disconnected set of techniques – a sort of jumbled toolbox in which you hope to find some procedure that will more or less meet your need of the moment. However, I will mention here a few books which in my opinion are authoritative but readable, give excellent coverage of the subject, and share my approach to the topics. They are: Clayton (1984), Ferguson (1989), Glenberg (1988), Gravetter and Wallnau (1988), Hays (1988) and Howell (1982, 1987). These are all intended for undergraduate use, though Ferguson, Hays or Howell would satisfy most graduate researchers too. A. D. Lovie (1986) has assembled some useful and important ideas which are not yet routine in psychological statistics, but are explained at a level accessible to most psychologists.

TYPES OF DATA

We have **data** when we represent aspects of the real world in a symbolic way; and if it is numbers that we use symbolically, we have **numerical data.** Often, numerical data are the result of **measurement,** but we must distinguish between the numbers themselves and the things we really want to know about. The numbers may allow us to make inferences and predictions about aspects of the world that concern us, but they are of little interest in isolation. Problems of data analysis most often turn out to be problems in deciding what the numbers actually tell us.

In Figure 1, we see one way of classifying types of data. The first division is into 'frequencies' and 'measures'. **Frequencies** are counts of the number of cases of a particular kind, and obviously must be whole numbers. **Measures** are numbers used to express the amount of something. They may be whole numbers, but they need not be. (In fact, the frequency of occurrence of something may be treated as a measure, though a measure may not be treated as a frequency.) **Distributions** of frequencies occur when various values of a single attribute are used to divide up the cases into their various categories – for example, if we count the number of children with black, with brown, with red and with fair hair. **Contingency tables** (also known as **cross-classifications**) are generated when two or more attributes are used to divide up the cases – for example, if we classify children as high, medium and low in anxiety, and simultaneously separate them out by hair colour as above, giving 12 categories in all.

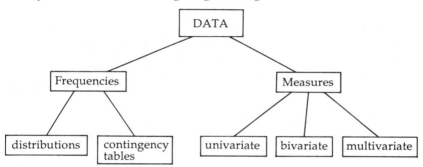

Figure 1. Some important types of data. The statistical methods appropriate to these types are very different.

Univariate measures vary in only one respect. Examples of univariate data are: age, score on a test, time taken to solve a problem, or the number of people voting anarchist in an election. **Multivariate** measures vary in several respects. For example, for each individual in our sample, we might know the age, the score made on a test and the number of times the person had voted anarchist. That ensemble of information about the individual is multivariate. Each measure is univariate when considered on its own, but the collection of measures is multivariate if we think of them as a composite description of the individual. Of course, we can treat such an assembly of measures as multivariate only if they are related together in some way – for example, if each measure comes from a single individual. **Bivariate** data are just a special kind of multivariate data with exactly two measures per individual. Many widely used techniques, such as the various forms of correlation, apply only to bivariate data.

Questionnaires are often best thought of as multivariate measures, because each respondent is free to give any pattern of answers and each different pattern may have a different meaning. For some purposes you might consider that all questions are, in effect, equivalent (all are comparable indicators of racial prejudice, say); and then you might take no interest in which particular questions were answered affirmatively, and so count only the *number* of affirmative answers. A total score obtained in that way would be univariate. Thus, the distinction between these types of data is not clear-cut, and is more an expression of our opinion about the meaning of the data than a matter of actual fact. However, if we take the view that our data are multivariate, we need different statistical techniques from those used with univariate data.

The classification of data types by Stevens (1946, 1951) is based on the relationship between the numbers constituting the data and the 'true' value of the thing measured. The numbers are said to conform to a **measurement scale** which is nominal, ordinal, interval, ratio or absolute. In a **nominal** scale, there is no relationship between the size of a number and the value of the thing 'measured' by it. A no. 14 bus need not exceed a no. 7 bus in any way – and you would certainly not think of catching two no. 7s if you really wanted a no. 14! All that you can tell from the numbers is whether two things are equivalent in some respect (because they have the same number) or are different (because they have different numbers). In ordinary language, that would hardly be called measurement at all, but it is convenient to use the same terminology for all the scale types. In an **ordinal** scale, the order of sizes of the numbers tells us the order of sizes of the things measured. If item *A* is assigned a larger number than item *B*, then *A* has more of the thing measured. For example, we can often be pretty confident that John is angrier than James (though both are furious) and Martha is angrier than Mary (though both are only mildly annoyed). But we probably have no way of deciding if *the difference* in anger between John and James is greater or smaller than the difference in anger between Martha and Mary. If we *can* put such differences in order, we have an **ordered metric** scale (a type which is fairly common but was not discussed by Stevens and is not often mentioned in general psychology). If, in addition, we can say when differences are *equal*, we have an **interval** scale. True interval scales are rather rare, because if we can compare differences between pairs of large values and pairs of small values well enough to say whether they are equal or not, we usually also know when the thing measured is completely absent, and then we have a **ratio** scale. In a ratio scale, the number zero denotes the absence of the thing measured; equal increases in number denote equal increases in the thing measured; and (as a consequence of these facts) equal ratios between numbers denote equal ratios in the thing measured. Most of the familiar measures of daily life (for example, weights or distances) are ratio scales, but ratio scales are rare for psychological variables. With **absolute** scales, even the units of measurement are fixed. For all practical purposes, they occur only when we count things rather than measure them.

In my classification, frequency data correspond to absolute scales, and measures correspond to ordinal, interval, ordered metric, or ratio scales. Most psychological data are measured on an absolute scale (counting) or an ordinal scale (measuring).

WHAT IS MEANT BY 'STATISTICS'?

The topics that psychologists think of as 'statistics' can be structured as shown in Figure 2. The first division is mainly one of *purpose:* do we want to summarize the results actually obtained (description), or are we interested in deducing things that we have not actually observed (inference)? Like the others, this division is not clear-cut. We usually want to: describe what we have observed; extract its interesting features; discard its uninteresting features; use the observations to infer answers about unobserved matters; make predictions about future observations or events. However, some ways of handling data emphasize description whereas others emphasize inference.

If we have studied 100 schoolchildren, we may want to say things about the particular individuals we have studied – put them in order of age, identify their individual strengths and weaknesses, and so on. These are **descriptions**, summarizing the data we actually obtained, and might be useful when advising the children or their teachers; but we do not expect to learn anything about other children we have not studied. Alternatively, we might be conducting an experiment to evaluate some teaching method. We then want the data to tell us something about the response of children in general. Because we cannot try out the method with all children, we must do so with a **sample** of children – perhaps 100 again. Our analysis now must try to use the information from the sample to make **inferences** about what to expect from children we have not studied. A wider group to which we hope to generalize our results is called a **population**.

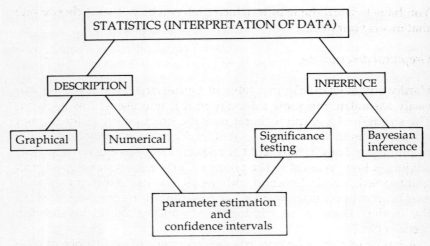

Figure 2. A structure for psychological statistics.

DESCRIPTIVE STATISTICS

Descriptive statistics serve to bring out interesting aspects of the data, by suppressing those thought uninteresting or by presenting the interesting aspects in a way more readily perceived. Numerical or graphical methods can be used for either purpose. Under the influence of a marvellous book by Tukey (1977), the approach has become known as exploratory data analysis (EDA). The techniques of data representation described in Tukey, and later by Hoaglin *et al.* (1983), are now found in several introductory texts and are often the best way to begin an analysis. Stem-and-leaf diagrams, box-and-whisker plots and smoothed graphs allow one to represent data in various ways in order to see 'what is really going on'. Tukey stresses that there are many different ways to graph one variable against another, and that each method will emphasize different properties of the relationship. For example, smoothing a graph discards erratic variation in order to make longer-term trends more prominent. But that is not always what you want to do. The opposite approach is to subtract the longer-term trends from the raw scores and plot the residuals (the part left over), and so focus particularly on *departures* from the trend. Which method is preferable depends on your belief about what the slowly changing trend and the swiftly changing departures from that trend actually mean in psychological terms. Again I emphasize that there is no single, 'correct' way to deal with data. The appropriateness of any analysis depends on your purpose.

You have to learn the uses to which each can be put, and choose one that meets your need.

Graphical descriptions

Hardly anyone can take in a table of figures at a glance, but we can easily assimilate the same information if it is presented as a graph. The strength of a graph is that it uses the great power of the human eye and brain to discern *patterns* that might not be detectable in a table of numbers. Tufte (1983) and Cleveland (1985) have given excellent advice on how to assist in the process. Tufte is more concerned with graphic design and Cleveland with the psychological interpretation of graphs, including ways of avoiding visual illusions that may mislead the reader. There is an admirable introduction by Cleveland and McGill (1985).

A **bar chart** shows on one axis the frequency of occurrence of each score (or group of scores) displayed along the other axis. Two or more bar charts can easily be compared if they are drawn using the same scales, and thus can reveal the differences among two or more sets of results. A **histogram** is a bar chart where the scores have a natural order; that is, where they are univariate measures on at least an ordinal scale. A histogram displays the **frequency distribution** of the measure, from which we can easily see the highest and lowest values that occurred and get a good idea of which scores were frequent and which were rare. More complex attributes such as **skew** (lack of symmetry) or **bimodality** (having two peaks) can also be seen easily. This type of description makes sense only when measurements are on at least an ordinal scale, because with a nominal scale there is no particular order in which the scores should be arranged, so that completely equivalent bar charts may have different shapes.

Cross-tabulated frequencies may not be easy to graph. Even if there are only two dimensions of cross-classification, the resulting frequency must be expressed on a third dimension. It is possible to draw a perspective view of a 3-D histogram where each slice is a normal histogram; or (if the frequencies vary smoothly) it may be useful to draw **contour plots,** using the conventions of mapmaking to represent the frequency as though it were a height. Alternatively, the frequency can be expressed as a number of dots, with the two classification dimensions forming the axes of a grid. When there are more than two dimensions of classification, it will usually be necessary to draw multiple graphs to represent the data adequately.

Bivariate measures can be expressed in **scatter plots** (also called

scattergrams), which treat each pair of numbers as the coordinates of one point on a graph whose scales are chosen to give about the same spread on each axis. Thus, the outline of the graph is approximately square. Relationships between the measures appear as systematic patterns in the points.

Figure 3 shows examples of various patterns that may result from scatter plots. In each of 3a, 3b and 3c, there is a tendency for scores on one variable to be large if scores on the other are large. In 3a, the tendency is strong, so that it is possible to be fairly confident about the value taken by one variable if we know the value of the other. In 3b, the tendency is much weaker. Knowing the value of one improves our prediction of the other – our best estimate of one is larger if the other is large, and smaller if the other is small – but many exceptions occur. In 3c, there is again a strong relationship, but it does not follow a straight line.

Multivariate measures can greatly benefit from our ability to recognize complex patterns. Each dimension of the data is represented by some attribute of a pattern, and the assembly of values forms a unity which can be recognized as a whole. Chernoff (1973) proposed the use of faces, where one data dimension might alter the size of the face, another the curvature of the mouth, another the spacing of the eyes, and so on. There are problems of avoiding undue emphasis on particular dimensions or inappropriate patterns, such as a smiling face to indicate a distressing combination of symptoms, but the approach is interesting. Advice on multivariate graphs can be found in Cleveland (1985), Everitt (1978), and Wainer and Thissen (1981).

Numerical descriptions

Numerical description may reduce the bulk of otherwise indigestible data by reducing many numbers to a few which describe the general nature of the results. With frequency distributions and univariate measures, a mean (expressing a typical value) and a standard deviation (expressing spread) may be enough to give a good idea of the sorts of numbers that occur. How much can be deduced about the original numbers from their mean and standard deviation depends on what we know about the way that the numbers are distributed. If we are prepared to assume that the numbers occur with frequencies that can be described by a particular mathematical curve (such as the normal distribution), the mean and standard deviation may tell us enough to recreate the whole distribution of raw data. Sometimes we

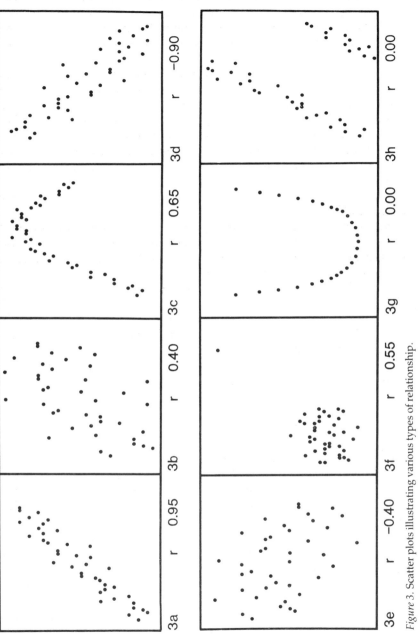

Figure 3. Scatter plots illustrating various types of relationship.

have no idea of the distribution, and then the summary given by a mean and standard deviation may tell us very little. The median (midpoint of the distribution) and interquartile range (the spread of the middle 50 per cent of the scores) always give a description that is easy to interpret.

Descriptive methods for cross-tabulated frequencies are usually concerned with establishing some relationship between the types of category that form the rows and columns of the table. In the example of hair colour and anxiety proposed earlier, we might be interested in discovering if those with one hair colour are more or less likely than those with another to be rated high on anxiety. Another example would be where two clinicians make independent assessments of the same clients. We might then be interested in characterizing the extent of agreement between the clinicians. Various measures can be used for each of these purposes, all with somewhat different meanings (Leach, 1979).

We tend to think of a straight-line graph as the simplest form of relationship between two variables, so we frequently calculate the product-moment correlation r, which is a measure of the goodness of fit of bivariate data to a straight-line plot on a scattergram. Practically all statistics textbooks discuss correlation, but Edwards (1976) is particularly relevant. Positive values of r indicate that the line slopes up, as in Figures 3a, 3b and 3c, and negative values that it slopes down, as in 3d and 3e. However, r does not measure any kind of relationship other than a straight line, and so its value should not be interpreted as measuring relatedness in general. For example, the value of r from the data of 3c indicates a weak linear relationship, although there is a strong relationship which is not linear. It is possible to have a close relationship between two variables, such that the value of one is entirely predictable from the value of the other, and yet for the correlation between them to be zero. Such a relationship is shown in 3g. The moral is that we must not interpret a small or zero correlation as showing that there is little or no relationship between the variables – it may be substantial but not linear.

A more subtle issue arises when we try to decide if the relationship between two variables is or is not linear. A curved relationship will usually *contain* a linear relationship, as in 3c; and if the data are plentiful, that linear component of the curved relationship may be highly significant. In fact, we can never prove that a straight line is *the best* description of the data, because allowing curvature always improves the fit! But if we can show that the improvement in fit is no more than would be expected by chance, we can conclude that a linear relationship is at least an adequate description.

If we believe that product-moment correlation underestimates the true extent of relatedness between measures because the variables are related in a non-linear way, we may use a variant called multiple correlation (or multiple regression) to express curvilinear relatedness. It can also be used to express the way that a single variable is related to several others. For example, success in a course might be separately predictable from intelligence, time spent studying, ambition to succeed, and previous knowledge of the subject. Knowing an individual's score on all four of these predictors would surely permit better prediction than any one of them on its own, and the multiple correlation of all the predictors with success would express the closeness of the agreement between prediction and outcome.

Individual values departing considerably from the rest of the data can have a marked effect on the value of r. For example, in 3f we see that for all the data other than the point in the top right corner, there is no relationship between the two variables. Nevertheless, there is a positive correlation, entirely as a result of that point. It often happens that such an exceptional point (termed an **outlier**) turns out to be different in other ways as well from those with which it has been grouped. If so, it will probably suit our purposes better to treat it as a special case. We would then describe the results as showing zero correlation, except for the existence of an outlier having scores higher than all the others on both dimensions. There are no firm rules for identifying outliers, but see P. Lovie (1986) and Tukey (1977).

There are particular problems when correlations are used to express the closeness of agreement between a theoretical model and the outcome of an experiment. Shanteau (1977) discusses the issues and shows that in at least three published studies, correlations provide a deceptive measure of fit.

There are many ways in which a correlation coefficient may misrepresent what is actually happening in bivariate data. We can easily see that in Figure 3h there are two groups of scores. In each group there is a strong correlation between the variables, but when the groups are lumped together to yield a single coefficient its value is zero. If we believe that our situation resembles Figure 3h, we should distrust any way of expressing the results that lumps together such disparate groups. The multivariate technique called **discriminant analysis** tries to separate individuals into groups on the basis of their scores on two or (usually) more variables.

INFERENTIAL STATISTICS

What psychologists usually think of as 'statistics' is the large body of techniques for drawing conclusions about the 'significance' or otherwise of results, though significance tests are just one form of statistical inference. They are needed because psychological data are rather variable, so it is always possible that when a result looks interesting, it is actually the unexplained variability that has caused it. In order to eliminate this disappointing explanation, significance tests calculate the probability of obtaining results like those actually obtained if chance alone is the true explanation. If the probability is small, then the explanation that chance alone is responsible seems less reasonable. Thus, if we are looking for some cause other than chance, a small probability is what we want; and if it is small enough, the result is said to be 'significant'. By convention, results are called significant if the probability is no larger than 0.05 (1 in 20), and for some purposes other levels such as 0.01 (1 in 100) or 0.001 (1 in 1000) may be quoted. There is no logical or mathematical reason for these values – they are a matter of convention and habit.

Frequencies

In the case of distributions, we are almost bound to be concerned with **measures of agreement**: does the distribution conform to some theoretical prediction? In the case of contingency tables, we may likewise want to evaluate agreement with a theoretical prediction, but are more likely to want to test **independence**. In the latter case, we see if the distribution on one variable is different for different values of another variable. Significance tests assess the probability of obtaining the results under one or other of these null hypotheses.

A style of analysis found in all basic texts calculates a statistic called X^2 (chi-squared). The calculations are easy, and the only problems are conceptual. The validity of the answers depends on certain conditions being met, principally independence of the outcomes and having an adequate amount of data. (Other methods allowing exact calculation of probabilities can be used if there are few observations.) It is, however, a serious error to apply any of these calculations to data which are not independent or not frequencies. The commonest cause of non-independence is having an individual contribute more than one unit to the count of frequencies, so a good rule of thumb is that the total of your observed frequencies should be the same as the number of individuals. Contravene this guideline only if you really know what you are doing!

Another style of analysis is called log-linear modelling. It is more versatile but less well known than applications of chi-squared. There is an introduction by Upton (1986), and there are books by Everitt (1977) and Upton (1978).

Univariate measures

For measurements, the most extensively developed set of methods is called analysis of variance or ANOVA (see Iversen and Norpoth, 1987). It differs from other methods mainly in complexity – for example, it allows one to test the existence of several different effects in the same set of data simultaneously, and it can also evaluate the extent to which one effect depends on (or **interacts** with) another. The price of its versatility is that it can be trusted only when certain assumptions are met; but these assumptions are not very restrictive, and in any case it is often possible to transform data before analysis so that they conform better to the requirements of ANOVA. A version of ANOVA for comparing just two sets of scores, called the *t*-test, was one of the first significance tests to become known in psychology and has been very prominent ever since.

Bivariate measures

The correlation coefficient *r*, discussed earlier as a descriptive technique for bivariate data, is conceptually related to ANOVA, and the square of *r* estimates the proportion of variance in one variable that can be predicted from knowledge of the other. It is not a test of significance, but the significance of a correlation coefficient can be tested. Our calculated *r* is a description of the data obtained, but we can ask if the true value of *r* in the population we are sampling from might plausibly be zero, using a form of ANOVA or *t*-test. Alternatively, we might ask if two values of *r* obtained from different samples might plausibly have been drawn from populations having the same value of *r*. This can be done using Fisher's *z* transform. It is also possible to calculate confidence limits for a correlation coefficient (and for any other descriptive measure).

Multivariate measures

I noted earlier that when data are considered to be multivariate, quite different analyses are required. Most textbooks of introductory statistics say little or nothing about multivariate methods such as MANOVA (multivariate analysis of variance), discriminant analysis, and factor analysis – perhaps judging that their complexity is such that they should be treated separately in specialist books. An unfortunate consequence is that many students who consider themselves weak in statistics and have difficulty with univariate and bivariate methods will blithely embark on the design and evaluation of questionnaires, or use other procedures where multivariate analysis should at least be considered.

The essential problem with multivariate data is that the number of possible *patterns* increases extremely rapidly when the number of measures increases. Thus, even if responses are only 'yes' and 'no', there are over a thousand possible patterns from ten questions and over a million patterns with only twenty questions. If all of these patterns potentially mean different things, it is difficult to obtain enough data to sample them to any satisfactory degree. Furthermore, it is difficult or impossible to *represent* them in any way that can be comprehended. In this situation, it becomes necessary to reduce the complexity of the results even more drastically than with univariate data.

I have said that multivariate data may be treated as univariate if all the components are considered to be equivalent, so that their total becomes a meaningful score. An intermediate approach is to characterize certain questions as measures of one topic, others as measures of a second topic, and so on for several topics. For each topic, its total score is used. Such results are still multivariate, but vary in fewer ways than the original responses, so it may be possible to summarize or graph them in ways that allow interpretation. Do not despise such an approach because it is informal and non-mathematical. Its justification comes from your beliefs about what the data *mean*, and anything a statistical approach can do is likewise dependent upon those beliefs. Mathematical methods, too, are valid only if your assumptions are appropriate – but the assumptions you need to make are largely hidden from view. A computer program used inappropriately will not necessarily warn you about the assumptions implied by the instructions you give it. It will just deliver some nicely formatted output – which may be the purest nonsense!

A good understanding of multivariate methods is almost impossible without some knowledge of matrix algebra. The one general principle I will state is that it is almost always invalid to embark on a multivariate analysis unless the number of individuals is substantially greater than the number of components in each multivariate measure. I shall not offer any detailed guidance. It is enough if I have managed to alert you to the nature of multivariate data and the need to seek advice if you want to analyze it in any way that needs a computer. As a first step, you could consult Harris (1985) or Tabachnick and Fidell (1989). Note that the topic called **multidimensional scaling** is related, but involves many additional issues and methods.

THE LOGIC OF STATISTICAL INFERENCE

A classical significance test assumes, for the purpose of argument, a **null hypothesis** that nothing other than chance is at work, and calculates from it the combined probability of the obtained result and of all more extreme results. If the calculated probability is lower than a preset criterion such as 0.05, the null hypothesis is rejected – not because it is unlikely but because it makes *the result* unlikely. The conclusion is exactly the same whether the probability is only slightly smaller than the criterion or very much smaller. If the null hypothesis is rejected we accept the outcome as support for an alternative, **experimental hypothesis**, which is some conclusion more interesting than mere chance.

---

a   Probability that (I visit Westminster Abbey) if (I am in London) = 0.01
b   Probability that (I am in London) if (I visit Westminster Abbey) = 1.0

c   Probability that (I get such results) if (chance is the only cause) = 0.05
d   Probability that (chance is the only cause) if (I get such results) = ?

Figure 4. Analogy showing that significance levels do not give the probability that the null hypothesis is true. It is clear that **a** and **b** are likely to have different values, therefore **c** and **d** need not have the same values. A test of significance gives the value of **c** but not of **d**.

The probability given by a test of significance is the probability of obtaining such results if chance is the only explanation. It is *not* the probability that chance *is* the only explanation. To clarify this point, consider the analogy presented in Figure 4. For everyone, the probability of being in London if they visit Westminster Abbey is 1.0. The probability of visiting Westminster Abbey when in London will be different for each person, and will hardly ever be 1.0. Therefore, the probabilities described by statements **a** and **b** are different. But the relationship between **a** and **b** is exactly the same as that between **c** and **d**, so the probabilities described by **c** and **d** are different also. A test of significance gives us a value for **c** but not for **d**.

It may seem pedantic to stress what appears to be a minor point of terminology, but it is not a minor point at all. Its importance becomes clear when we consider the inference to be drawn from a non-significant result. Suppose we have found that the probability of obtaining results like ours is *greater* than 0.05, so the result is judged to be non-significant. We cannot conclude that chance is therefore the sole cause of the results. Even if we find that there is a very high probability of obtaining results at least as extreme as these when chance is the only cause, we must not conclude that chance is likely to be the only cause. The significance test has shown that chance *can* explain the results but does not estimate the probability that it *did* give us these results. In fact, a conventional test of significance lets us conclude nothing useful if the result is not significant. If our aim is to show that two conditions in an experiment have different conse-quences, then a significant result is helpful, because it makes mere chance unattractive as an explanation. However, if our aim is to show that they are *not* different, a non-significant result is of no real help.

This limitation on the inferences to be drawn from significance tests is a serious one, and it is surprising that so little attention is paid in psychology to the two major ways of dealing with the problem: classical confidence intervals (discussed later) and Bayesian inference.

Bayesian inference

The **Bayesian** approach is different. Firstly, it attends only to the observed data and does not consider more extreme outcomes that did not occur. Secondly, it focuses on the likelihoods of explanations rather than of results. Thirdly, rather than testing one specific null hypothesis, Bayesian methods usually deal simultaneously with a range of hypotheses all of which are 'uninteresting' alternatives to an 'interesting' range of experimental hypotheses. In contrast to the huge number of books and papers about classical methods, there are few about Bayesian methods, and only one introductory textbook for psychologists – though a good one – by Phillips (1973).

Bayesian methods evaluate the likelihood of obtaining the observed data if hypothesis *A* is correct and of obtaining the same data if hypothesis *B* is correct. Either *A* or *B*, or both, may be a whole range of possible explanations for the data. The Bayesian approach requires us to make explicit our prior beliefs about the relative likelihood of possibilities *A* and *B*. The data and calculations then alter this previous opinion: if we were at first strongly convinced that *A* was correct, we need strong evidence to persuade us that *B* is more likely to be correct. Note that this evidence need not indicate that the results we obtained are actually *likely* if *B* is true – it need only show the results to be much less likely if *A* is true.

Some dislike the Bayesian use of prior beliefs, but I think this is a mistaken objection. Classical methods appear not to invoke prior beliefs, but if we ask what counts as 'significant' we find that in practice the answer depends on the plausibility of the experimental hypothesis. For example, we may well be convinced by a result significant at the 0.05 level that one training method or one therapy is better than another; but if an experiment is so well done that chance is the only reasonable alternative, many would accept chance as the explanation rather than take the same level of significance as proof of extrasensory perception. Similarly, most people consider a result which happens to reach the 0.01 level 'more convincing' than one which reaches the 0.05 level. This way of thinking goes against the logic of classical statistics, though it resembles the Bayesian view. In fact, most psychologists use classical methods and notation but interpret their results in a way that is almost (though inadequately) Bayesian.

There have been interesting recent developments in France using Bayesian logic. Most of the publications are in French, and the few English sources are rather difficult (for example, Rouanet and Lecoutre, 1983); but the approach seems to offer the possibility of addressing directly the questions that psychologists usually want to ask about data rather than adapting methods devised for other purposes.

The Classical and the Bayesian are not the only styles of statistical inference, but they have been the most widespread and influential.

Nonparametric statistics

Many writers about psychological statistics, such as Siegel (1956), have treated the Stevens classification of scale types as though it strictly determined the sorts of analysis to perform. In particular, they demand a style of significance testing called **nonparametric** for all data measured on ordinal scales. I disagree, but have discussed the issues at length elsewhere (MacRae, 1988) and will not repeat them here. That is not to say that I object to nonparametric methods.

Authors such as Bradley (1968), Leach (1979) and Mosteller and Rourke (1973) make a strong case for nonparametric methods in some circumstances, but on other and more valid grounds. Essentially, what they argue for is not specifically *nonparametric* methods but **robust** or **distribution-free** methods – what Mosteller and Rourke call 'sturdy statistics', whose answers are minimally dependent on assumptions.

Methods based on **ranks** (only the order and not the sizes of scores) can be used for descriptive and inferential statistics with univariate and bivariate data. The best known of them lack the ability of ANOVA and its relatives to deal in an integrated way with very complex data; but if your data and questions are appropriate, rank methods may serve your needs well, as Meddis (1984) shows. There has been recent expansion in methods based on a technique called **randomization** (Edgington, 1980). They usually require a computer, but can achieve something like the versatility of ANOVA without its assumptions.

Multiple comparisons: planned and unplanned

It is always important to be aware of what null hypothesis is being tested. A particular trap is to apply a method designed to compare two sets of scores to a situation where there are really several sets. If you measure two groups of people on 20 independent attributes, you should not be surprised if one of the comparisons reaches the 0.05 level of significance, because you can expect one case in 20 to reach that level by chance alone. If you intend to make 20 comparisons, you must test a null hypothesis that takes account of that intention. For the example just stated the procedure would be multivariate, but the problem can arise with univariate data too.

Suppose that you have completed an experiment with four different conditions, and have carried out an ANOVA (or something similar using ranks) which has not proved significant. Nevertheless, you observe that condition 2 has resulted in generally low scores while condition 4 has produced high ones. You compare conditions 2 and 4 using a *t*-test (or a test based on ranks) and find that the difference *is* significant. What has gone wrong?

The problem is that if you have two sets of data, as supposed by the *t*-test, there is only one comparison that can be made, and the test tells you the probability of obtaining such results from that comparison. When you have four sets of data, there are at least six comparisons that might be made: 1 – 2, 1 – 3, 1 – 4, 2 – 3, 2 – 4 and

3 – 4. The probability that at least one out of these six comparisons will produce such results is clearly higher than the probability that one particular comparison will do so. Thus, the result is more likely than the *t*-test seems to suggest (though not simply six times as likely!), and the result is not really significant.

Note that the situation may be even worse than I have said, because there are yet other comparisons that might be considered, such as 1 – (2+3) or 1 – (2+3+4). A technique which evaluates a true significance level where all possible comparisons can be considered is the Scheffé test. It will never be significant if the original ANOVA was not, so it is worth doing only if the ANOVA was significant and you are interested in seeing what aspect of the data caused the departure from the null hypothesis. If you are not interested in comparing groups of conditions with others but only pairs of single conditions, the Scheffé test is much too cautious. Tests such as Newman-Keuls, Duncan, and Tukey can be used instead.

The situation is different again if you know before looking at the data that you will be interested in particular comparisons. Provided that the comparisons are **orthogonal** (the outcome of one does not help us to predict another), the significance given by a standard test, such as a *t*-test, can be interpreted without adjustment; in fact, ANOVA can be thought of as a set of such **planned comparisons**. The essential difference is between comparisons selected on the basis of the data and comparisons selected on the basis of the design of the investigation. In the former case, if the data had turned out differently, other comparisons would have been made, giving other ways of obtaining a result of the size you have, whereas in the latter case there is only one way to obtain it.

PARAMETER ESTIMATION AND CONFIDENCE INTERVALS

There is a regrettable tendency in psychological statistics to focus on the *significance* of results rather than on their *importance* – a distinction nicely captured by Bolles (1962). It is true that unless you have managed to demonstrate significance in your results (cast doubt on chance as an explanation for them) it will be difficult to get others to take them seriously. However, your results may be highly significant and yet not important, even if the topic is an important one. The reason is that, with a large amount of data, significance can be demonstrated even for a very weak effect. Thus, in addition to significance, we must pay attention to **magnitude of effect** (see especially Howell, 1987). Various measures have been devised to describe the magnitude of effects, but the most intuitively appealing is the proposal by Levy (1967) to characterize an effect in terms of the proportion of individuals who would be correctly classified if the effect were used for the sorting. He offers the imaginary example of 250 psychologists being found significantly more psychopathic at the 0.05 level than 250 'normals'(!). Although the result is significant, you would be wrong 47 times in 100 if you tried to identify individuals as psychologists or normals on the basis of their scores. By chance you would expect 50 errors, so there is some improvement but hardly a useful one; and even if the significance level is 1 per cent rather than 5 per cent, the error rate only drops to 46 per cent.

The descriptive approach called **parameter estimation** focuses on the size of effect rather than on significance. Parameters are hypothetical characteristics of the population, and they are estimated from the data. Parameter estimates should not change systematically as the sample size changes, but significance does. It is the parameter estimate that shows the *importance* of an effect, because it shows the difference between the sets of scores being compared. The degree of success in deducing group membership from scores depends on that difference and not on the *significance* of the effect.

A **confidence interval** is a hybrid of a descriptive statistic and a significance test. The idea is that when you estimate a parameter – a population mean or correlation, for example – you also calculate a range of values (a confidence interval) within which you are reasonably confident that its true value lies. (There is no uncertainty about the mean of your sample of data, but you are uncertain about the mean of the population.) If you have a large amount of consistent data, the interval will be narrow and you will be sure of the value of the measure. If you have less data, or if the results are less consistent, the interval will be wider and you will be more uncertain about the true value of the measure.

The upper bound of the 95 per cent confidence interval is that value for the population parameter which, if it were the true value, would allow by chance an estimate at least as *low* as that obtained on 2.5 per cent of occasions. The lower bound is the value which would allow a result at least as *high* as the one observed on 2.5 per cent of occasions.

Confidence intervals are described in the better textbooks of psychological statistics, but less prominently than significance tests. When they are discussed it is usually in connection with ANOVA, and it is true that these are the easiest confidence intervals to calculate; but it is quite wrong to suppose that the technique is in any way limited to that situation. The classic paper by Clopper and Pearson (1934) applied them to proportions – the proportion of people who answer in a certain way, for example. The actual calculation of confidence intervals can be quite complex if the variability of the data cannot be described by a normal distribution, and this may explain their rarity in texts. It is disappointing that they figure so little in computer packages for data analysis, because if a computer is used the complexity of the calculation is virtually irrelevant. One which does give them the attention they deserve is ECDA (Dusoir, 1988), for Apple and IBM microcomputers.

Confidence intervals are usually the best way to analyse results when you hope to show that treatments or groups do not differ. Calculate a confidence interval for the size of the true difference. If it lies around and includes zero, then you have estimated the largest departures from zero (upward and downward) that can reasonably exist. If your data are consistent and plentiful, the confidence interval will be narrow, so you will know that any difference between the treatments must be small.

REFERENCES

Bolles, R.C. (1962) The difference between statistical hypotheses and scientific hypotheses. *Psychological Reports, 11*, 639–645.

Bradley, J.V. (1968) *Distribution-Free Statistical Tests.* Englewood Cliffs, NJ: Prentice-Hall.

Chernoff, H. (1973) The use of faces to represent points in k-dimensional space graphically. *Journal of the American Statistical Association, 68*, 361–368.

Clayton, K.N. (1984) *An Introduction to Statistics for Psychology and Education.* Columbus: Merrill.

Cleveland, W.S. (1985) *The Elements of Graphing Data.* Monterey, Ca: Wadsworth.

Cleveland, W.S. and McGill, R. (1985) Graphical perception and graphical methods for analyzing scientific data. *Science, 229*, 828.

Clopper, C.J. and Pearson, E.S. (1934) The use of confidence or fiducial limits illustrated in the case of the binomial. *Biometrika, 26*, 404–413.

Dusoir, A. (1988) *ECDA Exploratory and Confirmatory Data Analysis.* Hove, Sussex: Lawrence Erlbaum.

Edgington, E.S. (1980) *Randomization Tests.* New York: Marcel Dekker.

Edwards, A.L. (1976) *An Introduction to Linear Regression and Correlation.* San Francisco: Freeman.

Everitt, B.S. (1977) *The Analysis of Contingency Tables.* London: Chapman & Hall.

Everitt, B.S. (1978) *Graphical Techniques for Multivariate Data.* London: Heinemann.

Ferguson, G.A. (1989) *Statistical Analysis in Psychology and Education*, 6th ed. New York: McGraw-Hill.

Glenberg, A.M. (1988) *Learning From Data: An Introduction to Statistical Reasoning.* San Diego: Harcourt Brace Jovanovich.

Gravetter, F.J. and Wallnau, L.B. (1988) *Statistics for the Behavioral Sciences: A First Course for Students of Psychology and Education.* 2nd ed. St Paul, Minn.: West.

Harris, R.J. (1985) *A Primer of Multivariate Statistics.* 2nd ed. New York: Academic Press.

Hays, W.L. (1988) *Statistics*, 4th ed. New York: Holt, Rinehart & Winston.

Hoaglin, D.C., Mosteller, F. and Tukey, J.W. (eds) (1983) *Understanding Robust and Exploratory Data Analysis.* Chichester: Wiley.

Hoaglin, D.C. and Velleman, P.F. (1981) *Applications, Basics and Computing of Exploratory Data Analysis.* Boston: Duxbury.

Howell, D.C. (1982) *Fundamental Statistics for the Behavioral Sciences.* Boston: Duxbury.

Howell, D.C. (1987) *Statistical Methods for Psychology*, 2nd ed. Boston: Duxbury.

Huck, S.W. and Sandler, H.M. (1979) *Rival Hypotheses: Alternative Interpretations of Data Based Conclusions.* London: Harper & Row.

Huff, D. (1973) *How to Lie With Statistics.* Harmondsworth: Penguin.

Iversen, G.R. and Norpoth, H. (1987) *Analysis of Variance*, 2nd ed. Newbury Park, Ca: Sage.

Jaffe, A.J. and Spirer, H.F. (1987) *Misused Statistics: Straight Talk for Twisted Numbers.* New York: Marcel Dekker.

Leach, C. (1979) *Introduction to Statistics: A Nonparametric Approach for the Social Sciences.* Chichester: Wiley.

Levy, P.M. (1967) Substantive significance of significant differences between two groups. *Psychological Bulletin, 67,* 37–40.

Levy, P.M. (1981) On the relation between method and substance in psychology. *Bulletin of the British Psychological Society, 34,* 265–270.

Lovie, A.D. (ed.) (1986) *New Developments in Statistics for Psychology and the Social Sciences.* Leicester: The British Psychological Society; London: Routledge.

Lovie, P. (1986) Identifying outliers. In A.D. Lovie (ed.) *New Developments in Statistics for Psychology and the Social Sciences.* Leicester: The British Psychological Society; London: Routledge.

MacRae, A.W. (1988) Measurement scales and statistics: What can significance tests tell us about the world? *British Journal of Psychology, 79,* 161–171.

McGuigan, F.J. (1983) *Experimental Psychology: Methods of Research*, 4th ed. Englewood Cliffs, NJ: Prentice-Hall.

Meddis, R. (1984) *Statistics Using Ranks: A Unified Approach.* Oxford: Blackwell.

Mosteller, F. and Rourke, R.E.K. (1973) *Sturdy Statistics: Nonparametrics and Order Statistics.* Reading, Ma: Addison-Wesley.

Phillips, L.D. (1973) *Bayesian Statistics for Social Scientists.* London: Nelson.

Rouanet, H. and Lecoutre, B. (1983) Specific inference in ANOVA: From significance tests to Bayesian procedures. *British Journal of Mathematical and Statistical Psychology, 36,* 252–268.

Shanteau, J. (1977) Correlation as a deceiving measure of fit. *Bulletin of the Psychonomic Society, 10*, 134–136.

Siegel, S.J. (1956) *Nonparametric Statistics for the Behavioral Sciences*. New York: McGraw-Hill. (2nd ed.: 1988).

Stevens, S.S. (1946) On the theory of scales of measurement. *Science, 103*, 677–680.

Stevens, S.S. (1951) Mathematics, measurement and psychophysics. In S.S. Stevens (ed.) *Handbook of Experimental Psychology*. New York: Wiley.

Tabachnick, B.G. and Fidell, L.S. (1989) *Using Multivariate Statistics*. 2nd ed. New York: Harper & Row.

Tufte, E.R. (1983) *The Visual Display of Quantitative Information*. Cheshire, Ct: Graphics Press.

Tukey, J.W. (1977) *Exploratory Data Analysis*. Reading, Ma: Addison-Wesley.

Upton, G.J.G. (1978) *The Analysis of Cross-Tabulated Data*. Chichester: Wiley.

Upton, G.J.G. (1986) Cross-classified data. In A.D. Lovie (ed.) *New Developments in Statistics for Psychology and the Social Sciences*. Leicester: The British Psychological Society; London: Routledge.

Wainer, H. and Thissen, D. (1981) Graphical data analysis. *Annual Review of Psychology, 32*, 191–241.

SKILLS

John Annett

An item of behaviour is called *skilled*, or *a skill*, when it is (1) directed towards the attainment of a goal and (2) so organized that the goal is reliably achieved with economy of time and effort and (3) has been acquired by training and practice. Defined thus, the topic of skill embraces a very wide range of questions in theoretical and applied psychology. The characteristics and limits of human skilled performance have been of interest to occupational psychologists since the turn of the century with early studies of morse telegraphy (Bryan and Harter, 1897, 1899) and typing (Book, 1908) and later of flying skills (Bartlett, 1948; Fitts and Jones, 1947a, 1947b). In recent years, sport psychologists have provided many detailed studies (Glencross, 1978; Magill, 1985). There have been significant advances in the understanding of the neural mechanisms underlying movement stemming from the work of Bernstein (1967), Bizzi (1988), Evarts (1973), Jeannerod (1988), Paillard (1982), and others, whilst neurological disorders with motor implications in children (cerebral palsy) and the elderly (stroke and Parkinson's disease) have stimulated interest in assessment and rehabilitation (Wing, 1984).

Skills occur in great variety: from whole-body skills like gymnastics, to manipulative skills such as tying a bow, and complex intellectual skills such as running a nuclear power station. To analyse any skill it is necessary to consider at least three aspects. First, there are different *effector systems*, that is, functional units of the central nervous system (CNS) connected to various groups of muscles. Next, the skill must have an *object*, often some environmental variable, which is manipulated or changed by the operation of the effectors. Third, the particular way in which the effector system acts on the object is mediated by a *control system*. Although theoretically separable, these three aspects of skill are intimately related.

Research on motor skills has given pride of place to the hand as the effector system for manipulative and control skills and, of course, the trunk and limbs are the principal effectors in whole-body skills. Other important effectors include the ocular-motor (eye-movement) system and the vocal system. The skeletal effectors are essentially lever systems in which the angle of the joint is controlled by balanced groups of muscles, the agonists and antagonists. As mechanical systems, they have properties of mass and elasticity, which place important limitations on the movements which are physically possible and especially on the speed with which a change of joint angle can take place. The eye, however, has low inertia which enables it to make fast saccades to preselected locations. The vocal system, which includes the muscles of the diaphragm, larynx, jaw, tongue and lips, requires very precise integration and timing of movement sequences for the generation of speech.

In addition to these physical effector systems, there is a 'mental' effector system which controls images and thoughts and which shares some of the properties and probably the neuroanatomical bases of the physical effector systems (Cooper and Shepard, 1973; Roland *et al*, 1980a, 1980b). Purely mental skills are, however, beyond the scope of this short review.

The second aspect of skill, the properties of objects which are controlled, is also significant in determining the kind of control which is needed. For instance, Doyle (1988) has thrown some light on the control problem a cyclist has to solve by measuring performance on a bicycle specially designed to remove physical features which tend to give it stability. The normally curved front forks were replaced by straight vertical forks to remove the castor effect (the tendency of the front wheel to rotate about the axis of the forks) and a counter-rotating wheel to cancel out the gyroscopic effect. An ordinary bicycle ridden at reasonable speed is quite stable and all the rider has to do is control direction and forward speed, but the lack of vertical stability in Doyle's reconstructed bicycle meant that the rider must detect small deviations from the vertical and correct them by turning the handlebar into the direction of roll. Recordings of corrective movements showed that riders responded to the roll acceleration with a delay of between 0.06 and 0.12 seconds and that continuous correction was punctuated by intermittent bursts of corrective movement at frequencies of 1 Hz and 0.2 Hz. Clearly the physical properties of the object being controlled have profound consequences for the mechanism by which control is exerted and it is to theories of motor control that I now turn.

THE PROBLEM OF MOTOR CONTROL

The central issue for research on skill is how the effector mechanisms are successfully brought to bear on objects in the environment in order to fulfil the goals of the organism. The 'information processing' analysis of human skill, current from the 1950s (for example, Broadbent, 1958) until the mid 1970s (for example, Welford, 1976) has proved to be unsatisfactory as an account of motor control. In the basic model, sensory information is seen flowing through a channel, being filtered by attentional mechanisms, stored in temporary buffers and processed or transformed by central mechanisms into a motor output. This model followed the classic traditions of Helmholtz, Donders and Wundt, who used the principle of subtraction to deduce the time course of a sequence of hypothesized internal processes.

Donders (1868, translated 1969) measured the time a subject takes to repeat a syllable spoken by the experimenter. He used the five syllables 'ka', 'ke', 'ki', 'ko', 'ku' as stimuli. In simple or 'a-reactions', only one syllable is used in a block of trials, whilst in choice or 'b-reaction', all five are used, each requiring a matching response. For the 'c-reaction', all five stimuli are used but S is instructed to respond only to one, for example 'ki'. By subtracting RT(a) from RT(b), Donders obtained the time to discriminate the stimulus and select a response, the remaining time being attributed to peripheral sensory and motor neural transmission. Subtracting RT(a) from RT(c), gives a value for perceptual discrimination, and Donders then argued that $[(b-a) - (c-a)] = [b-c]$ = the time taken by 'an expression of the will', or, as we might put it nowadays, time to initiate a voluntary movement. This subtraction logic was pursued vigorously and with increasing degrees of sophistication for 100 years (Sternberg, 1969; Posner, 1978) in the search for a detailed account of the 'black boxes'. Limitations to performance were attributed principally to the capacity of the central channel and theorizing centred on the results of experiments on serial and choice reaction time, divided attention and performing two tasks at once. The capacity problem was not satisfactorily resolved within the framework of a static, linear model (Allport et al., 1972; Neisser, 1976) and more recent interpretations of the nature of motor control (Colley and Beech, 1989; Meijer and Roth, 1988) lead to quite different questions.

The neural basis of motor control

The pathways between sensory input and motor output are neither

LIMBIC SYSTEM | SENSORIMOTOR SYSTEM

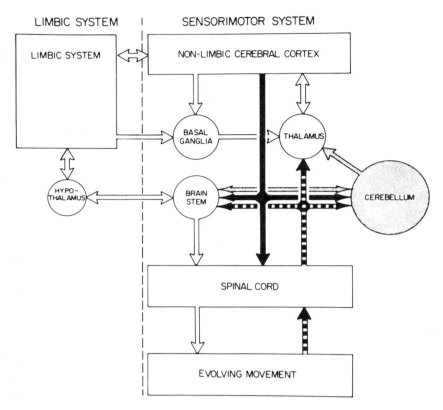

Figure 1. Principal pathways in the control of voluntary movement. (From Brooks, 1986.)

anatomically nor functionally linear and sequential. Figure 1 (from Brooks, 1986) shows the principal neural pathways involved in voluntary movement.

A number of different structures intervene between the senses and the muscles and there is a great deal of interaction between them. Information flows out from the cortex and other parts of the brain to the effectors but also back again to the higher centres. Figure 1 suggests that intentions or goals, driven originally by the motivational (limbic) system, are formulated in the association cortex, and developed into plans, principally in the frontal lobes. The formulation of a detailed executive program to achieve a goal which requires a postural change must relate body equilibrium to the direction and force of the intended action and here structures such as the basal ganglia, thalamus and lateral cerebellum make essential contributions by preparatory adjustments of muscular tone and by relating muscular forces to externally perceived space. The pyramidal cells of the primary motor cortex make synaptic connections direct to the motor neurons in the spinal cord and there are other direct connections from the brain stem (red nucleus). Furthermore, the motor cortex interacts with the intermediate cerebellum to relate efferent signals to the changing state of sensory information. At the spinal level, both descending systems (cortico- and rubro-spinal tracts) modulate semi-autonomous spinal reflexes which control the relationships between sets of muscles. The rate and extent to which muscles change their length is dependent on a number of factors including their starting position and load and the state of other muscles which are functionally related to them or form a 'synergy' or 'coordinative structure' (Bernstein, 1967). The messages coming down from the brain have been likened to advice rather than instructions since the influence of local conditions at the periphery can be strong and relevant information (about load, for instance) may not be directly available to the higher centres.

Motor consistency and variability

Highly skilled acts are characterized more by the constancy of their output or results than by the consistency of the muscular contractions used to achieve them. Whenever I aim to hit the 't' on my keyboard, my hand comes at it from a slightly different angle. I can pick up my coffee without first having to adopt precisely the same posture I used last time. A motor control system which depended on a centralized command structure would not be the most effective way of achieving constant goals under varying conditions. A complex joint like the shoulder is controlled by at least ten muscles, each containing a large number of motor units, that is, bundles of fibres controlled by a single nerve ending. If movements were centrally coded in terms of joint angles then the message specifying a new position of the upper arm would require the specification of ten different values or the control of ten 'degrees of freedom', to use the phrase of Bernstein (1967). A moderately complex movement involving just the arms, hand and fingers already involves a formidable number of degrees of freedom which would have to be specified in any centrally computed program. A robotics engineer designing a machine to mimic human action would look for a simpler solution; and recent debates in the motor skills field relate to proposed solutions.

Motor programs

Simple positioning tasks such as placing a peg in a hole (Fitts, 1954; Annett *et al.*, 1958, 1979) illustrate two types of control in one movement: a pre-programmed, ballistic or open-loop initial phase followed by a controlled or closed-loop second phase. The pre-programmed phase has been taken as evidence for a general mode of control by means of a *motor program*. Different authors have slightly different conceptions of the nature of motor programs (see Keele, 1975; Rosenbaum, 1985; Summers, 1981; Schmidt, 1988), but the core idea is of a pattern of motor impulses which may be computed on demand or may be drawn from a memory bank. A motor program for throwing a dart into the bullseye would constitute a pattern of arm acceleration and deceleration with the finger–thumb release being timed for a particular point in the cycle.

Evidence for the existence of motor programs comes from three main sources: (1) the degree to which it is possible to modify movement patterns which are subject to unforeseen mechanical forces or new information shortly after initiation, (2) the effects of feedback deprivation on the execution of the motor task and (3) the relationship between initiation time and the complexity of a prepared sequence of movements.

As an instance of the first type of evidence, Wadman *et al.* (1979) recorded changes in electrical potential of the muscles by electromyogram (EMG) associated with the acceleration/deceleration pattern of a rapid sequence of arm movements. The original pattern of muscle electrical activity was preserved even on trials when the physical movement was unexpectedly prevented, strongly suggesting pre-programmed control.

As regards feedback deprivation, Lashley (1917) noted that a patient who, due to a spinal injury, had no kinaesthetic sensation in his lower limbs could nonetheless reproduce movements accurately. He argued this would only be possible if there were a central memory for the motor command. Motor programs are implicated in the control of eye movements. When a pattern of excitation sweeps across the retina, the organism needs to know whether this is a result of movement in the external world or of the organism itself. On these grounds, von Holst and Mittelstädt (1950) argued that a copy of the original motor instruction, an 'efference copy', could be used to detect the difference between self-generated and externally generated visual movement. Experiments on the accuracy of movement in the absence of sensory feedback, due to surgical intervention (Taub and

Berman, 1968) or temporary ischemia (Laszlo, 1966, 1967), provide supportive evidence for motor program theory in the extent to which simple reaching movements can still be made in the absence of kinaesthetic feedback. However, fine control is typically lost, and there are many more actions in which transformations of external sensory feedback, such as delays and geometric transformations, seriously disrupt performance (Smith, 1962; Smith and Smith, 1962).

As regards the third type of evidence, Sternberg *et al.* (1978) found that the time to produce the first response in a pre-programmed sequence increased as a linear function of the total length of the sequence. The increased reaction time is taken to reflect the time taken to retrieve the program elements from memory. Rosenbaum *et al.* (1983) proposed a hierarchical structure for the components of a rapid sequence of finger movements and demonstrated a linear increase in reaction time with the number of nodes in the response hierarchy which would have to be activated to produce the sequence.

Critics of the motor program concept have argued that the amount of information which would have to be retained in memory to specify all the movements of which an adult is capable would exceed the storage capacity of the brain. However, the extent of the problem may have been overestimated. Vredenbregt and Koster (1971) were able to simulate cursive handwriting by using two DC motors to drive a pen across the writing surface. Carefully-timed discrete voltage pulses to the motors moving the pen in the horizontal and vertical directions produced recognizable letters due to the natural dynamics (inertia and viscosity) of the mechanical system. In other words, the information needed to specify the response is perhaps not as large as appears at first sight.

Some theories of motor control stress the role of peripheral factors; for example, a limb can be considered as a *mass-spring system*. The angle adopted by a joint depends on the relative tension in the agonist and antagonist muscles which themselves are elastic or spring-like. It has been suggested (for example, Bizzi, 1980, 1988) that the angle of a joint, and hence the position of a limb, can be specified in terms of the relative tension of the opposing muscles. If the initial position of the limb is disturbed by a temporary load, then it will automatically return to its former position when the load is released, just as a swing door will return to its closed position after being pushed open. Muscular tension, in turn, can be determined by the rate of firing of the neurons serving the opposing muscle groups. The particular significance of this solution is that external disturbances caused by sudden changes of load (for instance, by hitting a small object) do not affect the final position and do not require additional processing in the nervous system. The terminal position of a limb in space can also be determined by the relative tension of the opposing muscles.

Feedback control

It would be wrong to regard motor programs and feedback as mutually exclusive accounts of motor control. Actions require both some degree of pre-planning and some means of monitoring and adjusting the plan if the intended results are to be achieved under variable conditions. The operation of the feedback principle in the CNS was noted by Bell as long ago as 1825; but it is only since the 1940s, following the work of Craik and others (Craik, 1947; Hick and Bates, 1950) at Cambridge on the skills of pilots and gun layers, that its significance for motor control has been appreciated. The essential principle, illustrated in Figure 2, is that the output of a power source, for instance a motor or a muscle, is controlled by a signal derived from a discrepancy between the desired value of a variable and its current value. The humble thermostat which switches the boiler on when the temperature falls below the set point serves as a model for motor control in peg moving, bicycle riding and many other tasks. In a purely feedback-controlled system the only information which needs to be stored in the CNS is the set point or goal since it is the environment which holds the information necessary to control movement.

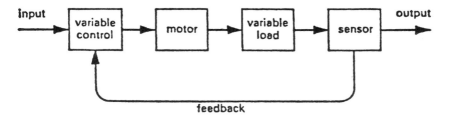

Figure 2. A simple servo. A 'motor' provides power which is applied to a variable load. The actual output is sensed and a signal is fed back to a variable control which resets the power to maintain constant output. (From Annett, 1969.)

Skills such as catching and hitting fast moving objects and steering towards or around fixed objects provide some particularly clear examples of direct feedback control of movement. When moving through the environment, the visual field represented on the retina expands outwards from the centre; and similarly, as an object approaches the observer, textural features on its surface move from central towards peripheral vision. Lee (1986) has shown, in a variety of interception tasks, that time to contact can be specified by the ratio of retinal size and expansion velocity of a textural feature and that this variable (tau) is used to control movement directly. For example, the graph of a long jumper's stride length over distance covered, in Figure 3, shows a steady increase as forward momentum is acquired but increasing variability as the takeoff point, which must be hit precisely, is approached. In a contrasting example, five-year-olds rapidly improve in their ability to judge whether they have sufficient time to cross a busy street when given practice in a safe simulation (Lee and Young, 1987). The process of coupling the visual cue to motor activity is something which must be learned but can be learned quite quickly.

The direct coupling of action to visual feedback is strikingly observed in tasks where mirrors, lenses or closed-circuit TV are used to change the familiar relationship between movement and the visual cues normally used to guide it. In tracing a star pattern seen in a mirror, subjects find it very difficult to change direction at the corners. They feel momentarily paralysed and further progress is only possible by decoupling the visual cue, that is, by not paying attention to it and allowing control to pass to the visual or kinaesthetic imagery system. Perceptual coupling is another way of relieving the motor system of its computational burden, and so we may conclude that both motor program theory and feedback theory have a range of possible answers to Bernstein's degrees of freedom problem.

Complex skills and control hierarchies

Feedback theory has been applied to a wider range of problems than just the control of simple motor acts. A complex skill, be it a straightforward sequence such as assembling a piece of equipment or a set of conditional actions such as might be employed in playing football or running a chemical plant, is characterized by a unique structure. Structured skills can be analysed into behavioural units called 'TOTE' units by Miller *et al.* (1960) or 'Operations' by Annett *et*

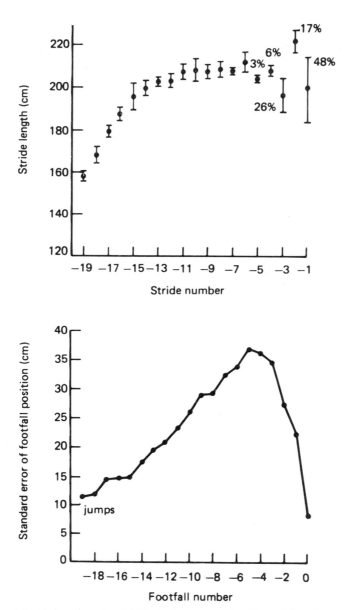

Figure 3. Stride length and variability in the run-up of an Olympic long jumper. The top graph shows stride length plotted against footfall, −1 being the last footfall before the takeoff board. The vertical bars show the amount of adjustment to stride length. The bottom graph shows variability of footfall location increasing up to the sixth stride before takeoff and decreasing rapidly over the last few strides. (From Lee *et al.*, 1982.)

al. (1971). Each unit is specified by a goal state of one or more variables, and the discrepancy between the goal state and the current state drives the action. Consider the series of steps required to tie a bow, from grasping the two ends to be tied together to the final tug which tightens the knot (Annett, 1986). Each step can be thought of as a goal to be attained – having one end in each hand is necessary before proceeding to twist them together, and so on. Tying a bow is a simple behavioural sequence but, at the same time, it has a vertical or hierarchical structure. A description of bow tying might refer to (1) making a half knot, (2) making two loops with the ends and (3) making another half knot with the two loops. Stage (1) might be further broken down into sub-operations such as (1.1) grasping the free ends, (1.2) twisting one over the other, (1.3) pulling the half knot tight, and so on. It is even possible to break down (1.1) into detailed finger movements, although it would be less useful to specify these in detail since factors such as the size and flexibility of the material to be tied could vary, making it necessary to change some of the details from one knot to the next.

When applied to complex industrial tasks (Annett *et al.*, 1971; Shepherd, 1985) this form of analysis yields a hierarchical structure with sub-operations 'nested' in superordinate operations as shown in Figure 4. Performing such a task depends not only on the ability to carry out each sub-operation but also on maintaining the essential overall structure. Clues about the nature of these structures can be found in the way skills break down in some circumstances such as under stress or inattention (Reason, 1980).

To assert that control of complex skills is hierarchically organized can give the misleading impression that all effective instructions issue from the 'highest' level and are passed down to the effector units unchanged. But not even military hierarchies work in this way. Generals are responsible for strategy, not tactics, and units in a well-organized army have some degree of autonomy. Shaffer (1980, 1981) analysed the performance of highly skilled pianists by having them play a piano wired to a computer which timed each keystroke. They played pieces from memory and by sight and in different tempi and moods. A statistical analysis of the variations in the timing of keystrokes revealed that the temporal structure was most constant at the level of the bar, with much of the detailed variation in timing of particular bars being repeated across performances. Expressive temporal features, such as rubato, could be varied between performances whilst others were left unchanged. Shaffer interprets these results as indicating that the temporal structure of the music is

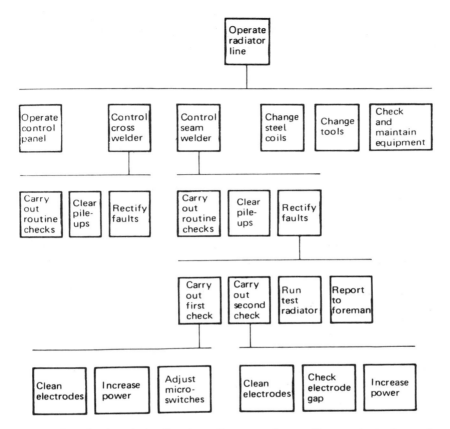

Figure 4. Partial task analysis of heating radiator manufacture. The operator in charge of the production line has various sub-tasks specified on the second line down. Of these, 'controlling cross welder' and 'controlling seam welder' are broken down into their constituent sub-operations in line 3. The 'rectify faults' sub-operation is further broken down into its sub-operations in lines 4 and 5 of the diagram. (From Annett *et al.*, 1971.)

represented at an abstract level and is not simply determined by the speed with which one keystroke follows the next. In this sense, the temporal features represent control at a relatively high level in the hierarchy.

A study in computer simulation of typing by Rumelhart and Norman (1982) illustrates another possible method of hierarchical control in a sequentially organized skill. The basic unit of the simulation is an *activation-triggered schema* (ATS). An ATS is a construct like a TOTE or Operation in that it represents the conditions for action. If its trigger conditions arise, it will fire until the activating condition is cancelled. For the purposes of the simulation, the input text is parsed by word schemas such that, when a particular word is presented, that word schema is activated. Nested within the word schemas are individual letter or keypress schemas. Figure 5 shows how the word schema 'very' drives the fingers of the two hands over a simulated QWERTY keyboard to type the individual letters v-e-r-y in the correct order.

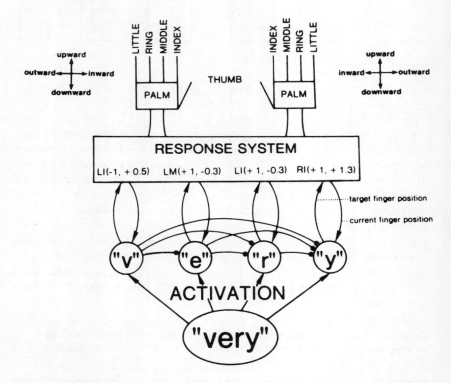

Figure 5. A typewriting simulation. The word schema 'very' activates the component keypress schemata. The left-to-right lines ending in filled circles indicate inhibition; thus, to begin with 'v' is not inhibited whilst 'y' is maximally inhibited. Within the response system L and R, I and M denote left and right index and middle fingers. The numbers in brackets indicate the momentary discrepancy between target and present finger position in the vertical and horizontal axes. The curved arrows indicate the feedback loops which act to reduce the discrepancy when each keypress schema is activated. (From Rumelhart and Norman, 1982.)

Schemas have the property of being able to activate or inhibit other schemas, and it is through this system of mutual inhibition and activation that control is passed from one schema to another. In typing words, this maintains the correct order of letters; but, since fingers are physically connected to hands, moving the left index finger to 'v' also has the consequence that the left middle finger is moved away from 'e'. The finger keypress schemas, once activated, are driven by a simple feedback loop which keeps track of the distance between the present position of the finger and its target key and initiates a press when it is within range. The diagram shows the word schema triggering all the letter schemas, but schema 'v' inhibits the other three (which also inhibit each other). The finger typing 'v' moves from its current position (which need not be initially specified) towards 'v' guided by the feedback loop, presses, and releases its inhibitory influence on 'e', which then also begins to move.

In the simulation, the activation values were made somewhat variable and the system made occasional mistakes. Set to type 2000 words, the simulation produced several common features of human typing. Keystroke intervals between hands are typically shorter than within hands and sometimes negative, accounting for some common reversal errors such as 'hte' for 'the'. A particularly interesting error is to double the wrong letter in a word, thus producing 'bokk' for 'book'. Rumelhart and Norman suggest that there may be a special 'doubling' schema which can be applied to individual keypress schemas. The disadvantage of the superficially simpler solution of repeating a letter schema is that, once activated, a schema switches itself off and, if this were the case, errors such as 'bok' would be much more common. If there are indeed letter-doubling schemas, then they may, because activation levels are variable, trigger the wrong letter schema.

Although the simulation does not mimic human typing in every detail, it is good enough to lend plausibility to this general type of model as an account of the way hierarchical control is maintained over a sequential skill. The model also illustrates the important principle of 'executive ignorance'. Each superior level triggers the subordinate schemas but does not issue detailed instructions. The word schema does not need to 'know' where the individual fingers happen to be when their schemas are activated, since the schemas themselves comprise an automatic homing mechanism. In much the same way, the person tying a bow does not need to 'know', and typically cannot say (Annett, 1986, 1988), which finger muscles are activated in what order to produce a particular result. Again, the hierarchical structure, in which features of the skill are represented at different levels of detail, puts a different complexion on what seemed like an impossibly difficult control problem.

THE ACQUISITION OF SKILLS

Skills are, by definition, learned, and in most cases must be specifically taught. The plasticity of skilled behaviour creates problems for theories of performance and is one of the main reasons for the abandonment of the 1950s-style linear information-processing model. The pivotal concept of a capacity-limited information-processing channel which could apparently account for choice reaction time data (Hick, 1952), the trade-off between speed and accuracy in rapid movement tasks (Fitts, 1954), and the division of attention between competing tasks (Broadbent, 1958), began to collapse when it was shown that extended practice changed the relationship between stimulus information and performance. The data collected by Mowbray and Rhoades (1959) from 20,000 trials of choice reaction time could no longer be fitted to Hick's equation $RT = K \log_2 (N +1)$; and Spelke *et al.* (1976) demonstrated that, after weeks of practice, two apparently conflicting tasks could be performed simultaneously.

Unfortunately, the investigation of learning was very closely identified with behaviourist concepts of stimulus, response and reinforcement; and, despite some early attempts to account for skill learning in information-processing terms (Annett and Kay, 1956, 1957), it was not until the end of the 1960s that non-S–R theories of skill acquisition began to emerge (Annett, 1969; Adams, 1971; Schmidt, 1975). These theories all referred to centrally stored data, the 'traces' of previous sensory and motor events, and reinterpreted knowledge of results as information feedback which changes behaviour rather than 'reinforcement' which acts by strengthening stimulus–response connections.

Mechanisms of learning

Practice results in both quantitative and qualitative changes in performance. Bryan and Harter (1899) plotted the first learning curves for skill in receiving morse telegraphy. The number of signals correctly transcribed per minute rises steadily over the first three or four months of practice, remains roughly constant for the next two months, and then begins to rise again. Bryan and Harter noted that the later acceleration in learning rate was accompanied by a change in method from transcribing single letters to receiving and writing down whole words. 'Grouping', as this process came to be known, is one of the common qualitative changes in performance which results from practice.

A quantitative change which occurs with practice in simple repetitive skills, including key pressing (Seibel, 1963), mirror drawing (Snoddy, 1926) and cigar rolling (Crossman, 1959) is that the logarithm of performance time is a linear function of the logarithm of the number of practice trials. This relationship is known as the 'log-log-linear law of learning' and its apparent simplicity suggests that there might be a single underlying learning process. Crossman (1959) suggested that each practice trial draws on a population of perceptual-motor processes and that these are evaluated in terms of the effort required to achieve the goal. On successive trials, each process is negatively weighted in proportion to the effort it entails, such that the probability of effortful processes being selected is progressively reduced. Newell and Rosenbloom (1981) believe that a power function provides a better fit to skill acquisition data, including results from both motor and mental skills, and they propose that the learning principle is 'chunking'. Information is said to be 'chunked' when it is dealt with as a single unit (for instance, the telegraphist dealing in whole words rather than single letters). In terms of the hierarchical theory described in the previous section, the lowest levels of the control hierarchy are chunked; thus a muscle synergy (a group of muscles operating together) would constitute a single chunk requiring only a single command rather than central specification of the activity in all the individual muscle units. It is hard to distinguish between the selection and the chunking theory on empirical grounds; but if one could look at changes in the detailed components of a skill as a function of practice, then the Crossman theory would predict that more effortful components progressively give way to less effortful, whilst the Newell and Rosenbloom theory would predict that relatively stable and consistent groups of components would emerge after practice.

A single process would provide the most parsimonious account of learning, but there is ample evidence to suggest that there are at least two broadly different types of learning process: one type which occurs as a result of repetition *per se* and another in which cognition plays a major role. Annett (1985) suggested that the log-log-linear law may well indicate not a single slow-acting process but a population of ways of learning which are successively drawn upon until exhausted. Thus, in the early stages, relatively rapid progress can be made by imitating the method of a skilled model or taking the advice of a coach, whilst much later in practice, when major sources of improvement have been exhausted, repetition may refine perceptual and temporal judgements, or, according to a classical theory, facilitate the connections between task elements (for example, MacKay, 1982).

Cognitive processes

Observational learning and verbal instruction play an important part in the early stages of learning new skills (Fitts, 1964), but a well-articulated theory of 'cognitive' motor learning is lacking, in part due to the lingering influence of behaviourism on theorizing about learning. Imitation is well documented in a variety of species (Goodall, 1963, in chimpanzees; Kawai, 1965, in macaques; Marler, 1970, in white-crowned sparrows), and in humans as young as 12 days (Meltzoff and Moore, 1977). Bandura's theory (Bandura, 1977), whilst providing a 'cognitive' framework for social learning, falls short of a detailed account of imitation in motor learning; but the hierarchical view of skill offers the possibility of a systematic 'cognitive' theory embracing both imitation and verbal instruction. The key to 'cognitive' motor learning lies in elucidating the way in which learned skills are represented in memory.

In classical learning theory there is only one level of representation and that is in a network of stimulus–response connections. The skilled person is different from the unskilled by virtue of a pattern of connections established by repetition and reinforcement. This meta-theory is compatible with the pure motor program theory discussed in earlier sections and dismissed in favour of one in which skilled actions are generated by the interaction of a stored hierarchy of representations with current information from the environment. The accounts of bow tying and typing given in the section on motor control are instances of this type of theory.

Coaching hints can exploit the human capacity to form represent-ations of objects and complex movement patterns. For example, one squash coach encourages his pupils to adopt a particular stance when receiving serve by instructing them to 'pretend to be a red indian on the warpath' (Annett, 1985). The phrase summons up an image of feet apart, knees slightly bent, right arm raised holding the racket/tomahawk head-high, and having a generally alert attitude. The fact that learners (and you, the reader) can both envisage the posture and adopt it is clear evidence of the existence of a high-level representation of a complex, but quite specific, movement pattern.

Annett (1982) hypothesized that such patterns, or 'action proto-types', are active in both the perception and production of actions, so if a pattern is perceivable it is (barring biomechanical limitations) producible. The theory that perception and action are served by the same rather than different processes has been entertained by a number of authors, particularly in relation to the skills of speech perception and production (Allport, 1984; MacKay, 1982), but also more generally (Neisser, 1985; Prinz, 1986; Scully and Newell, 1985; Weimer, 1977). There is strong evidence that, in perceiving the actions of other humans, certain invariant features are extracted from the complex stimulus array. In a technique developed by Johansson (1973) an actor, clad in dark clothes with small lights attached to the principal joints, is filmed in high contrast. When the actor is stationary, only a jumble of bright spots is seen, but when the actor moves, there is a distinct and immediate impression of human action. It has been shown (Cutting, 1978; Cutting and Proffitt, 1982) that accurate judgements can be made about the actor's sex and the weight of any object being carried.

A recent study by Whiting *et al.* (1987) of learning to ski illustrates how a learner can use an expert model as a source of information. The task was to learn a particular pattern of movement of the trunk and legs on a ski simulator. This device comprised a spring-loaded platform on which the learner stands and which slides from side to side over runners in response to leg and body movements. The movements were characterized by amplitude, frequency and 'fluency', the latter being a score derived from an idealized acceleration pattern. All subjects were given knowledge of results on the three scores (frequency, amplitude and fluency) and all improved with practice; but the subjects who observed the model quickly learned to match the fluency characteristic although, even after five practice sessions, few subjects were able to match the precise frequency and amplitude of the model's movements. This ability to abstract a particular higher-order description or representation of a complex activity is crucial to imitation (Scully and Newell, 1985), but more experimental studies are needed, particularly studies which relate the subjects' ability to perceive significant features of action with the ability to perform that action.

Practical studies of the use of demonstration and video-recording in training gymnasts and athletes have had mixed success (see Burwitz, 1981), but this may well be because learners lack practice in perceiving significant details of performance. There is some evidence (for example, Imwold and Hoffman, 1983) that specialists, such as experienced physical training instructors, see more in the recordings than those who ought to be learning from them; hence the expert model must be supplemented by other forms of instruction. [See also the chapter by Lew Hardy, in this volume, for a further discussion of training in sport.]

Verbal instruction

Motor *skill* is conventionally distinguished from verbal *knowledge,* and the former is often inaccessible to the latter. Annett (1985) found that skilled swimmers could not answer factual questions about the breaststroke any faster or more accurately than novices, whilst Berry and Broadbent (1984, 1987, 1988) have shown that subjects can learn to control complex systems, including simulated chemical plant and transportation systems, without being able to express the rules which govern their control decisions.

Neurological evidence points to the likelihood of separate encoding of verbal knowledge and motor capability in the central nervous system. Amnesics who cannot recall facts can learn and remember a motor skill (Corkin, 1968; Cohen and Squire, 1980); and one consequence of damage to the corpus callosum, which connects the two cerebral hemispheres, is that patients have difficulty in following verbal instructions to carry out simple tasks with the left hand, which is controlled by the right, non-verbal, hemisphere (Geschwind and Kaplan, 1962). The problem of how the verbal and non-verbal systems communicate (the action–language bridge: Annett, 1982) is a matter of conjecture, but it seems likely that the translation is effected through the mechanisms of high-level representations which include both images and abstractions. Experts asked (for the first time at least) to explain how a task is performed frequently resort to imagery, whilst instructors, as was shown in the 'red indian' example above, often resort to imagery-inducing language in order to convey information about postures and actions.

Knowledge of results

Perhaps the most extensive use of language in skill training is in the provision of knowledge of results (KR) and this topic has received very extensive coverage in the research literature (see summaries by Bilodeau, 1969; Annett, 1969; and Salmoni *et al.*, 1984). Informing the learner of the outcome of each response or trial typically gives the most rapid learning, whilst no-KR or practice-only conditions generally show poor learning or none at all. The rate and extent of learning is sensitive to the amount of information given – the more detailed the KR the better the learning, making it clear that the 'reinforcement' interpretation is inadequate.

Recent theories stress the informative properties of KR. Annett (1969) interpreted KR as a form of feedback used by the learner to adapt responses to the standard specified by the trainer. This very simple theory is represented as an algorithm in Figure 6, which shows how a subject might learn to make a simple linear movement of a specified extent without visual cues. The first attempt is guided only by a pre-existing concept of the required direction and amplitude, but the second attempt is based on (*i*) a (fading) trace of the first attempt, (*ii*) discrimination between internal feedback from a current response and the trace of the preceding response and (*iii*) a simple strategy such as: 'if the last response was shorter than required make the next one longer; if it was correct, reproduce it; if it was too long, make it shorter'. Evidence from the rate and extent of learning with different kinds and amounts of KR supports this basic model.

Adams's (1971) theory, also based on the concept of feedback, proposed a motor trace or record of the output specification of a response and a perceptual trace, a record of the sensory feedback (including KR) associated with that motor trace. Practice strengthens the perceptual trace such that the sensory consequences of motor outputs are anticipated. Outputs can then be preselected on the basis of their expected feedback.

Schmidt's 'schema' theory (Schmidt, 1975) extended Adams's 'closed loop' theory to account for the learning of classes of actions. The choice of motor output is related to expected sensory consequences by information about previous response specifications, previous sensory consequences and previous outcomes, that is, whether the sensory consequences signal a desired state of affairs. These sources of information are consolidated into a 'recognition schema' which encodes the relationships between sensory consequences and outcomes and a 'recall schema' which relates outcomes to response specifications. The particular merit of the schema theory is that it allows for generalized learning and it makes the specific prediction that learning is most effective when a variety of responses are made; thus practising throwing darts at different targets is as good as or better than just practising with the bullseye. This prediction is, by and large, fulfilled (Shapiro and Schmidt, 1982); but none of the three theories makes very strong differential predictions, and it can be argued that they provide only a general description of the learning mechanism, which might differ in details between different learning tasks. The corrective role of KR stressed in Annett's theory, which postulates only a short-term memory, is of primary importance when the learner is initially seeking to discover the main features of the permissible/desirable responses. The associative role,

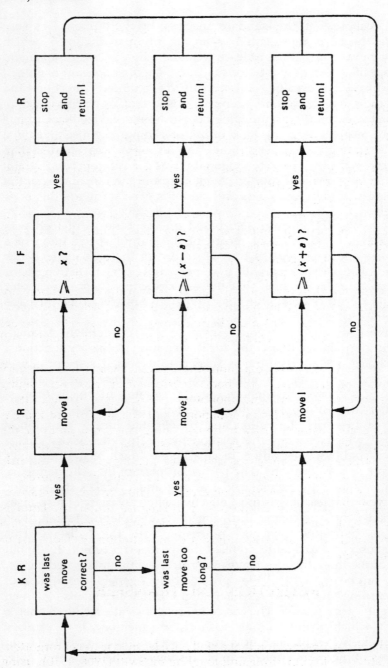

Figure 6. A strategy for learning a linear position response. KR = knowlege results, R = the next response, IF = feedback arising from that response, x = trace of magnitude of previous response, a = an arbitrary quantity on the same dimension. (From Annett, 1969.)

requiring long-term memory storage, will be particularly significant in the fine tuning of muscular adjustments when precision is required, but only in those tasks where relationships between sensory and motor events do not change, as would be the case in, say, adapting to an inverted visual field.

Much of the research on KR has used simple unidimensional positioning tasks; but in more complex skills, such as gymnastics, outcome information may be insufficient to identify critical features of the performance which need to be modified. Kinematic data may be helpful (Newell and McGinnis, 1985) but, as with video recordings, may need expert interpretation to establish the precise link between performance and outcome.

The associative or calibration role of KR which is central to schema theory is particularly important in the fine tuning of muscular adjustments when precision is required in tasks such as dart-throwing, which depends on learning the relation between the acceleration applied to the missile and its mass and the perceived distance and direction of the target. When these relations are changed, for instance by putting on distorting spectacles, both recall and recognition schemas must be relearned, a process which occurs rapidly with active experience (Held and Hein, 1958; Held and Freedman, 1963).

KR is often said to have a motivational role. Even when not very informative, KR seems to boost performance by encouraging persistence in effortful and monotonous tasks (see Annett, 1969, chapter 5). If KR provides information about goal attainment there is no need to postulate an additional 'energizing' function. In the context of current theories of skill as goal-directed action, it is unlikely that any activity which is not seen to be making progress towards some goal will be maintained, especially if it consumes resources of energy or information-processing capacity. Thus, in any comparison between KR and no-KR conditions, performance under the latter is likely to be less effortful, less concentrated and less persistent. The motivational effect of KR is simply a demonstration of 'feedback in action' (Annett, 1969).

RETENTION AND TRANSFER

Motor memory

It is a common observation that a skill once learned is never forgotten. Early studies of typewriting and juggling by Swift (1906, 1910), using the relearning or 'savings' method, showed that, after more than a year without practice, the level of performance originally reached after 45–50 days of practice was regained with about 10 days of retraining, a saving of 80 per cent of the original learning. Hill (1957), using himself as a subject, measured savings of 70 per cent in typing skill over a retention interval of 50 years. Retention of verbal material is typically less good (*cf.* Ansbacher, 1940; Lahey, 1941). A study by Leavitt and Schlosberg (1944) apparently confirmed the superiority of motor memory by comparing savings scores for pursuit rotor tracking and nonsense syllable learning after intervals of 1, 7, 28 and 70 days. They found retention of the motor task declined from near 90 per cent after a one-day retention interval to around 75 per cent after 70 days, whilst savings on the nonsense syllables declined from about 80 per cent after one day to 50 per cent after 70 days. This result is not, however, as clear-cut as it at first appears since the two tasks were not equated for ease of learning nor for the number of trials or repetitions, and both these factors are known to affect retention.

In studies of flight training, Ammons *et al.* (1958), Brown *et al.* (1963), Adams and Hufford (1962) and Mengelkoch *et al.* (1971) have all found that procedural tasks, comprising a sequence of discrete steps such as pre-flight instrument checks, decay over time without practice at a faster rate than the manual control element, such as maintaining altitude. The retention of procedures is of considerable practical importance in relation to training for emergency procedures where rehearsals, real or simulated, are often widely separated. Typically, a procedure fails because one important step, for instance checking the safety catch on a weapon, is forgotten. Procedures are quickly relearned, but in emergencies such loss of skill can be crucial (Annett, 1979).

Short-term retention of skills (short-term motor memory – STMM) has been studied largely through the medium of simple positioning tasks in which subjects attempt to reproduce movements of a specific extent, normally without the aid of vision (for reviews see E.A. Bilodeau, 1969; Smyth, 1984). Variables such as number of repetitions, duration of the retention interval and interference have yielded a body of information on 'kinaesthetic' memory, and the central, but not very conclusive, debate has been how movement information is encoded – for example, as action plans (motor programs) or sensory templates. Although absolute values of felt force, distance and direction can be retained with moderate accuracy for short periods, it is unlikely that we rely on simple sensori-motor memory to remember how to do things. The world in which we live and the actions we need to take are far too variable for it to be worthwhile to memorize precise movement information. It is rather through a set of outline plans organized so as to achieve criterion conditions, which may be abstractly defined, that we are able to remember how to solve familiar motor problems (Annett, 1988).

Transfer of training

The element of non-specificity in skill learning makes it possible to transfer the benefits of experience in one situation to others which are related. Having learned to drive a Mini, only a little more training is needed to master a Jaguar or a Rolls, and indeed the whole system of education and training is based on the presumption of transfer. Transfer of training, like retention, can be measured in terms of the 'savings' in learning task B which can be attributed to prior experience on task A. According to Woodworth (1938), E.H. Weber, the father of psychophysics, reported in the 1840s that skills learned with the right hand transferred to the left and vice versa, and that a surgeon trained his students to carry out difficult operations with the left hand so that they would be better able to perform them with the right.

The traditional theory of transfer was that practice on any task will develop one or more abilities and that the transfer task will benefit to the extent that it also depends on the same ability. This 'formal discipline' theory was at the basis of educational practice, popular at least since the time of John Locke, which insisted on learning poetry to develop the memory and mathematics to develop logical thinking. Thorndike and Woodworth (1901) proposed a new theory of 'identical elements', that is, that transfer occurs only when the original learning task and the transfer task share some common feature or element. Although it was not their intention, the elements soon came to be understood as stimuli and responses, and from this narrow interpretation arose the paradox of 'negative transfer'.

Negative transfer occurs when previous experience interferes with the learning or performance of a skill, and this can happen when transferring between tasks which are similar in all but a few important respects, such as transferring from a right-hand-drive car to a left-hand-drive, or even changing from driving on the left side of the road to driving on the right. In such cases, almost every element is identical. However, as Osgood (1949) pointed out, a problem can arise when near-identical stimuli must be linked to different responses, for example moving a lever in the opposite direction to that orginally learned. For transfer to occur, not only is it important that the two tasks should have common stimuli and responses but they should also have common stimulus–response connections.

Even with this modification, the identical elements theory is not entirely satisfactory because of the occasional failure of transfer even when the tasks concerned have important common elements (Annett and Sparrow, 1985; Brown and Campione, 1986). Fotheringhame (1984), for example, found no significant transfer between two measurement tasks employing the same principles (the use of micrometers and vernier height gauges) unless the principle linking the two was explicitly taught. Again, this problem is better understood in the context of the theory of skill which assigns importance to the overall structure of goals and plans in the execution of a skill. Annett and Sparrow (1985) suggest that transfer between related tasks can involve two kinds of problem. If the overall plan of the new task is similar to an existing plan, the latter is likely to be run off as a whole, sometimes resulting in error due to negative transfer (Reason, 1980). However, if the overall plan of the new skill is (or appears to be) quite different, it would not be surprising that the learner does not notice that a sub-skill, which has already been learned in a different context, is relevant. The additional, and perhaps essential, factor in transfer is an awareness of features or elements common to the old and the new task, and here the trainer or educator can employ training techniques likely to enhance useful transfer (Annett and Sparrow, 1985).

Flavell and Wellman (1971) suggested that learning often occurs at two levels, a 'cognitive' and a 'metacognitive' level. Metacognition refers to awareness of one's own cognitive processes; thus it is possible both to learn a skill and to know something about how one is doing it and to have a learning strategy. Less able learners, and those who show poor generalization and transfer, typically have underdeveloped metacognitive skills (Brown and Campione, 1986; Downs and Perry, 1984, 1987), and training programmes in metacognitive skills are being developed (Segal et al., 1985; Chipman et al., 1985) for use in schools and the training of less able school leavers. The role which metacognition might play in the acquisition and transfer of perceptual-motor skills is, however, relatively unexplored territory.

CONCLUSION

Any introductory review of such a broad and active field as human skill is bound to be incomplete. Little has been said in this survey about the problems which technological advances bring to modern industrial skills, as discussed, for example, by Goodstein *et al.* (1988) and Patrick and Duncan (1988). Important symposia have recently been devoted to neuropsychological aspects of skill (Roy, 1985), to the skills of the mentally handicapped (Wade, 1986) and to developmental aspects of motor skills (Wade and Whiting, 1986; Whiting and Wade, 1986). Some forty years ago, researchers in motor skills were amongst the first to see the relevance of information-processing concepts to our understanding of human motor performance. In doing so, they provided an important building block for modern cognitive psychology; but it is only recently that relations between cognition and skill are being explored in depth. The Cartesian dichotomy of body and mind would relegate motor skill to mere mechanism, not involving truly psychological processes, but a conception of skill is emerging which interprets the mechanisms of movement in the context of meaningful action (see especially Colley and Beech, 1989; Heuer and Fromm, 1986; Meijer and Roth, 1988; Prinz and Sanders, 1984). This recognition of the importance of cognitive processes in the generation and control of action and in the acquisition of skill is leading to exciting new research prospects.

REFERENCES

Adams, J.A. (1971) A closed loop theory of motor learning. *Journal of Motor Behaviour, 3,* 111–150.

Adams, J.A. and Hufford, L.E. (1962) Contribution of a part task trainer to the learning and relearning of a time-shared flight maneuver. *Human Factors, 4,* 159–170.

Allen, G.I. and Tsukuhara, N. (1974) Cerebrocerebellar communication systems. *Physiological Review, 54,* 957–1006.

Allport, D.A. (1984) Speech production and comprehension: One lexicon or two? In W. Prinz and A.F. Sanders (eds) *Cognition and Motor Processes.* Berlin: Springer.

Allport, D.A., Antonis, B. and Reynolds P. (1972) On the division of attention: A disproof of the single channel hypothesis. *Quarterly Journal of Experimental Psychology, 24,* 225–235.

Ammons, R.B., Farr, R.G., Bloch, E., Neuman, E., Dey, M., Marion. R. and Ammons, C.H. (1958) Long term retention of perceptual-motor skills. *Journal of Experimental Psychology, 55,* 318–328.

Annett, J. (1969) *Feedback and Human Behaviour.* Harmondsworth: Penguin.

Annett, J. (1979) Memory for skill. In M.M. Gruneberg and P.E. Morris (eds) *Applied Problems in Memory.* London: Academic Press.

Annett, J. (1982) Action, language and imagination. In L. Wankel and R.B. Wilberg (eds) *Psychology of Sport and Motor Behaviour: Research and Practice*. Edmonton: University of Alberta Department of Physical Education and Leisure Studies.

Annett, J. (1985) Motor learning: A review. In H. Heuer, U. Kleinbeck and K.-U. Schmidt, *Motor Behaviour: Programming, Control and Acquisition*. Berlin: Springer.

Annett, J. (1986) On knowing how to do things. In H. Heuer and C. Fromm, *Generation and Modulation of Action Patterns*. Berlin: Springer.

Annett, J. (1988a) Motor learning and retention. In M.M. Gruneberg, P.E. Morris and R.N. Sykes (eds) *Practical Aspects of Memory: Current Research and Issues. Volume 2: Clinical and Educational Implications*. Chichester: Wiley. Also in J. Patrick and K. D. Duncan (eds) *Training, Human Decision Making and Control*. Amsterdam: North-Holland.

Annett, J. (1988b) Imagery and skill acquisition. In M. Denis, J. Engelkamp and J.T.E. Richardson (eds) *Cognitive and Neuropsychological Approaches to Mental Imagery*. Dordrecht: Martinus Nijhoff.

Annett, J., Annett, M.E., Hudson, P.T.W. and Turner, A. (1979) The control of movement in the preferred and non-preferred hands. *Quarterly Journal of Experimental Psychology, 31*, 641–652.

Annett, J., Duncan K.D., Stammers, R.B. and Gray, M.J. (1971) *Task Analysis*. Department of Employment Training Information Paper 6. London: HMSO.

Annett, J., Golby, C.W. and Kay, H. (1958) The measurement of elements in an assembly task – the information output of the human motor system. *Quarterly Journal of Experimental Psychology, 10*, 1–11.

Annett, J. and Kay, H. (1956) Skilled performance. *Occupational Psychology, 30*, 112–117.

Annett, J. and Kay, H. (1957) Knowledge of results and skilled performance. *Occupational Psychology, 31*, 69–79.

Annett, J. and Sparrow, J. (1985). Transfer of training: A review of research and practical implications. *Programmed Learning and Educational Technology, 22*, 116–124.

Ansbacher, H.L. (1940) On the permanence of college learning. *Journal of Educational Psychology, 31*, 622–624.

Bandura, A. (1977) *Social Learning Theory*. Englewood Cliffs, NJ: Prentice-Hall.

Bartlett, F.C. (1948) The measurement of human skill. *Occupational Psychology, 22*, 31–38 and 83–91.

Bernstein, N. (1967) *The Coordination and Regulation of Movements*. Oxford: Pergamon Press.

Berry, D.C. and Broadbent, D.E. (1984) On the relationship between task performance and associated verbalisable knowledge. *Quarterly Journal of Experimental Psychology, 36A*, 209–231.

Berry, D.C. and Broadbent, D.E. (1987) Explanation and verbalisation in a computer-assisted search task. *Quarterly Journal of Experimental Psychology, 39A*, 585–609.

Berry, D.C. and Broadbent, D.E. (1988) Interactive tasks and the implicit–explicit distinction. *British Journal of Psychology, 79*, 251–272.

Bilodeau, E.A. (1969) Retention under free and stimulated conditions. In E.A. Bilodeau and I. McD. Bilodeau (eds) *Principles of Skill Acquisition*. New York: Academic Press.

Bilodeau, I. McD. (1969) Information feedback. In E.A. Bilodeau and I. McD. Bilodeau (eds) *Principles of Skill Acquisition*. New York: Academic Press.

Bizzi, E. (1980) Central and peripheral mechanisms in motor control. In G.E. Stelmach and J. Requin (eds) *Tutorials in Motor Behavior*. Amsterdam: North-Holland.

Bizzi, E. (1988) Theoretical and experimental approaches to motor control. Bartlett Lecture, Experimental Psychology Society, Edinburgh, 1988. Unpublished.

Book, W.F. (1908) *The Psychology of Skill: with special reference to its acquisition in typewriting*. University of Montana Publications in Psychology, Bulletin No. 53, Psychological Series No. 1.

Broadbent, D.E. (1958) *Perception and Communication*. London: Pergamon Press.

Brooks, V.B. (1986) *The Neural Basis of Motor Control*. Oxford: Oxford University Press.

Brown, D.R., Briggs, G.E. and Naylor, J.C. (1963) *The retention of discrete and continuous tasks as a function of interim practice with modified tasks*. Technical Documentary Report No. 63–35. Wright-Patterson Airforce Base, Ohio: Aerospace Medical Research Laboratories.

Brown, A.L. and Campione, J.C. (1986) Training for transfer: Guidelines for promoting flexible use of trained skills. In M.G. Wade (ed) *Motor Skill Acquisition of the Metally Handicapped*. Amsterdam: North-Holland.

Bryan, W.L. and Harter, N. (1897) Studies in the physiology and psychology of the telegraphic language. *Psychological Review, 4*, 27–53.

Bryan, W.L. and Harter, N. (1899) Studies in the telegraphic language: The acquisition of a hierarchy of habits. *Psychological Review, 6*, 345–375.

Burwitz, L. (1981) The use of demonstrations and video-tape recorders in sport and physical education. In I.M. Cockerill and W.W. McGillivary (eds) *Vision and Sport*. Cheltenham: Stanley Thornes.

Chipman, S.F., Segal, J.W. and Glaser, R. (eds) (1985) *Thinking and Learning Skills. Volume 2: Research and Open Questions*. Hillsborough: Lawrence Erlbaum.

Cohen, N.J. and Squire, L.R. (1980) Preserved learning and retention of pattern analysing skill in amnesia: Dissociation of knowing how and knowing that. *Science, 210*, 207–210.

Colley, A.M. and Beech, J.R. (1989) *Cognition and Action in Skilled Behaviour*. Amsterdam: Elsevier Science Publishers.

Cooper, L.A. and Shepard, R.N. (1973) Chronometric studies of the rotation of mental images. In W.G. Chase (ed.) *Visual Information Processing*. New York: Academic Press.

Corkin, S. (1968) Acquisition of motor skills after bilateral medial temporal lobe excision. *Neuropsychologia, 6*, 255-265.

Craik, K.J.W. (1947) Theory of the human operator in control systems. 1. The operator as an engineering system. *British Journal of Psychology, 38*, 56–61.

Crossman, E.R.F.W. (1959) A theory of the acquisition of speed skill. *Ergonomics, 2*, 153–166.

Cutting, J.E. (1978) Generation of synthetic male and female walkers through the manipulation of a biomechanical invariant. *Perception, 7,* 393–405.

Cutting, J.E. and Proffitt, D.R. (1982) The minimum principle and the perception of absolute, common and relative motion. *Cognitive Psychology, 14,* 211–286.

Donders, F.C. (1868) On the speed of mental processes. Reprinted in W.G. Koster (ed.) (1969) *Attention and Performance II, Acta Psychologica 30,* 412–431.

Downs, S. and Perry, P. (1984) *Developing Skilled Learners: Learning to Learn in the YTS.* Sheffield: Manpower Services Commission R&D No. 22.

Downs, S. and Perry, P. (1987) *Developing Skilled Learners: Helping Adults to Become Better Learners.* Sheffield: MSC R&D No. 40.

Doyle, A.J.R. (1988) The essential human contribution to bicycle riding. In J. Patrick and K.D. Duncan (eds) *Training, Decision Making and Control.* Amsterdam: North-Holland.

Evarts, E.V. (1973) Motor cortex reflexes associated with learned movement. *Science, 179,* 501–504.

Fitts, P.M. (1954) The information capacity of the human motor system in controlling the amplitude of movement. *Journal of Experimental Psychology, 47,* 381–391.

Fitts, P.M. (1964) Perceptual motor skill learning. In A.W. Melton (ed) *Categories of Human Learning.* New York: Academic Press.

Fitts, P.E. and Jones, R.E. (1947a) Analysis of factors contributing to 460 'pilot error' experiences in operating aircraft controls. Report TSEAA–694–12, Air Material Command, Wright-Patterson Air Force Base, Dayton Ohio. Reprinted in W. H. Sinaiko (ed) (1961) *Selected Papers in Human Factors in the Design and Use of Control Systems.* New York: Dover.

Fitts, P.M. and Jones, R.E. (1947b) Psychological aspects of instrument display. 1: Analysis of 270 'pilot error' experiences in reading and interpreting aircraft instruments. Report TSEAA–694–12A, Air Material Command, Wright-Patterson Air Force Base, Dayton Ohio. Reprinted in W.H. Sinaiko (ed) (1961) *Selected Papers in Human Factors in the Design and Use of Control Systems.* New York: Dover.

Flavell, J.H. and Wellman, H.M. (1971) Metamemory. In R.V. Kail and J.W. Hagen (eds) *Perspectives in the Development of Memory and Cognition.* Hillsdale, NJ: Lawrence Erlbaum.

Fotheringhame, J. (1984) Transfer of training: A field investigation. *Occupational Psychology, 57,* 239–248.

Geschwind, N. and Kaplan, E. (1962) A human cerebral disconnection syndrome. *Neurology, 12,* 675–685.

Glencross, D.J. (1978) *Psychology and Sport.* Sydney: McGraw-Hill.

Goodall, J. van L. (1963) *In the Shadow of Man.* London: Collins.

Goodstein, L.P., Andersen, L.P. and Olsen, S.E. (1988) *Tasks, Errors and Mental Models.* London: Taylor & Francis.

Held, R. and Freedman, S.J. (1963) Plasticity in human sensori-motor control. *Science, 142,* 455–462.

Held, R. and Hein, A. (1958) Adaptation of disarranged hand–eye coordination contingent upon reafferent stimulation. *Perceptual and Motor Skills, 8,* 87–90.

Heuer, H. and Fromm, C. (eds) (1986) *Generation and Modulation of Action Patterns*. Berlin: Springer.

Hick, W.E. (1952) On the rate of gain of information. *Quarterly Journal of Experimental Psychology*, 4, 11–26.

Hick, W.E. and Bates, J.A.V. (1950) *The Human Operator of Control Mechanisms*. Ministry of Supply Permanent Records of Research and Development. No. 17–204.

Hill, L.B. (1957) A second quarter-century of delayed recall or relearning at eighty. *Journal of Educational Psychology*, 48, 65–68.

Holst, E. von, and Mittelstädt, H. (1950) Das Reafferenzprinzip. Wechselwirkung zwischen Zentralnervensystem und Peripherie. *Naturwissenschaften*, 37, 464–476. (Translated by R.D. Martin as 'The reafference principle. Interaction between the central nervous system and the periphery'. In C.R. Gallistel (1980) *The Organisation of Action*. Hillsdale, NJ: Lawrence Erlbaum.

Imwold, C.H. and Hoffman, S.J. (1983) Visual recognition of a gymnastic skill by experienced and inexperienced instructors. *Research Quarterly for Sport and Exercise Sciences*, 54, 149–155.

Jeannerod, M. (1988) *The Neural and Behavioural Organization of Goal-Directed Movements*. Oxford: Oxford University Press.

Johansson, G. (1973) Visual perception of biological motion and a model for its analysis. *Perception and Psychophysics*, 14, 201–211.

Kawai, M. (1965) Newly acquired precultural behavior in the natural troupe of Japanese monkeys on Koshima islet. *Primates*, 6, 1–30.

Keele, S.W. (1975) The representation of motor programs. In P.M.A. Rabbitt and S. Dornic (eds) *Attention and Performance, Volume V*. New York: Academic Press.

Lahey, M.F.L. (1941) Permanence of retention of first-year algebra. *Journal of Educational Psychology*, 32, 401–413.

Lashley, K.S. (1917) The accuracy of movement in the absence of excitation from the moving organ. *American Journal of Physiology*, 43, 169–194.

Laszlo, J.I. (1966) The performance of simple motor task with kinaesthetic sense loss. *Quarterly Journal of Experimental Psychology*, 18, 1–8.

Laszlo, J.I. (1967) Kinaesthetic and exteroceptive information in the performance of motor skills. *Physiology and Behavior*, 2, 359–365.

Leavitt, H.J. and Schlosberg, H. (1944) The retention of verbal and motor skills. *Journal of Experimental Psychology*, 34, 404–417.

Lee, D.N. (1986) Gearing action to the environment. In H. Heuer and C. Fromm (eds) *Generation and Modulation of Action Patterns*. Berlin: Springer.

Lee, D.N., Lishman, J.R. and Thomson, J.A. (1982) Regulation of gait in long jumping. *Journal of Experimental Psychology: Human Perception and Performance*, 8, 448–459.

Lee, D.N. and Young, D.S. (1987) Training children in road-crossing skills using a roadside simulation. *Accident Analysis and Prevention*, 19, 327–341.

Mackay, D.G. (1982) The problem of flexibility, fluency and speed–accuracy trade-off in skilled behavior. *Psychological Review*, 89, 483–506.

Magill, R.A. (1985) *Motor Learning: Concepts and Applications*. Dutuque, Iowa: Wm C. Brown.

Marler, P. (1970) Birdsong and speech development: Could there be parallels? *American Scientist*, 58, 699–673.

Meijer, O.G. and Roth, K. (1988) *Complex Movement Behaviour: The 'Motor-Action' Controversy*. Amsterdam: North-Holland.

Meltzoff, A.N. and Moore, M.K. (1977) Imitation of facial and manual gestures. *Science, 198*, 75–80.

Mengelkoch, R.F., Adams, J.A. and Gainer, C.A. (1971) The forgetting of instrument flying skills as a function of the level of initial proficiency. *Human Factors, 13*, 397–405.

Miller, G.A., Galanter, E. and Pribram, K. (1960) *Plans and the Structure of Behavior*. New York: Holt, Reinhart & Winston.

Mowbray, G.H. and Rhoades, M.V. (1959) On the reduction of choice-reaction times with practice. *Quarterly Journal of Experimental Psychology, 11*, 16–23.

Neisser, U. (1976) *Cognition and Reality*. San Francisco: W.H. Freeman.

Neisser, U. (1985) The role of invariant structures in the control of movement. In M. Frese and J. Sabini (eds) *Goal-Directed Behavior: The Concept of Action in Psychology*. Hillsdale, NJ: Lawrence Erlbaum.

Newell, A. and Rosenbloom, P.S. (1981) Mechanisms of skill acquisition and the law of practice. In J.R. Anderson (ed) *Cognitive Skills and their Acquisition*. Hillsdale, NJ: Lawrence Erlbaum.

Newell, K.M. and McGinnis, P.M. (1985) Kinematic information feedback for skilled performance. *Human Learning, 4*, 39–56.

Osgood, J. (1949) The similarity paradox in human learning. *Psychological Review, 47*, 419–427.

Paillard, J. (1982) Apraxia and the neurophysiology of motor control. *Philosophical Transactions of the Royal Society of London, B298*, 111–134.

Patrick, J. and Duncan, K.D. (1988) *Training, Human Decision Making and Control*. Amsterdam: North-Holland.

Posner, M.I. (1978) *Chronometric Explorations of Mind*. Hillsdale, NJ: Lawrence Erlbaum.

Prinz, W. (1986) Modes of linkage between perception and action. In W. Prinz and A.F. Sanders (eds) *Cognition and Motor Processes*. Berlin: Springer.

Prinz, W. and Sanders, A.F. (eds) (1984) *Cognition and Motor Processes*. Berlin: Springer.

Reason, J. (1980) Actions not as planned: The price of automatisation. In R. Stevens and G. Underwood (eds) *Aspects of Consciousness*. London: Academic Press.

Roland, P.E., Larsen, B., Lassen, N.A. and Skinhoj, E. (1980) Supplementary motor area and other cortical areas in organization of voluntary movements in man. *Journal of Neurophysiology, 43*, 118–136.

Roland, P.E., Skinhoj, E., Lassen, N.A. and Larsen, B. (1980) Different cortical areas in man in organization of voluntary movements in extrapersonal space. *Journal of Neurophysiology, 43*, 137–150.

Rosenbaum, D.A. (1985) Motor programming: A review and scheduling theory. In H. Heuer, U. Kleinbeck and K.-H. Schmidt (eds) *Motor Behavior: Programming, Control and Acquisition*. Berlin: Springer.

Rosenbaum, D.A., Kenny, S. and Derr, M.A. (1983) Hierarchical control of rapid movement sequences. *Journal of Experimental Psychology: Human Perception and Performance, 9*, 86–102.

Roy, E.A. (ed) (1985) *Neuropsychological Studies of Apraxia and Related Disorders*. Amsterdam: North-Holland.

Rumelhart, D.E. and Norman, D.A. (1982) Simulating a skilled typist. A study of skilled cognitive-motor performance. *Cognitive Science, 6,* 1–36.

Salmoni, A.W., Schmidt, R.A. and Walter, C.B. (1984) Knowledge of results and motor learning: A review and critical appraisal. *Psychological Bulletin, 95,* 355–386.

Schmidt, R.A. (1975) A schema theory of discrete motor skill learning. *Psychological Review, 82,* 225–260.

Schmidt, R.A. (1988) Motor and action perspectives on motor behavior. In O.G. Meijer and K. Roth (eds) *Complex Movement Behavior: The 'Motor-Action' Controversy.* Amsterdam: North-Holland.

Scully, M. and Newell, K.M. (1985) Observational learning and the acquisition of motor skills: Towards a visual perception perspective. *Journal of Human Movement Studies, 11,* 168–186.

Segal, J.W., Chipman, S.F. and Glaser, R. (1985) *Thinking and Learning Skills, Volume 1: Relating Instruction to Research.* Hillsdale, NJ: Lawrence Erlbaum.

Seibel, R. (1963) Discrimination reaction time for a 1,023-alternative task. *Journal of Experimental Psychology, 66,* 215–226.

Shaffer, L.H. (1980) Analysing piano performance: A study of concert pianists. In G.E. Stelmach and J. Requin (eds) *Tutorials in Motor Behavior.* Amsterdam: North-Holland.

Shaffer, L.H. (1981) Performances of Chopin, Bach and Bartok: Studies in motor programming. *Cognitive Psychology, 13,* 326–376.

Shapiro, D.C. and Schmidt, R.A. (1982) The schema theory: Recent evidence and developmental implications. In J.A.S. Kelso and J. E. Clark (eds) *The Development of Movement Control and Coordination.* New York: Wiley.

Shepard, R.N. and Cooper, L.A. (1982) *Mental Images and their Transformations.* Cambridge, Mass.: MIT Press.

Shepherd, A. (1985) Hierarchical task analysis and training decisions. *Programmed Learning and Educational Technology, 22,* 162–176.

Smith, K.U. (1962) *Delayed Sensory Feedback and Behavior.* Philadelphia: Saunders.

Smith, K.U. and Smith, W.M. (1962) *Perception and Motion: An Analysis of Space-Structured Behavior.* Philadelphia: Saunders.

Smyth, M.M. (1984) Memory for movements. In M.M. Smyth and A.M. Wing (eds) *The Psychology of Human Movement.* London: Academic Press.

Snoddy, G.S. (1926) Learning and stability. *Journal of Applied Psychology, 10,* 1–36.

Spelke, E., Hirst, E. and Neisser, U. (1976) Skills of divided attention. *Cognition, 4,* 215–230.

Sternberg, S. (1969) The discovery of processing stages: An extension of Donders' method. In W.G. Koster (ed) *Attention and Performance II, Acta Psychologica, 30,* 276–315.

Sternberg, S., Monsell, S.L., Knoll, R.L. and Wright, C.E. (1978) The latency and duration of rapid movement sequences: Comparisons of speech and typewriting. In G.E. Stelmach (ed) *Information Processing in Motor Control and Learning.* New York: Academic Press.

Summers, J.J. (1981) Motor programs. In D.H. Holding (ed) *Human Skills.* Chichester: Wiley.

Swift, E.J. (1906) Memory of skilful movements. *Psychological Bulletin, 3,* 185–187.

Swift, E.J. (1910) Relearning a skilful act: An experimental study of neuromuscular memory. *Psychological Bulletin, 7,* 17–19.

Taub, E. and Berman, A.J. (1968) Movement and learning in the absence of sensory feedback. In S. J. Freedman (ed) *The Neuropsychology of Spatially Oriented Behavior.* Homewood, Ill.: Dorsey.

Thorndike, E.L. and Woodworth, R.S. (1901) The influence of improvement in one essential function on the efficiency of other functions. *Psychological Review, 8,* 247–261.

Vredenbregt, J. and Koster, W.G. (1971) Analysis and synthesis of handwriting. *Philips Technical Review, 32,* 73–78.

Wade, M.G. (ed) (1986) *Motor Skill Acquisition of the Mentally Handicapped.* Amsterdam: North-Holland.

Wade, M.G. and Whiting, H.T.A. (eds) (1986) *Motor Development in Children: Aspects of Coordination and Control.* Dordrecht: Martinus Nijhoff.

Wadman, W.J., Denier van der Gon, J.J., Geuze, R.H. and Moll, C.R. (1979) Control of fast goal-directed arm movements. *Journal of Human Movement Studies, 5,* 3–17.

Weimer, W.B. (1977) A conceptual framework for cognitive psychology: Motor theories of the mind. In R. Shaw and J. Bransford (eds) *Perceiving, Acting and Knowing: Towards an Ecological Psychology.* Hillsdale, NJ: Lawrence Erlbaum.

Welford, A.T. (1976) *Skilled Performance: Perceptual and Motor Skills.* Glenview, Ill.: Scott, Foresman & Co.

Whiting, H.T.A., Bijlard, M.J. and den Brinker, B.P.L.M. (1987) The effect of the availability of a dynamic model on the acquisition of a complex cyclical action. *Quarterly Journal of Experimental Psychology, 39A,* 43–59.

Whiting, H.T.A. and Wade, M.G. (eds) (1986) *Themes in Motor Development.* Dordrecht: Martinus Nijhoff.

Wing, A.M. (1984) Disorders of movement. In M. M. Smyth and A. M. Wing (eds) *The Psychology of Human Movement.* London: Academic Press.

Woodworth, R.S. (1938) *Experimental Psychology.* London: Methuen.

NON-VERBAL COMMUNICATION
Peter Bull

THE CONCEPT OF NON-VERBAL COMMUNICATION

For an area of study which has become so popular, the definition of 'non-verbal communication' is surprisingly vague. If the term 'verbal' is taken as meaning only the actual words used, then non-verbal communication can refer to vocal features such as intonation, stress, speech rate, accent and loudness. It can also refer to facial movement, gaze, pupil size, body movement and interpersonal distance. It can refer as well to communication through touch or smell, through various kinds of artefacts such as masks and clothes, or through formalized communication systems such as semaphore. Because the term 'non-verbal' is a definition only by exclusion, the number of features of human communication which can be included within this rubric are virtually limitless.

However, in this review I intend to focus discussion on one aspect of human non-verbal communication – that of bodily movement. The reasons for this are both practical and conceptual. The sheer range of phenomena embraced by the term 'non-verbal communication' is so vast that to do justice to the subject some degree of specialization is necessary. At the same time, the features which can be included under the term 'body movement' do constitute a separate and distinctive form of communication. The term refers, in effect, to communication through visible forms of body movement – through movements of the facial muscles, the eyes, the pupils and the limbs, and movements of the body in relation to other people.

The definition of what behaviours constitute communication presents even more problems. Ekman and Friesen (1969a) argued that only those non-verbal behaviours which are *intended* to be communicative can be regarded as forms of non-verbal communication. A radically different view stems from the work of Watzlawick *et al.*

(1968), who dismiss intentionality as totally irrelevant; they argue that, since all behaviour conveys information, all behaviour can be seen as communication. Consequently, according to this view, all behaviour defined as non-verbal can be regarded as non-verbal communication; for example, the man in the passenger compartment of a train who looks straight ahead, avoiding the gaze of the other passengers, can be said to be communicating just as much as if he were talking to them, since those nearby usually 'get the message' and leave him alone.

Both these views of communication were challenged in an important theoretical paper by Wiener *et al.* (1972), who criticized the view that all behaviour can be seen as communicative on the grounds that a basic and necessary distinction should be made between signs and communication. Signs, they maintain, imply only an observer making an inference from or assigning significance to an event or a behaviour; in contrast, communication implies a socially shared signal system or code through which an encoder makes something public which is responded to systematically and appropriately by a decoder. Hence, in these terms, it needs to be shown that information is both transmitted and received through non-verbal behaviour if it is to be regarded as non-verbal communication. Wiener *et al.* also challenge the view that the only non-verbal behaviours which can be regarded as communicative are those which are intended as such, arguing that it is often difficult to establish exactly what a person does intend to communicate. If only those behaviours which a person *says* are intended to communicate are defined as communicative, then there is no problem; but once it is acknowledged that a person may be mistaken, deceitful, or simply unaware of his or her intentions, Wiener *et al.* maintain, there is no basis in the behaviours themselves for deciding whether or not they should be regarded as intentional communications.

It is also my own view that neither intention to communicate nor awareness of the significance of specific non-verbal cues are necessary for regarding communication as having taken place (Bull, 1987). Communication may take place without any conscious intention to communicate, or indeed, even against the best intentions of the encoder. For example, in one series of studies, I found that boredom is systematically associated with leaning back, dropping the head, supporting the head on one hand and stretching the legs. A person in an audience may show these behaviours, without any conscious intention to communicate that he is bored; nevertheless, this may well be the message the speaker receives! The person in the audience may even seek to suppress these tell-tale cues of boredom by trying hard to appear attentive, but still be incapable of stifling the occasional yawn. To the speaker, he may still communicate that he is bored, despite his best intentions not to do so (Bull, 1987).

Nor is it my view that awareness of non-verbal cues is necessary for them to be regarded as communicative, in the sense that neither encoder nor decoder need be able to identify the specific non-verbal cues through which a particular message is transmitted. So, for example, people may be left with the feeling that someone was upset or angry without being able to state precisely what behaviour was responsible for creating that impression. Indeed, it can be argued that a great deal of non-verbal communication takes this form, and that a primary task of the researcher is to try and identify in more detail the cues which underlie such perceptions.

However, this is not to argue that all non-verbal behaviour is communicative, and this is where the encoding/decoding distinction is of importance. Communication requires both encoding and decoding, but encoding can take place without decoding, while decoding can itself be inaccurate. These distinctions imply three different kinds of status for non-verbal cues.

First, if an emotion, for example, is encoded by particular non-verbal cues, but is not decoded appropriately by other people, then this suggests that non-verbal cues may be a valuable source of information about others which is generally neglected. This kind of approach has been particularly associated with some psychoanalysts; for example, Deutsch (1947) described how one female patient held her hands under her neck when fearful of being punished for masturbation, lifted her right hand and held her left hand protectively over her head when she was angry with men, and lifted both arms when she was angry with both parents. Deutsch argued that an awareness of postural expression is of great value to the psycho-analyst in providing clues to psychodynamics, and to the patient in allowing awareness of repressed feelings through the analyst's interpretation of the particular postures adopted. According to this view, non-verbal cues are significant not because they constitute a generalized system of communication, but as a source of valuable information which only a skilled perceiver can learn to understand through careful observation. The same kind of assumption can also be seen to underlie the popular literature on 'body language' (for example, Fast, 1970), which seeks to instruct people on tell-tale signs, for example, of sexual availability.

A second possibility is that non-verbal cues are commonly

perceived as conveying meanings which they do not in fact possess (decoding errors); in this case, their social significance will be quite different. They might in fact be of considerable social importance, but in the sense that they lead people to make erroneous attributions about others, and possibly to act upon those mistakes. For example, it is commonly assumed that non-verbal cues tell us a great deal about personality, but empirical research has provided little support for this belief (for example, Bull, 1983, pp. 79–87); this may well be an example of a decoding error. Research has also shown substantial individual differences in people's ability to decode non-verbal cues (for example, Rosenthal *et al.*, 1979), so that the extent to which these cues operate as a communication system will vary substantially according to the perceptiveness of the decoder. In fact, many studies of non-verbal cues have relied upon decoding designs alone; there is a real danger that, in the absence of satisfactory encoding studies, the evidence obtained from decoding alone may be quite misleading. For example, decoder judgements of emotional expressions may reflect popular stereotypes of their significance rather than an accurate representation of the way in which emotions are actually expressed.

The third possibility is, of course, that non-verbal cues may be both encoded and decoded appropriately, and that in this case their significance lies in their role as a means of communication. The importance of the preceding discussion is that the social significance of non-verbal behaviour does not necessarily lie in communication. For this reason, the encoding/decoding distinction always needs to be considered in evaluating research on non-verbal behaviour, and as such it formed the basis of my previous review of the non-verbal communication literature (Bull, 1983).

THE ROLE OF NON-VERBAL CUES IN
SOCIAL INTERACTION

Non-verbal cues can be said to communicate information about emotion, speech, individual differences and interpersonal relationships; their significance also needs to be considered in specific social contexts (Bull, 1983).

(i) Emotion

Particular importance is commonly ascribed to non-verbal cues in the communication of emotion, stemming from the observations of

Charles Darwin (1872), who argued that the facial expressions of emotion constitute part of an innate, adaptive, physiological response. Evidence relevant to the innate hypothesis can be summarized as follows. First, there are the results of cross-cultural studies (for example, Ekman *et al.*, 1972), which show that facial expressions associated with six emotions (happiness, sadness, anger, fear, disgust, surprise) are decoded in the same way by members of both literate and pre-literate cultures. However, as Ekman (1973) acknowledges, the demonstration of universals in decoding does not necessarily prove that the facial expressions of emotion are inherited; it simply increases the probability that this explanation is valid. The only hypothesis necessary to account for universal decoding in facial expression is that whatever is responsible for common facial expressions is constant for all humankind; thus, common inheritance is one such factor, but common learning experiences could equally well be another.

Second, there is the evidence from the study of children born deaf and blind. The ethologist Eibl-Eibesfeldt (1973) has filmed a number of such children, and claims that they show the same kinds of basic facial expression in appropriate situational contexts as do children born without such handicaps. Again, a likely explanation for these observations is that such expressions are inherited, but it is still possible that they may be learned through some form of behaviour shaping.

Third, there is evidence from studies of non-handicapped children which shows that the facial musculature is fully formed and functional at birth. Oster and Ekman (1977), using Ekman and Friesen's (1978) Facial Action Coding System, have shown that all but one of the discrete muscle actions visible in the adult can be identified in newborn infants, both full-term and premature. Again, however, this does not prove that the association of particular facial expressions with particular emotions is innate. Smiling can be called a universal gesture in the sense that it is an expression which human beings are universally capable of producing, but this does not mean that it is innately associated with the emotion of happiness, nor that it has a universal meaning.

Thus, although the evidence is consistent with the innate hypothesis, it is by no means conclusive. Nevertheless, if the hypothesis is accepted as valid, then it suggests that facial expression is of particular importance in communicating information about certain emotions. However, this is not to imply that all facial expressions of emotion are innate. The learned and innate aspects of emotional expression have been neatly reconciled by Ekman (1972) in what he calls his neuro-cultural model, according to which he assumes the existence of at least six fundamental emotions with innate expressions which can be modified through the learning of what he calls display rules; display rules refer to norms governing the expression of emotions in different contexts, and may take the form of attenuation, amplification, substitution or concealment of particular expressions.

The proposal that facial expressions of emotion may be both innate and learned has important implications for the significance which we ascribe to facial expression (Bull, 1984). For example, it means that no simple answer is possible to the question of the relative importance of different cues in communicating information about emotion, since it may depend on whether we are discussing deliberate or spontaneous expressions. Ekman and Friesen (1969b) describe what they call 'non-verbal leakage', whereby information about deception is revealed more through body movement than facial expression; they argue that, because of the greater repertoire of facial movement, people may be more careful to control their faces when trying to deceive others, and hence are more likely to give themselves away inadvertently through bodily movements. But if we are comparing different types of spontaneous expression, it still seems likely that the face constitutes the prime non-verbal source of information about emotion. Facial muscle changes are rapid; the face is usually clearly visible; and there are at least six universal expressions probably innately associated with different emotions. The eyes and the pupils lack the variety of facial movement and are also less easily discernible. It has yet to be shown that pupil dilation or gaze enable us to distinguish between different emotions; they probably convey information about intensity of emotion rather than the nature of emotion as such (Bull, 1983, pp. 2–9, 43–46). The evidence on posture and gesture is much less clear-cut, since it is possible to distinguish between emotions and attitudes on the basis of posture alone (Bull, 1987).

(ii) Body movement and speech

The prime importance of non-verbal cues in the communication of emotion has led some writers to regard body movement as an alternative system to speech, offering a more reliable indicator of people's feelings. This has been especially true of the popular literature on 'body language', in which it seems to be suggested that non-verbal communication represents a kind of 'royal road to the unconscious', providing a vital source of information about people's 'real' feelings and attitudes. For example, Fast (1970) maintains that body language conveys an emotional message to the outside world which is more reliable than the spoken word: 'if the spoken language is stripped away and the only communication left is body language, the truth will find some way of poking through' (p.92).

One particular danger of this viewpoint is that it neglects the extent to which speech and body movement complement one another in communication; indeed, it may be the case that incidences in which non-verbal communication conflicts with speech are the exception rather than the rule. For example, Condon and Ogston (1966) described on the basis of a frame-by-frame analysis how the body of the speaker moves closely in time with his speech, a phenomenon which they called self-synchrony. Condon and Ogston's observations were not simply confined to hand gestures; it was movements of all parts of the body which they found to be closely synchronized with speech. At the same time, it does not appear to be the case that every bodily movement is related to discourse. Freedman and Hoffman (1967) claimed from a study of psychotherapy sessions that it was essentially non-contact hand movements (movements which do not involve touching the body) which are related to speech. In a quite different context (that of political speech-making), Bull (1986) also found that it was primarily non-contact rather than contact hand movements which were related to vocal stress.

Non-verbal behaviour has been shown to be related to speech in terms of syntax (Lindenfeld, 1971), vocal stress (Pittenger *et al.*, 1960) and meaning (Scheflen, 1964, 1973). Lindenfeld investigated the relationship between body movement and syntax by analysing the speech of a patient in a psychotherapy session. She took observations of the number of postural shifts, leg movements and foot movements, and noted whether or not they coincided with syntactic boundaries. A movement was scored as coinciding with syntax if it took place within the duration of one clause, and as not coinciding with syntax if it took place across more than one clause. Lindenfeld found that most of the body movements she observed fell within syntactic boundaries, and hence concluded that body movement is closely related to syntax.

Discourse has a discernible structure based on strings of words which seem to be spoken as a unit. This unit was identified by Trager and Smith (1951) and named the phonemic clause or tone group. The phonemic clause consists of a group of words, averaging five in length, in which there is only one primary (or tonic) stress indicated by changes in pitch, rhythm or loudness, and which is terminated by a juncture, where these changes in pitch, rhythm and loudness level off before the beginning of the next phonemic clause. Pittenger *et al.* (1960) observed that most speakers of American English accompany their primary stresses with slight jerks of the head or hand. Scheflen (1964) notes Birdwhistell's demonstration that junctures are accompanied by a movement of the head, eyes or hands. Bull and Connelly (1985) found in a study of informal conversation that over 90 per cent of tonic stresses were accompanied by body movements; these were not only movements of the head or hands, but also trunk movements and movements of the legs and feet. In a study of political speeches (Bull, 1986), I found that a large proportion of the speakers' hand movements were related to vocal stress. I also found that repeated movements, where for example the speaker extends and flexes the forearm two or more times in sequence, always occurred within the duration of a tone group and never violated tone group boundaries. These repeated movements seemed to serve a dual function: they both pick out stressed words and demarcate the extent of the tone group.

Scheflen (1964, 1973) maintained that posture is related to structural units larger than the phonemic clause. He discusses three such units – the point, the position and the presentation. Scheflen maintains that the speaker changes the position of his head and eyes every few sentences; this attitude is held for a few sentences, and then shifted to another position. Each of these shifts, according to Scheflen, marks the end of a structural unit in discourse at the next level higher than the syntactic sentence (just as the paragraph represents a higher unit than the sentence in text). He calls the unit a 'point', because it corresponds roughly to a point made in a discussion. A sequence of several points goes to make up a 'position', which corresponds roughly to a point of view that a person might take in a conversation; the position is marked by a gross postural shift involving at least half the body. The largest unit Scheflen employs is the 'presentation', which consists of the totality of one person's positions in a given interaction. Presentations may last from several minutes to several hours, and are terminated by a complete change in location.

Scheflen's observations find some support in a study by Kendon (1972), who carried out a detailed analysis of a film of a conversation in a London pub. Kendon found that the trunk and leg movements of one speaker occurred only with changes of what he called a 'locution cluster'; this refers to a change in what the speaker is talking about, and appears to be very similar to Scheflen's concept of the position. Bull (1987) found that two BBC television newsreaders both made use of particular hand movements when moving on to a new item of news, thus clearly marking out topic changes in the broadcast through specific changes in posture. Bull and Brown (1977) carried out a study of informal conversation, in which they found that speech which introduced new information was significantly more likely to be accompanied by certain changes in posture than speech which was less informative. This is consistent with Scheflen's concept of a 'programme', according to which new stages in social interaction are indicated by postural markers.

It has also been argued that non-verbal behaviour serves a variety of functions in relation to speech which can be divided, according to Ekman and Friesen (1969a), into emblems, illustrators and regulators. The term 'emblem' they derived from Efron (1941), to refer to those non-verbal acts which have a direct translation, such as nodding the head when meaning 'Yes', or shaking the head when meaning 'No'; their function is communicative and explicitly recognized as such. Emblems are generally assumed to be specific to particular cultures or occupations, but there do appear to be pan-cultural emblems such as the 'eyebrow flash', where a person raises his eyebrows for about a sixth of a second as a greeting; Eibl-Eibesfeldt (1972) claims to have observed this in many different cultures. Morris *et al.* (1979) mapped the geographical distribution of 20 emblems across western and southern Europe and the Mediterranean. Their findings showed that, whereas some emblems were specific to one culture, others showed a high degree of generality across cultures. For example, an emblem which they call the cheek-screw, in which a straightened forefinger is pressed against the centre of the cheek and rotated, is a gesture of praise in Italy; it is little known elsewhere in Europe. Another gesture which they call the nose-thumb, in which the thumb touches the tip of the nose with the fingers pointing upwards spread out in a fan, is widely known throughout Europe as a form of mockery. The meaning of other emblems varies between cultures. For example, a gesture which Morris *et al.* call the ring, where the thumb and forefinger touch to form a circle, means in Britain that something is good, in parts of France that something is worthless, while in Sardinia it is an obscene sexual insult! Ekman and Friesen argue that the particular importance of emblems stems from the fact that they are often used when speech is difficult or impossible, and hence function as an alternative system to speech. For example, the policeman directing traffic or the deaf-and-dumb person using sign language can both be said to be using emblems in situations where speech is not possible. A number of the emblems described by Morris *et al.* are insults; the advantage of insulting people at a distance is presumably that it is more difficult for the insulted person to retaliate!

Illustrators are movements which are directly tied to speech, and it is maintained by Ekman and Friesen that they facilitate communication by amplifying and elaborating the verbal content of the message. Whether illustrators do in fact facilitate communication was tested in an experiment by Rogers (1978). Rogers prepared a silent film of various actions being performed, such as a car making a series of turns. Observers were asked to view these actions and to describe them to another person who was unable to see the film. These descriptions were videotaped and played back to a second group of observers in three ways: with sound and vision, with sound only, or in a modified audio-visual condition where the contrast was reduced to obliterate facial information and hence prevent lip-reading. Comprehension was found to be significantly better in the modified audio-visual condition than in the audio condition only, which suggests that illustrators do facilitate speech comprehension independently of the information obtained from lip-reading.

Regulators are movements which are assumed to guide and control the flow of conversation, influencing both who is to speak and how much is said. The most intensive set of studies of turn-taking has been carried out by Duncan and his associates (for example, Duncan, 1972; Duncan and Niederehe, 1974; Duncan and Fiske, 1977). Duncan found that attempts by the listener to take over the turn could be effectively prevented by the speaker continuing to gesture; Duncan called this the attempt-suppressing signal. His observations also showed that ceasing to gesture was one of six turn-yielding cues, signals that offer a speaking turn to the other person. Duncan maintained that the effect of these six cues is additive: his observations showed a linear relationship between the number of turn-yielding cues displayed and a smooth switch between speakers. The other cues were the completion of a grammatical clause, a rise or fall in pitch at the end of a clause, a drawl on the final syllable, stereotyped expressions such as 'but uh' and 'you know', and a drop in pitch or loudness associated with one of these stereotyped expressions. (Subsequently, however, Duncan and Fiske (1985) have omitted drop in pitch or loudness associated with stereotyped expressions from their list of turn-yielding cues.)

Ekman and Friesen's threefold distinction between emblems,

illustrators and regulators is useful in that it serves to highlight some of the different functions of gesture in relation to speech. However, a major implication of their typology is that gesture is essentially secondary to speech, either serving as a substitute form of communication when speech is difficult or impossible, or serving to support the spoken message. An alternative view stems from Kendon (1985), who points out that gesture, as a silent, visual mode of expression, has very different properties from those of speech, and consequently that it is suitable for a different range of communication tasks. Thus, gesture may be useful when speech is difficult or impossible because of noise or distance. Gesture may be used to comment on an interaction without interrupting the flow of speech. This may be done cooperatively or critically, so that the commentator does not have to take a speaking turn. Gesture may be used to make comments 'en passant', to avoid entering into focused interaction. Some things may be too delicate to put into words and so are better left unsaid: gesture may be preferred to communicate this kind of information. The value of Kendon's analysis is the emphasis that he places on the distinctive properties of gesture: because it is a silent, visual medium, it is particularly useful for conveying certain kinds of information. In fact, Kendon maintains that gesture is as fundamental as speech for the representation of meaning, that it is separate, in principle equal with speech, and joined with speech only because it is used simultaneously for the same purpose (Kendon, 1983).

(iii) Individual differences

An extensive literature has also developed on individual differences in both the encoding and decoding of non-verbal behaviour. With regard to encoding, non-verbal cues not only encode information about individual differences, but there are also individual differences concerning the extent to which people transmit information through non-verbal cues: some people may transmit a great deal through these cues, others relatively little (Bull, 1985). For example, Hall (1979) reviewed 26 studies in which comparisons were made of sex differences in encoding – nine showed a significant gender difference, and eight showed that women were clearer encoders. Hence, in this sense, women can be seen as more expressive; that is, they transmit more information through non-verbal cues. Men and women also differ in the kinds of non-verbal behaviour they use. A recent review of the literature by Hall (1984) showed a number of consistent non-verbal sex differences. Women both smile more and gaze more at other people; they prefer closer interpersonal distances and are approached more closely than men; they also use smaller and less open body movements and positions. Given that people can make quite subtle judgements about the sex-role attitudes of others on the basis of their non-verbal behaviour alone (Lippa, 1978), it can be argued that such behaviours can be used as a code for communicating information about masculinity and feminity (Bull, 1985). Thus, individual differences in encoding may be important not only in that people may differ in the extent to which they transmit information through non-verbal cues, but also in that the non-verbal cues they do employ may encode significant information about aspects of personality.

Individual differences in decoding constitute a second important theoretical issue. A number of studies have been carried out to investigate whether groups differ in their decoding ability, whether, for example, women are superior to men in this respect, or whether psychiatric patients are disadvantaged in comparison to the normal population. An extensive body of research has been carried out by Rosenthal et al. (1979), based on a test of decoding non-verbal cues called the Profile of Non-Verbal Sensitivity (PONS); results using the PONS show a number of significant effects due to age, sex, culture and psychopathology. The importance of these findings with regard to the communicative status of non-verbal behaviour is that, although non-verbal cues may encode information about, say, emotion, speech or individual differences, such information may not always be accurately decoded; if certain groups of people fail to decode non-verbal cues appropriately, then the significance of those cues as a form of communication must inevitably vary according to the sensitivity of the decoders.

(iv) Interpersonal relationships

Non-verbal behaviour also varies as a function of the relationships between people. A number of experiments have been carried out in which observers are asked to make judgements about the identity of an unseen conversational partner on the basis of viewing the non-verbal behaviour of one of the conversationalists alone. For example, Benjamin and Creider (1975) showed that observers were able to perform this task successfully in terms of the age, sex and acquaintanceship of the unseen conversational partner. Studies by Abramovitch (Abramovitch, 1977; Abramovitch and Daly, 1979) have shown that even very young children are capable of accurately discerning the relationship between people from non-verbal cues alone. Benjamin and Creider also identified certain differences in facial expression which varied according to the type of relationship. When adults talked to children, their muscle tonus was low, the skin beneath the eyes and over the cheek bones hanging loosely down except during broad smiles, whereas when adults talked to other adults, their skin was bunched and raised. There also appear to be significant differences in the activity rate between same-age and different-age conversations, conversations between people of the same age appearing to be much more animated. These studies show both that non-verbal behaviour varies according to the nature of the relationship, and that decoders can utilize such information to discern the relationship between people in terms of sex, age and acquaintanceship.

Scheflen (1964) claimed that posture can tell us a great deal about social relationships. He argued that similarity of posture (called postural congruence) indicates similarity of views or roles in the group; conversely, non-congruence of posture is used to indicate marked divergences in attitude or status. A number of quantitative studies have been carried out to test Scheflen's observations that postural congruence is indicative of rapport, and hence may be regarded as encoding designs. However, there have also been studies carried out to investigate how postural congruence is perceived, which may be regarded as decoding designs.

For example, Charny (1966) analysed a film of a psychotherapy session. Charny categorized postures as congruent or non-congruent; he also distinguished between mirror-image congruent postures, where one person's left side is equivalent to the other's right, and identical postures, where right matches right and left matches left. He found that as the interview progressed, there was a significant trend towards spending more time in mirror-congruent postures. He also found that the speech associated with these postures was more positive, concluding that they may be taken as indicative of rapport or relatedness. Identical postures rarely occurred during the session, so were not included in the final analysis.

LaFrance has investigated whether postural congruence is related to rapport in American college seminars. In one study, LaFrance and Broadbent (1976) found a significant positive correlation between mirror-congruent postures and a questionnaire intended to measure rapport; a significant negative correlation between non-congruent postures and rapport; and no significant relationship between identical postures and rapport, although the correlation was positive.

In a second study, LaFrance (1979) measured posture and rapport during the first week (time 1) and the final week (time 2) of a six-week seminar course, to investigate the probable direction of causality between mirror-congruent postures and rapport, using a method of statistical analysis known as the cross-lag panel technique (Kenny, 1975). To use this technique, mirror-congruent postures at time 1 are correlated with rapport at time 2, while rapport at time 1 is correlated with mirror-congruent postures at time 2. The difference between these two correlations can then be used to investigate which of the two variables has causal priority over the other. For example, if postural congruence determines rapport, then the correlation between postural congruence at time 1 and rapport at time 2 should exceed the correlation between rapport at time 1 and postural congruence at time 2. In fact, both correlations were positive and statistically significant, although the results did not show a significant difference between these two correlations; however, the direction of the effect suggested that it is postural congruence which may be influential in establishing rapport.

Thus, for the most part, encoding studies of postural congruence suggest that it is related to rapport. Another way of investigating the phenomenon is to see whether postural congruence is decoded as conveying rapport. For example, Trout and Rosenfeld (1980) set up an experiment to investigate the perception of postural congruence in simulated therapist–client interactions. They arranged for two male American graduate students to play the roles of therapist and client, and to adopt either mirror-congruent or non-congruent postures. Videorecordings of these interactions were shown to judges, although there was no sound-track, and the faces were blocked out of the tape. The results showed that the mirror-congruent postures were rated as indicating significantly more rapport than the non-congruent postures.

Dabbs (1969) investigated how postural congruence would affect the ratings of an interviewee in a simulated interview. He arranged for pairs of American students to interview a confederate of the experimenter who was in fact a trained actor, and had been instructed to mimic the postures and gestures of one student selected randomly by the experimenter from each pair. At the conclusion of the 'interview', the students completed a questionnaire evaluating the confederate. They showed no awareness of the mimicry, nor did the mimicked students rate the confederate as significantly more similar in postures and gestures. But the confederate was evaluated significantly more favourably by the mimicked students; in particular, they considered that he 'thought more like they did', and said that they 'identified' with him. Dabbs made no effort to distinguish between mirror-image and identical postures, although his findings are clearly consistent with Scheflen's observations concerning postural congruence; indeed, they also support LaFrance's hypothesis that the use of postural congruence can be an influential means of establishing rapport.

PRACTICAL APPLICATIONS OF NON-VERBAL COMMUNICATION RESEARCH

There is no doubt that the systematic study of non-verbal behaviour does have considerable practical significance. A particularly important influence has been the social skills model of social interaction, according to which social behaviour can be seen as a kind of motor skill, involving the same kinds of processes as, for example, driving a car or playing a game of tennis (Argyle and Kendon, 1967). The advantage of this approach, Argyle and Kendon maintain, is that we know a great deal about motor skill processes, and consequently can apply ideas and concepts developed in the study of skills to the study of social interaction.

Argyle and Kendon list six processes which they claim are common to motor skills and social performance: distinctive goals, selective perception of cues, central translation processes, motor responses, feedback and corrective action, and the timing of responses. Social performance can be seen as having distinctive goals; for example, an interviewer has the main goal of obtaining information from the interviewee, and sub-goals such as establishing rapport. Selective perception of cues refers to the process whereby individuals pay particular attention to certain types of information which are relevant to achieving their particular objectives. Central translation processes prescribe what to do about any particular piece of information; people learn behavioural strategies with which to respond to certain types of perceptual information. Motor responses refer to the actual social behaviours which are implemented as a consequence of the central translation processes. Feedback and corrective action refers to the ways in which an individual may modify his behaviour in the light of feedback from others; Argyle and Kendon argue that non-verbal cues are a particularly important source of feedback. Finally, the timing of responses is of importance; for example, choosing the right moment to make a point in a group discussion.

One major implication of the social skills model of social interaction is that, if social behaviour is seen as a skill, then it is possible for people to improve their social performance through learning, just as it is possible for them to improve their performance on any other skill. This learning might take the form of a systematic course in social skills training (for example, Trower *et al.*, 1978), or it might be the case that simply reading a book on non-verbal communication may be sufficient to improve the quality of a person's social relationships (as is typically claimed in the popular literature on 'body language').

However, there is no reason why skilled decoding should automatically result in improved social effectiveness. The selective perception of cues has to be transformed through central translation processes into effective motor responses; in terms of the social skills model, it is perfectly possible for someone to be highly perceptive without being able to translate that perceptiveness into appropriate social behaviour. In this sense, the claims of the body language literature should be treated with caution – even if reading such books does substantially change people's social awareness, it will not automatically improve the quality of their social relationships.

Another important qualification on the claims made for the practical advantages of an awareness of 'body language' is the role of social context. The impression is sometimes given that we have only to master the dictionary of 'body language' in order to understand the meaning of subtle non-verbal cues. But non-verbal behaviour is not simply an expression of the individual's biological endowment; it takes place within a social context, and is influenced by the norms which govern behaviour both in the society at large and in particular social situations. Hence, meaning is dependent upon an understanding of context; practical applications of non-verbal communication research must be considered with regard to specific situations and the constraints which operate on people in those situations.

Thus, research on non-verbal behaviour does have considerable practical significance, if it is applied in a sophisticated manner; but it is only too easy to fall into the trap of regarding such research as a panacea for all problems in interpersonal communication – as a kind of hieroglyphics, whose mysteries once deciphered reveal to the skilled observer the subtle intricacies of human relationships in all their infinite variety. Nevertheless, the significance of non-verbal communication should not be underestimated. Research over the past few decades has demonstrated its considerable importance; as a consequence of that research, our concept of what constitutes communication has been substantially enhanced, while a more profound and sophisticated understanding has been acquired of the processes and practice of social interaction.

REFERENCES

Abramovitch, R. (1977) Children's recognition of situational aspects of facial expression. *Child Development, 48,* 459–463.

Abramovitch, R. and Daly, E.M. (1979) Inferring attributes of a situation from the facial expression of peers. *Child Development, 50,* 586–589.

Argyle, M. and Kendon, A. (1967) The experimental analysis of social performance. In L. Berkowitz (ed.) *Advances in Experimental Social Psychology, 3.* New York: Academic Press.

Benjamin, G.R. and Creider, C.A. (1975) Social distinctions in non-verbal behaviour. *Semiotica, 14,* 52–60.

Bull, P.E. (1983) *Body Movement and Interpersonal Communication.* Chichester: Wiley.

Bull, P.E. (1984) The communication of emotion. Paper presented to the Annual Conference of the British Psychological Society, University of Warwick.

Bull, P.E. (1985) Individual differences in non-verbal communication. In B.D. Kirkcaldy (ed.) *Individual Differences in Movement.* Lancaster: MTP Press.

Bull, P.E. (1986) The use of hand gesture in political speeches: Some case studies. *Journal of Language and Social Psychology, 5,* 103–118.

Bull, P.E. (1987) *Posture and Gesture.* Oxford: Pergamon Press.

Bull, P.E. and Brown, R. (1977) The role of postural change in dyadic conversation. *British Journal of Social and Clinical Psychology, 16,* 29–33.

Bull, P.E. and Connelly, G. (1985) Body movement and emphasis in speech. *Journal of Nonverbal Behaviour, 9,* 169–187.

Charny, E.J. (1966) Psychosomatic manifestations of rapport in psycho-therapy. *Psychosomatic Medicine, 28,* 305–315.

Condon, W.S. and Ogston, W.D. (1966) Sound film analysis of normal and pathological behaviour patterns. *Journal of Nervous and Mental Disease, 143,* 338–347.

Dabbs, J.M. (1969) Similarity of gestures and interpersonal influence. *Proceedings of the 77th Annual Convention of the American Psychological Association, 4,* 337–338.

Darwin, C. (1872) *The Expression of the Emotions in Man and Animals.* London: Murray.

Deutsch, F. (1947) Analysis of postural behaviour. *Psychoanalytic Quarterly, 16,* 195–213.

Duncan, S. (1972) Some signals and rules for taking speaking turns in conversations. *Journal of Personality and Social Psychology, 23,* 283–292.

Duncan, S. and Fiske, D.W. (1977) *Face-to-Face Interaction: Research, Methods and Theory.* Hillsdale, NJ: Lawrence Erlbaum.

Duncan, S. and Fiske, D.W. (1985) *Interaction Structure and Strategy.* New York: Cambridge University Press.

Duncan, S. and Niederehe, G. (1974) On signalling that it's your turn to speak. *Journal of Experimental Social Psychology, 10,* 234–247.

Efron, D. (1941) *Gesture and Environment.* New York: King's Crown Press. (Current ed.: *Gesture, Race and Culture.* The Hague: Mouton, 1972.)

Eibl-Eibesfeldt, I. (1972) Similarities and differences between cultures in expressive movements. In R.A. Hinde (ed.), *Non-Verbal Communication.* Cambridge: Cambridge University Press.

Eibl-Eibesfeldt, I. (1973) The expressive behaviour of the deaf-and-blind born. In M. von Cranach and I. Vine (eds) *Social Communication and Movement.* London: Academic Press.

Ekman, P. (1972) Universal and cultural differences in facial expression of emotion. In J.R. Cole (ed.) *Nebraska Symposium on Motivation, 1971.* Lincoln, Nebraska: University of Nebraska Press.

Ekman, P. (1973) Cross-cultural studies of facial expression. In P. Ekman (ed.) *Darwin and Facial Expression.* New York: Academic Press.

Ekman, P. and Friesen, W.V. (1969a) The repertoire of nonverbal behaviour: Categories, origins, usage and coding. *Semiotica, 1,* 49–98.

Ekman, P. and Friesen, W.V. (1969b) Non-verbal leakage and clues to deception. *Psychiatry, 32,* 88–106.

Ekman, P. and Friesen, W.V. (1978) *Facial Action Coding System.* Palo Alto: Consulting Psychologists Press.

Ekman, P., Friesen, W.V. and Ellsworth, P. (1972) *Emotion in the Human Face: Guidelines for Research and an Integration of Findings.* New York: Pergamon.

Fast, J. (1970) *Body Language.* New York: Evans.

Freedman, N. and Hoffman, S.P. (1967) Kinetic behaviour in altered clinical states: Approach to objective analysis of motor behaviour during clinical interviews. *Perceptual and Motor Skills, 24,* 527–539.

Hall, J.A. (1979) Gender, gender roles and non-verbal communication skills. In R. Rosenthal (ed.) *Skill in Non-Verbal Communication: Individual Differences.* Cambridge, Ma: Oelgeschlager, Gunn and Hain.

Hall, J.A. (1984) *Nonverbal Sex Differences: Communication Accuracy and Expressive Style.* Baltimore: Johns Hopkins University Press.

Kendon, A. (1972) Some relationships between body motion and speech. In A.W. Siegman and B. Pope (eds) *Studies in Dyadic Communication.* New York: Pergamon.

Kendon, A. (1983) Gesture and speech: How they interact. In J.M. Wiemann and R.P. Harrison (eds) *Nonverbal Interaction.* Beverly Hills, Ca: Sage.

Kendon, A. (1985) Some uses of gesture. In O. Tannen and M. Saville-Troike (eds) *Perspectives on Silence.* New Jersey: Ablex.

Kenny, D.A. (1975) Cross-lagged panel correlation: A test for spuriousness. *Psychological Bulletin, 82,* 887–903.

LaFrance, M. (1979) Non-verbal synchrony and rapport: Analysis by the cross-lag panel technique. *Social Psychology Quarterly, 42,* 66–70.

LaFrance, M. and Broadbent, M. (1976) Group rapport: Posture sharing as a non-verbal indicator. *Group and Organisation Studies, 1,* 328–333.

Lindenfeld, J. (1971) Verbal and non-verbal elements in discourse. *Semiotica, 3,* 223–233.

Lippa, R. (1978) The naive perception of masculinity–femininity on the basis of expressive cues. *Journal of Research in Personality, 12,* 1–14.

Morris, D., Collett, P., Marsh, P. and O'Shaughnessy, M. (1979) *Gestures: Their Origins and Distribution*. London: Jonathan Cape.

Oster, H. and Ekman, P. (1977) Facial behaviour in child development. In A. Collins (ed.) *Minnesota Symposium on Child Psychology, Vol 11*. Minneapolis: Minnesota University Press.

Pittenger, R.E., Hockett, C.F. and Danehy, J.J. (1960) *The First Five Minutes: A Sample of Microscopic Interview Analysis*. Ithaca, NY: Martineau.

Rogers, W.T. (1978) The contribution of kinesic illustrators toward the comprehension of verbal behaviour within utterances. *Human Communication Research, 5*, 54–62.

Rosenthal, R., Hall, J.A., DiMatteo, M.R., Rogers, P.L. and Archer, D. (1979) *Sensitivity to Non-Verbal Communication: The PONS Test*. Baltimore: Johns Hopkins University Press.

Scheflen, A.E. (1964) The significance of posture in communication systems. *Psychiatry, 27*, 316–331.

Scheflen, A.E. (1973) *Communicational Structure: Analysis of a Psychotherapy Transaction*. Bloomington: Indiana University Press.

Trager, G.L. and Smith, H.L. Jr (1951) *An Outline of English Structure*. Studies in Linguistics: Occasional Papers, 3. Norman, Okla.: Battenberg Press. (Republished: New York: American Council of Learned Societies, 1965.)

Trout, D.L. and Rosenfeld, H.M. (1980) The effect of postural lean and body congruence on the judgement of psychotherapeutic rapport. *Journal of Nonverbal Behaviour, 4*, 176–190.

Trower, P., Bryant, B. and Argyle, M. (1978) *Social Skills and Mental Health*. London: Methuen.

Watzlawick, P., Beavin, J.H. and Jackson, D.D. (1968) *Pragmatics of Human Communication*. Faber & Faber.

Wiener, M., Devoe, S., Robinson, S. and Geller, J. (1972) Nonverbal behaviour and nonverbal communication. *Psychological Review, 79*, 185–214.

DISCOURSE ANALYSIS
Mansur Lalljee and Sue Widdicombe

Nineteen eighty-five saw the publication of a set of four volumes of the *Handbook of Discourse Analysis*, edited by Teun van Dijk. The first volume, which is sub-titled *Disciplines of Discourse*, includes chapters from the wide variety of perspectives that contribute to 'discourse analysis'. These include linguistics, artificial intelligence, philosophy, anthropology and sociology as well as various aspects of psychology. Van Dijk suggests that discourse analysis is potentially an interdisciplinary area, although it has not yet emerged as a unified field. At present it is marked by a wide diversity of theoretical orientations, methods and problems.

Propp's work on the structure of folktales (Propp, 1958, originally published 1928) is heralded by van Dijk as the seminal text in the recent history of discourse analysis. Work subsequent to its appearance was dominated by structuralist ideas and primarily concerned with the analysis of myths and folktales and with textual material. The 1960s, however, saw the beginnings of the influence of Austin's work on speech acts on philosophy, linguistics and psychology. It also marked the beginning of the analysis of everyday speech by anthropologists such as Dell Hymes and conversation analysts like Harvey Sacks. This emphasis was in marked contrast to the formal grammatical models being worked upon at the time under the dominating influence of Chomsky's linguistics.

Social psychologists have generally ignored language (though there are important exceptions; see Fraser and Scherer, 1982). In 1954, the first edition of Gardner Lindzey's *Handbook of Social Psychology* was published and further editions, edited by Lindzey and Aronson, were published in 1969 and 1985. Handbooks provide exhaustive summaries of the state of the art and point to directions for future work. They are generally seen as milestones in the development of the subject – though they occasionally serve as tombstones as well! The

1954 *Handbook of Social Psychology* has a chapter on the young discipline of 'psycholinguistics' but little space is given to the consideration of psychological processes, and none to social ones. This situation was slightly amended in the second edition 15 years later with the inclusion of a section on 'social psycholinguistics' in the equivalent chapter. The third edition of the *Handbook*, however, carries a substantial chapter by Clark entitled 'Language Use and Language Users'. Clark points out that there have been great advances in the understanding of language from an essentially individualistic perspective, but that the social foundations of language – and the study of language in interaction – have largely been ignored, particularly by social psychologists. Indeed much of the work Clark reviews comes from philosophy, linguistics, anthropology and sociology. Clark stresses the view that talk should be seen as cooperative communicative activity and studied as an interest in its own right, not as a source of information about something else. This general theme forms the basis for the present chapter. Interestingly, such a view of language is closer to the view proposed in an earlier *Handbook of Social Psychology* published in 1935, edited by Carl Murchison.

It is beyond the competence of the present authors and the scope of the present chapter to provide the reader with even the briefest overview of the various themes that pass under the general banner of discourse analysis. We write as social psychologists interested in talk, and this orientation has guided our choice of material. Rather than attempt to deal in detail with one approach or issue, we have tried to incorporate a diversity of ideas and methods that we think are of particular relevance for social psychology. After providing a cursory view of some of Austin's ideas concerning speech acts, the chapter will look at some recent work on discourse and consider its implications for the concept of attitude. We will then describe some of the research on conversation analysis and on categories in talk and end by discussing some of the theoretical and methodological ways in which such analyses differ from those that are generally preferred in social psychology.

SPEECH ACTS

Social psychologists have usually distinguished between talk and behaviour. Talk is usually 'just talk' or 'mere talk'. Behaviour is real. It's what people DO. Behaviour is what we really want to understand.

Talk may give us some insight into a person's inner state, but that smacks of introspectionism; and we are all familiar with the limitations of that! But is language essentially to be seen as a way of making statements, either about our inner states or more generally about the world, that are true or false? Is the distinction between talk and behaviour really a satisfactory one? Developments in philosophy over the last few decades have contributed to a fundamental change in attitude towards language which has crucial relevance for social psychology. This change is generally associated with the ideas of J.L. Austin, who was Professor of Moral Philosophy at Oxford. We will explore some of Austin's ideas and look at the way in which they have changed the focus of our understanding of language.

Consider the following sentences:

A   It is raining.
B   The earth is round.
C   Mary is Jo's sister.

Compare them with these:

D   I promise I will return your book tomorrow.
E   I bet England will win the next Test match.
F   I now pronounce you man and wife.

One difference between sentences *A–C* and sentences *D–F* is that the former make propositions about the world that are true or false. Analyses of the truth conditions of propositions have been a dominant philosophical concern for a long time. The latter group seem to be different. They do not seem to be making assertions about the world in anything like the same sense. They seem to be changing the world in some way – they seem to be doing things themselves.

Austin elaborated these ideas in an influential series of the prestigious William James lectures at Harvard University which were published, in 1962, under the title *How To Do Things With Words*. In these lectures, Austin elaborated on the properties of such sentences. After considering possible differences between these apparently different types of utterance, Austin concluded that 'doing things' is not simply a property of a small restricted class of utterance, but that all utterances 'do things'. In *A–C* above, the speaker is making an *assertion* about the state of the weather, about the shape of the earth, and about the relationship between Mary and Jo. Austin also distinguished between the act performed (warning, questioning, accusing, stating or whatever) and the effects of the act on other people. Warning someone may, for example, have the effect of making the person aggressive or uncooperative; or asserting that 'the world is round' may lead to reactions of incredulity. It is the former of these, the act being performed rather than its consequences, to which the term *speech act* usually refers.

Austin's ideas marked a major departure from conventional ways of considering language. Language, it seems, is a way of doing things: a way of giving verdicts, ordering, warning, advising, apologizing, challenging and so forth. If we agree that these are crucially important SOCIAL acts, then it is clear that social psychologists must pay more attention to language. Maybe we can discover what people are trying to achieve during social interaction through the analysis of their speech acts. Perhaps speech acts can form the cornerstone of our understanding of social interaction.

How, then, do we know what social act is being performed by a particular utterance? One candidate for the stuff of which the bridge between language and social action may be built has been grammar. Perhaps different grammatical features may map on to speech act categories – the interrogative grammatical form on to questions, for instance. But even this apparently simple suggestion is fraught with difficulties. We can ask questions without using the interrogative, and we can use the interrogative without asking a question. Consider the following example from Schegloff (1984, p. 31):

(1) *A1:* Why don't you <u>come</u> and see me some ⌐times
     B1:   ⌐I would
         like to
     A2: I would like you to. Lemme ⌐just
     B2:   └I don't know just
         where the-us-this address <u>is</u>.

Here, the first utterance is not seen as a question, nor is it responded to as one in *B1*. If *B* had got *A*'s intended interpretation wrong, this may have been evident from the subsequent interaction, where *A* might engage in repair work. *B2*, on the other hand, sounds like a question (and *A* later provides the relevant directions). Schegloff and his conversation analysis colleagues look to the interaction and, in particular, to the previous conversational context as indicators of whether an utterance is a question or an assertion, and to the responses within the interaction to see if the interpretations are correct, that is, whether they are shared by the participants. Moreover it is not even obvious that terms such as 'I promise' or 'I bet' are typically used in the way implied at the beginning of this section. Take, for example:

G. I promise he left an hour ago.
H. I bet that's all there was to it.

The first is clearly not a promise in the sense of a commitment to future action; and the second may be more a way of ending a particular topic of conversation rather than offering a bet. Schegloff and his colleagues have warned that the use of examples and utterances in isolation leads to a misguided view of the nature of conversation.

Even though we may not be able to say how people put utterances into speech act categories, and a grammatical approach to this question seems highly inadequate, in everyday talk we readily interpret what people say as questioning, advising, warning and so on. Conversations seem to be coherent and well-ordered events. After all, greetings are generally followed by greetings, requests with acceptances or refusal, and questions with answers. Labov and Fanshel (1977, p. 2) provide the following example:

(2) A: What is your name?
     B: Well, let's say you might have thought you had something from before, but you haven't got it anymore.
     A: I'm going to call you Dean.

This extract of a conversation between a doctor and a schizophrenic patient seems to support the view that there are rules, which perhaps the mental patient is not following, which underlie the orderly nature of conversation. The analogy is with sentence grammar, where particular classes of words are expected to occur in certain positions with regard to other words. Just as linguists and psychologists have attempted to understand the structure of a sentence, perhaps discourse analysts can write the grammar of conversation.

Several attempts have been made to explore this issue using the notion of speech acts. For instance, Labov and Fanshel have proposed that if *A* 'Challenges' *B*, then *B* has essentially three options (at least in the context of psychotherapy): to 'Defend', 'Admit' or 'Huff', after which *A* can either 'Retreat' or 'Mitigate'. However, when they actually analyse 15 minutes of an interview between a patient and a therapist, they find that life is considerably more complex than that.

Levinson (1983) has pointed out that there are many fundamental difficulties with any attempt to understand the sequential nature of conversation simply in terms of the relationships between speech act categories. Besides the difficulties in specifying how many speech acts there are, and how to map utterances on to speech acts, it is also the case that an utterance may perform several speech acts. For instance, 'Would you like a cup of coffee?' may be an offer as well as a suggestion concerning greater intimacy. This makes the business of writing sequencing rules for the interrelationship between speech acts a much more complex affair.

There are also other difficulties. *B*'s response to *A*'s speech act may be a function of its effect. If, at a party, *A* says to *B*, 'It's getting late', *B*'s response may depend not just on what speech act *A* is performing (a 'Suggestion' perhaps), but on the effects of such a Suggestion on *B*. If *B* becomes concerned, the reply might be, 'Aren't you enjoying yourself?', while if *B* becomes irritated, the reply might be 'Don't be such a stick-in-the-mud'. The point is that the relations being described are no longer solely relations between speech acts. There are a vast range of possible effects of a particular act, which a theory solely based on speech acts cannot take into account.

Further, as Levinson and others have pointed out, contextual information can generally disambiguate apparently incoherent conversational sequences. He cites the following example (p. 292):

(3) *A:* I have a fourteen year old son
     B: Well that's all right
     C: I also have a dog
     D: Oh I'm sorry

This apparently bizarre sequence (which he quotes from a lecture by Harvey Sacks) makes perfectly good sense when you know that it is in the context of renting an apartment.

Finally, the speech act performed by a particular utterance is not just an abstract label that can be imposed without consideration of the *subsequent* events in the conversation. What makes an utterance a question, for instance, may be the way in which it is dealt with in the interaction. It is a joint product of the participants. Thus, the possibility of writing general sequencing rules of conversation based on speech acts has been shown to be fundamentally inadequate, and it is to other orientations that we must look in order to investigate the coherence of conversation. This issue is taken up again in the section on 'Conversation Analysis'.

ATTITUDE TALK

The work reported in this section follows Austin in that it takes talk as social activity that is of interest in its own right rather than as an index of something else. We will contrast this approach with one of the dominant traditional concepts in the social psychological literature – that of attitudes.

The concept of attitude has been one of the central concepts of social psychology. In the post-war history of the concept, an 'attitude' has generally been seen as an internal predisposition to respond in an evaluatively positive or negative way towards a class of objects. Attitudes are thus seen as 'internal' factors that cause behaviour. They are usually measured through questionnaire items or through interviews where respondents are asked to indicate the extent of their agreement with a range of statements about the attitude object. The traditional goal of attitude measurement has been to locate each respondent's attitude towards a given entity on a bipolar dimension of favourableness. Though this concept has been seen as a cornerstone of social psychology, the traditionally poor prediction of behaviour from attitude measures has led to considerable disappointment, and attempts to reconceptualize the concept have been made. (It should be noted in passing that there have also been various other moves in order to clarify the relationship between attitudes and behaviour, but these are not relevant to our present concerns.) Rather than see attitudes as internal predispositions, Lalljee *et al.* (1984) propose they should be seen as communicative acts. Thus, statements such as 'I approve (or disapprove) of persons of type *x*' would be the clearest statements of attitude towards that group. They argue that the proper study of attitudes should be concerned with the way attitudes are displayed and maintained through talk.

Van Dijk (1987) reports details of a study on racist talk in Holland. From the interviews that he and his colleagues conducted with white Dutch people, he suggests that such talk attempts to express negative attitudes about minority groups while at the same time rebutting the charge of racism. Take the following example from an interview with a woman whose son cannot get an apartment:

(4)   And those foreigners they take people with them when coming
      back from their vacation, also the children of other people, and
      they get a house right away, you know, and many Blacks, not
      because they are Blacks of course, I have never disliked them,
      NOW I do. Now I dislike them very much, I live here. Just for fun

you have to come and live here for a week when we move, but then you shouldn't sleep at night. (p. 295)

Van Dijk suggests that the following strategic moves are discernible in the statement above:

Credibility-enhancing moves: reports of own experience in detail and an appeal to the interviewer to try it for himself to establish the validity of the facts.

Positive self-presentation: denial of racist motives and showing 'good reasons' for disliking blacks; own group presented as victims of unfair competition.

Negative other-presentation: the description of negative and perhaps illegal behaviour of the other group.

The message sent is: 'I'm not prejudiced, but anyone can see the facts about the negative characteristics of the minority group'.

The display of attitudes towards minority groups is also explored by Wetherell and Potter (1988) who stress the variability of such talk and the inadequacy of conceptualizing its range in terms of a single bipolar evaluative dimension. They report interviews carried out with white European New Zealanders concerning their attitudes towards Maori culture and its role in the school system. Rather than attempting to assess their respondents' attitudes towards this issue, and then attempting to predict what their respondents would 'do' when faced, for instance, with a petition about support for, or opposition to, more money being spent on fostering Maori culture in schools, Wetherell and Potter analyse the various types of response that people make to these issues, and suggest that they use three main repertoires:

(i) **Culture fostering**: This includes the idea that Maori culture should be encouraged because of its own particular character- istics and also because of the importance of the sense of identity which it encourages in the Maori people. Broadly it sounds like a repertoire that supports multiculturalism. For instance:

(5) I'm certainly in favour of a bit of Maoritanga it is something uniquely New Zealand. I guess I'm very conservation minded and in the same way as I don't like seeing a species go out of existence I don't like seeing a culture and a language and everything else fade out. (p. 179)

(ii) **Pragmatic realism**: This emphasizes the importance of keeping up with the modern world and equipping people to succeed in it. For instance:

(6) I actually object to um them bringing um massive Maori culture curricula into schools etcetera . . . because I do feel that this doesn't equip them for the modern world at all. (p. 180)

(iii) **Togetherness**: This emphasizes the commonality of people and the artificiality of the distinctions being promoted. This may sound laudable and egalitarian, but it becomes clear that, in this context, the respondents' definition of 'New Zealand' is basically white and European. For instance:

(7) I wish that we could stop thinking about Maori and European and think about New Zealanders and to hell with what colour people are. (p. 180)

People use more than one repertoire in their talk about Maoritanga. Almost all of them talk in terms of culture fostering, but this was mainly combined with another repertoire, and about 10 per cent of respondents used all three. Thus, the charge of racism can be rebutted by displaying 'culture fostering', while 'pragmatic realism' enables the respondent to oppose change and diffuse Maori protest, and 'togetherness' can be invoked to accuse others of being needlessly divisive.

The concept of repertoire used by Wetherell and Potter derives from the work of Gilbert and Mulkay (1984). In 1979/1980, they interviewed 34 scientists about fundamental changes that had taken place in their discipline. Rather than use the interviews as a way of writing a definitive account of what really happened, Gilbert and Mulkay were interested in the way in which scientists account for their own 'correct' views, and also explain why other eminent members of their discipline got it wrong! They find that one's own correct beliefs were generally explained in terms of what they call the 'empiricist repertoire': an explanation in terms of the facts. Here were a series of experiments that gradually built up the evidence clearly in support of one theory and against the other. But if the facts are so clear-cut, why did not all the scientists working in the field share the same view?

The interviewees explain the false beliefs of their colleagues not in terms of the ambiguity of the data but in terms of what Gilbert and Mulkay call the 'contingent repertoire', that is, in terms of the personal inclinations and social positions of the individuals involved.

They were too pig-headed, too dogmatic, and had vested too much of their egos in the old approach. Incidentally, Gilbert and Mulkay's account fits in nicely with actor–observer differences in attribution – the tendency for actors to explain their own behaviour in terms of the situation while explaining the behaviour of others in terms of the personality of the other. Gilbert and Mulkay's scientists account for the beliefs of others in terms of their personalities, and their own beliefs in terms of the facts – external situational factors. Note, however, that this work on attitude talk does not pay attention to conversation as being a joint coordinated product. Though it provides analysis of the interviewee's talk, there is no account of the interviewer's talk. In the case of Gilbert and Mulkay's scientists, it is crucial to know whether the asymmetrical accounting they report can be explained in terms of the behaviour of the interviewer. Gilbert and Mulkay do raise this question and claim they found no evidence that this was the case. However, the reader might want detailed support for such as assertion.

Gilbert and Mulkay's work illustrates several of the central features of discourse analysis. It takes talk as an area of interest in its own right and sees it as a way of achieving goals, rather than looking at it in terms of an index of reality, or of the person's inner states or whatever. It does not attempt to arrive at a single account by suppressing variability, and it attempts to put the variability into some kind of order. It also raises a whole range of questions concerning the ways in which people seek to establish the validity of their beliefs and opinions. The scientists seem to do it in terms of the empiricist repertoire, the appeal to the facts, and incidentally believe that even though others may dissent because, for instance, of their personalities, in the long run the truth will out. Thus the empiricist repertoire wins in the end. But what about other arenas of social life? What about social and political beliefs? Does the empiricist repertoire reign supreme in those domains or is there a resort to value concepts as the ultimate arbitrator? And religious beliefs? Is the empiricist repertoire relevant at all? Nearly 40 years ago, Leon Festinger (1950) underlined the importance of believing one is correct in one's central beliefs. He noted that relatively few of our important beliefs can be sorted out simply by reference to the facts, that is, those derived from physical reality. He claimed that most of them were validated with reference to the beliefs of others, particularly others of our own group, that is, with reference to social reality. Though the idea of social reality is regularly invoked as an explanatory concept in social psychology, the question how people establish this validity has largely been ignored. Current interest in the analysis of talk may lead to a resurgence of interest in this much neglected issue.

CONVERSATION ANALYSIS

The central theme of the preceding section has been to emphasize the importance of studying talk in its own right and not just as an index of something else. But the investigators referred to show marked differences in their orientation to their data. Van Dijk draws on cognitive and motivational processes that are conventional in social psychology to understand racist talk. Wetherell and Potter emphasize the variability of talk and the functions it fulfils. They claim that discourse analysis offers a non-cognitive orientation to social psychology (Potter and Wetherell, 1987; but see Bowers, 1988, for a critique). Gilbert and Mulkay's account emphasizes the orderliness underlying the variability of discourse. It is primarily descriptive and there is little recourse to cognitive, motivational or functional explanation.

The research reported in the present section is marked by a conceptual and methodological coherence which originates in a series of lectures given by Harvey Sacks between 1964 and 1971. In these lectures, which were transcribed by Gail Jefferson, Sacks argued for three methodological orientations to the study of talk (see Sacks, 1974). First, that ordinary talk is systematically, sequentially and socially organized. Second, that its analysis should be based upon naturally occurring data. Third, that analytic interests should not be constrained by external considerations. Each of these points is worth considering briefly.

First, the idea that ordinary talk is orderly contrasted with the prevailing models of language at that time. For example, Chomsky tried to develop an idealized model of people's competence, or what they *can* do. What they actually *do* in their talk was assumed to be a degenerate version of these idealized models. Sacks argued that *ordinary* talk could be formally described in terms of socially organized, culturally available rules and procedures. It should be studied not as a deviant version of people's competence, but as orderly in its own right. One important way in which talk is organized is on a turn-by-turn basis. Sequences, and turns within sequences, are the primary units of analysis for conversation analysts and *not* isolated utterances. The importance of this observation is twofold. First, as mentioned in the section on speech acts, some utterances derive their character entirely from their sequential placement. The second important aspect of the sequential organization of conversation is that whatever a first speaker says, the recipient must display some understanding of that utterance in his/her next turn. That is, the recipient must display to the first speaker that he or she understood the utterance to be, say, a question which demands an answer. In this way, the first speaker may appreciate that his/her question was understood as a question. Adjacency pairs like question–answer, greeting–greeting and invitation–acceptance/rejection lay strong constraints on next speakers regarding what type of utterance is appropriate next. Even where the appropriateness of a particular next turn is not strongly constrained by the adjacency pair format, it is still necessary for speakers to display some understanding of the prior turn's talk. Cases of ambiguity occur where this process of understanding breaks down. The following (from Schegloff, 1984, p. 28) is an extract from a radio phone-in programme in which a boy (*B*) is complaining about his history teacher's views on the morality of American foreign policy:

(8) *B:* He says, governments, an' you know he keeps –
        he talks about governments, they sh- the thing
        that they sh'd do is what's right or wrong.
    A: For <u>whom</u>.
    B: Well he says – ⌜he
    A: ⌞By what <u>stan</u>dard.
    B: That's what – that's exactly what I mean. he s-
        but he says . . .

In this extract, it is clear that *B* interprets *A*'s initial utterance 'for whom' as a question, to which he begins to provide an answer. This answer is interrupted early on by *A* whose analogous comment, 'By what standard', is a display of agreement with the initial complaint (that right and wrong are relative). In his final utterance, *B* displays his understanding of the nature of *A*'s comment as being one of agreement. Thus, it is through the use of adjacent positioning that appreciations, failures, corrections and so on, can themselves be understandably attempted (Schegloff and Sacks, 1973). Moreover, the observation that a recipient must display some understanding of the prior speaker's talk is a useful analytic resource, not just in cases of ambiguity, but in understanding what is going on in the conversation. Thus, in the following two sequences, *J* is the recipient of information from different co-participants about the recent arrival of furniture:

(9) A: the two beds'v come this morning . the new
         beds. And uh b't on ⌐ly one
     J: └Ih b't that wz quick that
         w'z quick them coming.
     A: Not too bad. B't thez only one mattress with
         it.

(10) I: the things 'ev arrived from Barker 'n
         Stone 'ou ⌐ se
     J: └Oh
         Oh c'n ah c'm round ⌐
     I: └Yes please that's w't I
         wantche tih come round.

While the two 'informings' are rather similar in character, J's subsequent treatment of them shows very different analyses of their implications. She treats the first as the occasion for a comment about the speed with which the beds arrived, and she treats the second as implying that her informant wants her to come and inspect or admire the new furniture by pre-empting a possibly forthcoming invitation. The point is that however a recipient analyses these informings and whatever the conclusion arrived at through this analysis, some conclusion will be displayed in the recipient's next turn at talk (Atkinson and Heritage, 1984). These authors also point out that although a convenient 'intentionalist' language is employed in conversation analytic work, a relatively agnostic stance is taken by workers in this area on the question of how far the speaker consciously aimed at some particular interpretation. A further point to note is that whether an utterance is an invitation or not cannot be predefined according to certain features of that utterance. Rather, invitations and the like are *interactionally constructed*. An invitation is such, in one sense, because that is how it is treated by the recipient, and this interpretation is accepted by the other.

These observations relate to Sacks's second methodological point that the analysis of talk should be based on naturally occurring data. For example, we can only begin to understand what is ambiguous and how it is resolved by seeing how alternative interpretations of an utterance are dealt with by the co-participants. The meaning of the first utterance in extracts 9 and 10 was not ambiguous, whilst in extract 8, 'for whom' was. Thus, all utterances and turns must be analysed and understood within their natural interactional context. Basing an understanding of human interaction on naturally occurring conversation has an important advantage to social psychologists for the simple reason that one can record the *actual* happenings of the conversation. This is in contrast to studying reports of other events, for instance through diaries or interviews, which are of questionable accuracy. Indeed, this was one of Sacks's main motivations in electing to study talk. That is, conversations can be recorded then and there, and they can be transcribed to produce a fairly accurate record of what actually happened. The conversation can then be analysed and reanalysed in the light of new findings. Thus, analysing conversation is one means of understanding human interaction as it actually happens.

The focus on naturally occurring data relates to Sacks's third methodological point, which is that analytic interests should not be constrained by external considerations. To illustrate this point, it is useful to consider how research generally proceeds within social psychology. It begins with the definition of a problem, for example, the conditions under which people act in terms of their group membership. The researcher then goes on to formulate an appropriate method for investigating the problem. Then data are collected, analysed and interpreted as a solution to that problem. Conversation analysis, on the other hand, begins with the talk or data itself. The analyst may first read through transcripts of naturally occurring conversations to identify common patterns in the data. These common patterns are then taken to be a solution to some interactional problem and the analytic question then becomes one of trying to identify the problem.

To take just one example, Paul Drew (1987) found that teases in conversation are not responded to in accordance with the humour of the tease. In many cases, even where recipients of teases do respond by laughing, they do so, almost always, either as a preliminary to, or in the course of, making a serious response. Drew called this phenomenon 'po-faced' receipts of teases. The following example is taken from a dinner-time conversation between members of a family who are being video-recorded:

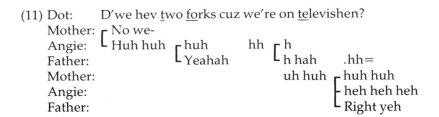

(11) Dot: D'we hev two forks cuz we're on televishen?
Mother: ⌈ No we-
Angie: └ Huh huh ⌈ huh   hh ⌈ h
Father: └ Yeahah   └ h hah   .hh=
Mother: uh huh ⌈ huh huh
Angie: ⊢ heh heh heh
Father: └ Right yeh

```
           pro ⌐bly the answer r't th ⌐re
Angie:         Leh hah hah
Mother:                              Lhhh. You have pie
           You have pie tunight.
```

(From Drew, 1987, p. 221)

In this extract, Mother begins by making a serious response to the tease that two forks are laid simply because of the presence of the video camera. She abandons this response and joins in with the laughter initiated by her other daughter, Angie. On completion of the laughter, and Father's facetious rejoinder to the tease, Mother goes on to complete her po-faced correction with an explanation for the setting of two forks. Mother's laughter indicates that she (or, in general, the recipient of a tease) may recognize the tease and recognize that it is intended as a humorous remark or proposal, but nevertheless respond seriously to it.

As a preliminary, Drew asks what it is about the statement 'D'we hev two forks cuz we're on televishen' that makes it recognizable as a tease. One possibility is that it involves gross exaggeration (that is, 'being on television' contrasted with 'being videoed'). Drew then notes that teases typically follow things like complaining, boasting and so on which have the property of being overdone. They are seconds or responses to such activities which display some scepticism about the teased's claims. In some sense, in rejecting or correcting the tease, recipients counter any scepticism by holding on to the truth or validity of their original claims. However, a further motivation for responding seriously to a tease is that teases attribute some kind of deviant activity or category to the person who is teased. In the example above, the tease-implicated deviant identity is that of being phoney or pretentious, of laying out two forks simply because of the presence of the video camera. The seriousness of the response therefore serves to reject the implied deviant identity. Teases serve a social control function in interaction because they follow overdone activities and, because of their social control function, are likely to be met with resistance through a po-faced receipt.

Conversation analysts, then, look for common patterns or procedures in people's talk which are used for getting certain things done. They are interested in details of how people do things like teasing and what it accomplishes. One aim is to elucidate these common patterns or procedures. And this, of course, relates to the previous point about the orderliness of conversation. Not only is conversation ordered sequentially but there are ways of doing things like teasing which follow an orderly and identifiable pattern which is socially recognizable.

CATEGORIES IN TALK

Categories and attributions of blame and responsibility have been regarded very differently by social psychologists and conversation analysts. To social psychologists, categories are cognitive things, and attributions of blame and responsibility are the result of cognitive and motivational processes. Typically, social psychologists have been interested in the content of categories (for example, the stereotypical attributes associated with a particular category) through the use of adjective checklists. They have also been interested in the consequences of categorization, that is, in the question of what happens when people are categorized in a particular way. These are usually carried out in experimental contexts. To study attributions of blame and responsibility, psychologists have generally presented subjects with brief descriptions of hypothetical events and elicited their responses on rating scales. In this way, hypotheses about the effects of the nature of the person performing an act, or the severity of the consequences on attributions of blame, can be tested. For conversation analysts, on the other hand, categories are commonsense things and blame an interactional accomplishment. They study actual instances of category use and attributions of blame in settings such as courtrooms and police interrogations.

Sacks (1964) describes membership categories as ordinary-language equivalence classes for the description and identification of persons; that is, they are commonsense designations which serve to make reference to persons. Sacks elucidated some conventional procedures which society members use in categorization activities. One procedure is the 'economy rule': A single membership category will serve as adequate reference for one or more persons for practical conversational activities. It may be noted that in describing these as conventional procedures, Sacks is *not* suggesting that they are hard-and-fast rules. As we shall see later, these conventions can be exploited to bring about certain interactional effects. Generally, however, one label is sufficient to refer to a person or group of people in any one context, even though everyone belongs to a potentially infinite number of categories. Consider the following extract, taken from a police interrogation of a white male accused of killing a black male:

(12) P: Why did you shoot at this G . . . ?
     S: He's a nigger.
          (*29 lines omitted*)
     P: Well then did you know that you were shooting
          at G . . . or did you shoot at him just because he
          was coloured period?
     S: He's a nigger.
     P: And that's why you shot him and er.
     S: That's why I shot him.

(Taken from Watson, 1983, p. 44)

In this account, the victim is referenced by a single category, 'nigger'. Watson (1983) points out that in using this label, the suspect is implicitly avowing his motive for the offence. In reasoning about the motive behind an offence, we must categorize both the victim and the offender. In the example above, the use of the term 'nigger' projects the relevance of a second category, 'white person', and enables us to impute a cross-racial motive for the murder.

A further point to note about the above account is how the police officer's reference to the victim as 'coloured' is affirmed by the suspect, except that he uses a different label to describe the victim – 'nigger'. This illustrates an important point about categories which is that they typically bear more than one label. People have a choice between these category labels and it is clear that these labels are not all equivalent; they may be ranked in a hierarchy such that some might ordinarily count as a downgrading and others as an upgrading label. The selection of a downgraded label can work to achieve a debasing reference or some other subordination. Hearers may typically draw inferences about the motivated nature of speakers' selection of one label rather than other candidate labels for a category so as to account for particular deeds committed against members of certain categories. Thus, in changing the label from 'coloured' to 'nigger', the suspect downgrades the victim and this confirms the cross-racial motive behind the murder since it allows hearers to imply that the suspect hates blacks. It is interesting to note, however, that amongst young black males in some ghetto cultures in the USA, 'nigger' is used as an upgrading label, implying solidarity, shared category membership and so on. Thus, the status of utterances and descriptions can only be interpreted within the interactional context in which they occur.

'Black' and 'white' are what Sacks (1972) calls a 'standard relational pair' because, in many interactional contexts, the relevance of one can be inferred from a mention of the other. Relational pairs are one way in which categories are organized. A related mode of organization of membership categories is membership categorization devices. Membership categorization devices are collections of categories. For example, the membership categorization device 'family' contains the categories 'mother', 'father', 'aunt' and so on. Other devices do not have such straightforward labels, such as 'sexual orientation', which may include the categories 'homosexual', 'heterosexual' and 'bisexual'. A procedure which is used in connection with these collections or devices is termed the 'consistency rule' (Sacks, 1974). This procedure is: If two or more categories occurring proximately in a conversational sequence can be heard as coming from the same collection or device, then hear them that way. The consistency rule formulates one principle for the co-selection of membership categories.

Some membership categorization devices have the special property of duplicative organization, that is, they possess a 'team-like' quality. 'Family' and 'members of a gang' may be seen to possess team-like properties of sticking, or acting, together and of ingroup loyalty. Similarly, relational pairs of categories drawn from a duplicatively organized device can also be treated as duplicatively organized (for example, 'brother'–'sister') and, consequently, as sticking together. Derivatively, the invocation of such ingroup loyalties also intensifies the potential for highlighting *dis*loyalty and can therefore be used in accusations, complaints, excuses and other blame negotiations as well as in imputing motive (Watson, 1983). The following provides an example of this. It comes from a police interview of a witness regarding a black male allegedly killing a black female:

(13) Then he turned off the ignition then the one in the back he said 'alright who doing the whoring around here?' Then (S . . .) said well if you want money, I don't have money so the one in the back said we don't want your money, he said we weren't going to be lucky enough to tell what happened and then he said 'we disgusted him everytime one of his black sisters goes to bed with white men and was going to put a stop to it'. He asked (S . . .) again why she went to bed with the white men and she told him she had 3 kids and he said was a God damn liar and punched her in the face and about the body a couple of times. (From Watson, 1983, p. 50)

The pivotal aspect of this account lies in the use of the categories 'white men' and 'black sisters'. 'White' and 'black' form a relational pair and imply some cross-racial motivation in the woman's murder.

The categories 'men' and 'sister' are used to emphasize this motive. 'Sister' comes from the membership categorization device 'family' which, as mentioned above, possesses duplicative organization. The relational pair of 'sister' is 'brother', and the latter category may be seen to apply to the offender. Given that 'sister' and 'brother' belong to the membership categorization device 'family', it follows that one should expect loyalty and 'sticking together' from their members. In sleeping with 'white men', the victim was being disloyal. From this, a recipient can infer that the motive for the offence was the breaking of the loyalty or solidarity that the victim should have had with the racial category of which she is a member. The use of 'sister' in conjunction with 'black' therefore emphasizes or reinforces the victim's and offender's co-membership of the latter categorization, as well as emphasizing the need to stick together. The complex relational pairing of 'white man'–'black sister', then, does a great deal of economical and persuasive work in imputing motive, for it preserves the cross-racial element in the motivation of an offence even if it occurs between members of the same race. At the same time, it disavows one possible candidate motivation, the financial one. Thus, as mentioned above, the economy rule can sometimes be exploited for specific interactional effects.

Sacks also noted that, in ordinary conversation, there are typically a great many references to actions or deeds. Moreover, he observed that some activities (and attributes) are conventionally tied to a membership category (or to a restricted set of categories). Reference can be made to a particular membership category by outlining the activities or attributes conventionally tied to it without the category itself being explicitly mentioned. Similarly, inferences can be made about people and their behaviours on the basis of the membership categorizations used to identify them (Wowk, 1984). This process is illustrated in a study of an account given by the alleged offender of a female's murder (Wowk, 1984). The offender describes the woman's activities in the following ways: 'she propositioned me', 'she asked if I would like to get laid' and 'she called me a prick a no good sonofabitch and threw what was left of a bottle of beer at me'. The recipient can make inferences as to 'what kind of girl' would do this and one available solution is, for example, 'tramp' or 'slut'. In tying these attributes or activities to one particular category (or subset of categories) from the membership categorization device 'moral types of female', society members are making moral assumptions and involved in doing the groundwork for the ascription of motive, blame, innocence, provocation, responsibility and so on. This is important because, in attributing some blame to the victim, the suspect is thereby able to present himself as less blameworthy. In summary, motives are closely bound to categories, relational pairs and to membership categorization devices. Watson (1983), moreover, makes the point that it seems analytically preferable to treat motives as constitutive features of the description of deeds and of accounts 'surrounding' those descriptions rather than as *causes* of action. While this work has highlighted the often subtle and economical ways in which categories and category-bound activities are used in interrogations and courtroom interaction, the study of category use in everyday conversation seems so far to have been neglected.

CONCLUSIONS

Throughout this chapter we have stressed that talk is not 'just talk' but a form of social action and that conversational activities are systematic and orderly enterprises which are the joint products of the participants. From this account, it can be seen that the methodological orientation and style of much work on talk is very different from that of psychology in general. Its prime source of data is conversation – either in naturalistic settings or in interviews – and it eschews experimentation. Its orientation is mainly inductive and data-driven – it avoids hypothesis testing. The emphasis on naturally occurring data contrasts with many of the traditional methods of social psychology. For example, it differs in important ways from the use of interviewing techniques in which verbal reports of the respondents are treated as acceptable surrogates for actual observation. It also contrasts with observational studies in which data are recorded in field notes or through the use of a pre-defined coding schedule. And it differs from the emphasis in much social psychological research on experimentation. In experiments the behaviour of the subject is manipulated or directed by the experimenter. Behavioural variation is limited to those aspects selected for investigation under controlled conditions. It is the experimenter who must determine the relevant dependent and independent variables, and these will tend to be restricted to what the experimenter deems to be important on a theoretical basis.

The orientation underlying the work in this chapter, and the observations that such work has produced, raise important questions for the concepts and methods underlying social psychology. Take, for instance, the concept of attitude and the assumptions underlying attitude measurement. Here, talk has generally been seen as an index of the internal predisposition to respond, and the arbitrary distinction between talk and behaviour accepted. Its measurement ignores the fact that, as we have seen, the very act of asking a question in an interview, or on a questionnaire, implies an answer. The implications of the work reported for our conventional concepts of categorization and on attributing blame have not been clearly worked out. This is hardly surprising given the paucity of work in the area. And it is only after further research that its implications for these concepts will be properly understood and the implications for the theories and methods involved in social psychology properly evaluated.

Studying talk is a way of studying the actual happenings of a phenomenon, and the work described shows how it is possible to study the coherence and systematic nature of talk. Its orientation has been observational and inductive and many of the researchers deny the relevance of cognitive explanations and focus on descriptions of procedures rather than on building predictive models. Its inclusion in social psychology will properly cause debate and controversy. However, the place of such an orientation may not be determined so much by its abstract features, but by the ability of the approach to deliver interesting answers to the sort of issues which absorb social psychologists.

Acknowledgement. We would like to thank Rob Wooffitt for his assistance in preparing this chapter.

Note on transcription notation. This chapter contains a number of extracts of conversation which have been taken from a variety of sources. We have followed whatever notational convention has been used in the various texts.

REFERENCES

Austin, J.L. (1962) *How To Do Things With Words.* Oxford: Oxford University Press.
Atkinson, J.M. and Heritage, J. (1984) *Structures of Social Action: Studies in Conversation Analysis.* Cambridge: Cambridge University Press.
Bowers, J. (1988) Review essay on discourse and social psychology: Beyond attitudes and behaviour. *British Journal of Social Psychology, 27,* 185–192.
Clark, H.H. (1985) Language use and language users. In G. Lindzey and E. Aronson (eds) *Handbook of Social Psychology, Volume 2.* New York: Random House.

Drew, P. (1987) Po-faced receipts of teases. *Linguistics, 25,* 219–253.
Gilbert, G.N. and Mulkay, M. (1984) *Opening Pandora's Box: A Sociological Analysis of Scientists' Discourse.* Cambridge: Cambridge University Press.
Festinger, L. (1950) Informal social communication. *Psychological Review, 57,* 271–282.
Fraser, C. and Scherer, K.R. (1982) *Advances in the Social Psychology of Language.* Cambridge: Cambridge University Press.
Labov, W. and Fanshel, D. (1977) *Therapeutic Discourse: Psychotherapy as Conversation.* New York: Academic Press.
Lalljee, M., Brown, L.B. and Ginsburg, G.P. (1984) Attitudes: Disposition, behaviour or evaluation? *British Journal of Social Psychology, 23,* 233–244.
Levinson, S. (1983) *Pragmatics.* Cambridge: Cambridge University Press.
Lindzey, G. (ed.) (1954) *Handbook of Social Psychology.* Cambridge, Mass.: Addison-Wesley.
Lindzey, G. and Aronson, E. (eds) (1969) *Handbook of Social Psychology.* Cambridge, Mass.: Addison-Wesley.
Lindzey, G. and Aronson, E. (eds) (1985) *Handbook of Social Psychology.* New York: Random House.
Murchison, C. (ed.) (1935) *A Handbook of Social Psychology.* Worcester, Mass.: Clark University Press.
Potter, J. and Wetherell, M. (1987) *Discourse and Social Psychology: Beyond Attitudes and Behaviour.* London: Sage.
Propp, V. (1958) *Morphology of the Folktale.* Bloomington, In.: Indiana University Press. (Original work published 1928.)
Sacks, H. (1964) Unpublished transcribed lectures, University of California, Irvine.
Sacks, H. (1972) An initial investigation of the usability of conversational data for doing sociology. In D. Sudnow (ed.) *Studies in Social Interaction.* London: The Free Press.
Sacks, H. (1974) On the analysability of stories by children. In R. Turner (ed.) *Ethnomethodology.* Harmondsworth: Penguin. (Also published in J.J. Gumperz and D. Hymes (eds) (1972) *Directions in Sociolinguistics.* New York: Holt, Rinehart and Winston.)
Schegloff, E.A. (1984) On some questions and ambiguities in conversation. In J.M. Atkinson and J. Heritage (eds) *Structures of Social Action: Studies in Conversation Analysis.* Cambridge: Cambridge University Press.
Schegloff, E.A. and Sacks, H. (1973) Opening up closings. In R. Turner (ed.) *Ethnomethodology.* Harmondsworth: Penguin.
Van Dijk, T.A. (ed.) (1985) *Handbook of Discourse Analysis.* London: Academic Press.
Van Dijk, T.A. (1987) *Communicating Racism: Ethnic Prejudice in Thought and Action.* Newbury Park, Ca: Sage.
Watson, D.R. (1983) The presentation of victim and motive in discourse: The case of police interrogations and interviews. *Victimology, 8,* 31–52.
Wetherell, M. and Potter, J. (1988) Discourse analysis and the identification of interpretative repertoires. In C. Antaki (ed.) *Analysing Everyday Explanation: A Casebook of Methods.* London: Sage.
Wowk, M. (1984) Blame allocation, sex and gender in a murder interrogation. *Women's Studies International Forum, 7,* 75–82.

KNOWLEDGE REPRESENTATION
John T. E. Richardson

Like many ideas in psychology, the concept of knowledge representation has a long history. Classical philosophical theories about human
memory postulated some persisting 'idea' or 'image' that was
structurally similar to that which is remembered; in the words of
William James (1890, p. 651), remembering involves 'a very complex
representation'. As Malcolm (1977, pp. 127–128, 218) pointed out, this
entity was supposed to be an abstract propositional thought rather
than any literal image, and accounts of this nature were not refuted
by the commonplace observation that remembering frequently occurs
in the absence of any specific mental event. Malcolm also noted that
the concept of memory representation played a similar role in
physiological theories of the memory 'trace', which go back at least to
Aristotle. The principal difference between the two viewpoints is that
the philosophical accounts postulated mental representations in
order to explain how memory could be the source of justified
knowledge claims, whereas the physiological accounts posited neural
states and processes as the hypothetical causes of occurrences of
recognition and remembering (Malcolm, 1977, pp. 167–168).

In contemporary psychological research, theories of human cognition are equally based upon the idea that some sort of internal
representation mediates observable behaviour (Kohlberg, 1969;
Fodor, 1975, p. 9). To a large extent, this is a consequence of the
widespread use of the structure and function of the digital computer
as a metaphor in theorizing about cognitive function; as Fodor (1975,
p. 27) commented, 'Computation presupposes a medium of computation: a representational system'. Fodor (1981, ch. 7) subsequently
argued that any adequate theory of human cognition (or, at least, of
'propositional attitudes' such as believing, thinking, and knowing)
must be expressed in terms of a system of internal representations.
These have semantic properties, and to that extent contemporary

cognitive psychology is 'a revival of the representational theory of mind' (Fodor, 1981, p. 203). They also have causal properties, since they mediate both conscious experience and observable behaviour. In this chapter I shall consider the development and current status of modern thinking on the representation of knowledge. This originated in studies of coding processes and organization within episodic memory and also in research into artificial intelligence, and these will first be briefly reviewed. Theoretical discussions within contemporary research have been concerned with the relative importance of propositional, imaginal, and procedural represent-ations, and with the merits of different conceptualizations of the modular organization of knowledge structures, such as schemata, frames, scripts, cognitive maps, and mental models. These ideas have found application in a number of cognate fields, including anthro-pology, linguistics, and abnormal psychology, and some researchers also refer to knowledge representation when discussing the properties of particular neurophysiological systems in the brain. Nevertheless, I shall conclude by pointing out that there are fundamental conceptual problems in the notions of neural and mental represent-ation which have yet to be adequately addressed.

CODING AND CODING PROCESSES

The notion of coding processes in human cognition was first introduced by Miller (1956a). In his classic paper entitled 'The magical number seven, plus or minus two', Miller argued that the capacity of immediate memory was determined by the number of items to be remembered and not by their informational content. He then showed that the apparent memory span could be increased by grouping the items to be remembered into units or 'chunks', attaching new names to these chunks, and then remembering the new names rather than the original items. Miller commented that 'in the jargon of communication theory, this process would be called *recoding*', and he claimed that 'this process is a very general and important one for psychology. . . . In one form or another we use recoding constantly in our daily behavior' (pp. 93, 95).

This account of human memory differed from traditional associative views in so far as it emphasized the integrated hierarchical organiz-ation of encoded items rather than direct associative connections (Johnson, 1972). Nevertheless, it is important to note that encoding – in the literal sense of *encryption* – is not tantamount to the production of a representation, internal or otherwise. As Jackson (1986, p. 29) has noted, a piece of code preserves any lexical or structural ambiguities that are inherent in the original message. For instance, the sentence 'Visiting relatives can be a nuisance' would be just as ambiguous in an encrypted form as it is in English, and would be no more intelligible than the original message. In contrast, a representation would be expected to provide a perspicuous interpretation of the intended meaning (or, at the least, to distinguish explicitly between the message's alternative interpretations). Conversely, understanding a message written in clear text normally demands no process of encoding or decoding because there is nothing which has been encoded or decoded (Hacker, 1987, p. 496).

Be that as it may, Miller (1956a) went on to argue that 'the most customary kind of recoding that we do all the time is to translate into a verbal code. . . . When we witness some event we want to remember, we make a verbal description of the event and then remember our verbalization' (p. 95; cf. Bower, 1972). It would thus appear that Miller himself was using the word 'code' in an extended sense, in much the same way that researchers in other disciplines talk about 'genetic' or 'chemical' codes (cf. Hacker, 1987, p. 497). One should also note that communications researchers (for example, Hall, 1980) and neuroscientists (cf. Young, 1978, p. 43) sometimes use the term 'decoding' to refer to the extraction of information from a message. In retrospect, it would perhaps have been more appropriate to talk about 'compiling', by analogy with the translation of the statements in a computer program into machine *code* (cf. Fodor, 1975, p. 67). However, researchers in cognitive psychology found Miller's proposals very attractive, so that by the early 1970s it was widely agreed that coding was a central feature of all human information processing. Melton and Martin (1972, pp. xii–xiii) defined the basic principles of this approach:

> The core intent of this idea is that between the external world and a human's memorial representation of that external world there operate certain processes that translate external information into internal inform-ation. . . . The critical determinants of learning and remembering are to be found in the coding response to an experienced event, pair of events, or sequence of events. Further, it is implied that coding responses have their components and structure determined by the preexisting structure of the brain.

These researchers were clearly using the term 'coding' to refer to the generation of 'internal' representations (see Newell, 1972). They were also using it to cover the variety of different operations or transformations that might be carried out upon material which was to be remembered (Bower, 1972; Underwood, 1972). This focus upon coding and coding processes was heuristically interesting and important because it encouraged researchers to investigate the diversity of operations by which information is registered in memory. It also provided a means of conceptualizing the manner in which different events are analysed by the information-processing system, the extent to which different memories interfere with one another, and the effectiveness with which other events act as retrieval cues (Bower, 1972). Nevertheless, the analysis of coding processes in human memory was intrinsically restricted to a linear model of encoding–storage–retrieval (Underwood, 1972). Newell (1972, p. 392) objected that 'it is only in a pure communication system that matters are so simple, where the only use made of the code is to decode it at the other end of the line'. In a real cognitive system, on the other hand, all kinds of processing operations are carried out upon the code itself. In order to handle the rich diversity of human cognition, therefore, this model needs to be elaborated and extended to accommodate the variety of uses of internal representations.

There is a second reason why the literal interpretation of encoding as encryption is of limited value as a theoretical metaphor: a message which is recorded or stored in an encrypted form is no easier to retrieve than the original clear text. An adequate representation of such a message would instead be expected to render its contents accessible and easy to apply in a more or less direct way; in other words, representation implies organization (Jackson, 1986, p. 29). In his original paper, Miller (1956a, p. 93) did emphasize 'the importance of grouping or organizing the input sequence into units or chunks' using simple substitution rules. He also suggested that the development of a hierarchical organization of this sort would explain the phenomenon of associative clustering in free recall (p. 95). Elsewhere (Miller, 1956b), he elaborated upon the notion that organizing the material to be remembered into a hierarchy of symbols or 'cognitive units' would permit a more efficient use of human memory.

Tulving (1962, 1964) suggested that chunking or unitization, as envisaged by Miller, was just one example of the processes of 'subjective organization' underlying the formation of higher-order memory units. He argued that such processes would be manifested in a tendency for subjects to produce items from the same units together during recall, and that the functional significance of the development of these units was to be found in the increased accessibility of individual items. Similar ideas were adopted by other researchers (for example, G. Mandler, 1967), so that by the early 1970s it was similarly agreed that organization was a central feature of human memory (Tulving and Donaldson, 1972). Unfortunately, this research did not lead to more sophisticated ideas about the representational format in which that organization was to be described. Organizational processes were often discussed informally in terms of the concept of an association, but this in itself has little explanatory power and does not constitute an adequate formalism for describing the nature of the relationships amongst the items within higher-order memory units (Anderson, 1972).

KNOWLEDGE REPRESENTATION IN ARTIFICIAL INTELLIGENCE

The problem of knowledge representation also arose naturally in the field of computer science during the 1960s. Computers can obviously be used to record and store information in an electronic medium rather than in books or filing cabinets. However, with the development of computer languages that enabled non-numeric computations to be carried out on data structures expressing large bodies of knowledge, the attention of researchers turned to the question of how that knowledge might most conveniently be stored for the purposes of symbolic computation. Early work was concerned with specific tasks such as theorem proving or machine translation, but it was soon appreciated that knowledge representation is fundamental to the whole enterprise of developing intelligent artificial systems. Indeed, B.C. Smith (1985, p. 33) identified a 'knowledge representation hypothesis' at the heart of contemporary work on artifical intelligence:

> Any mechanically embodied intelligent process will be comprised of structural ingredients that a) we as external observers naturally take to represent a propositional account of the knowledge that the overall process exhibits, and b) independent of such external semantical attribution, play a formal but causal and essential role in engendering the behaviour that manifests that knowledge.

An extensive collection of papers tracing the development of research on knowledge representation in artificial intelligence has been edited by Brachman and Levesque (1985).

Three main types of convention have been used for codifying human knowledge in artificial systems: production rules, structured objects, and predicate logic. A good introduction to the principles underlying these different approaches has been given by Jackson (1986). The use of production rules stems from automata theory and the development of formal grammars, and has dominated research on expert systems, where they are sometimes described as 'condition-action rules' (see Davis and King, 1977). Each rule consists of a set of conditions or premises, together with a set of actions to be carried out if the relevant conditions hold. A production system consists of a collection of such rules, an interpreter which decides when and how to apply the rules, and a working memory which holds data, goals, or intermediate results. The best-known implementation of such a system is MYCIN, which provides consultative advice on the diagnosis and treatment of infectious diseases (Davis *et al.*, 1977).

The origins of structured-object representations lie in graph theory and the development of associative networks. In general terms, a graph consists of a set of nodes, together with a set of links connecting them. A network is a graph in which the links are directed and labelled. In the case of 'associative' or 'semantic' networks, the nodes stand for concepts and the links stand for relationships between them (Findler, 1979). The earliest application of this approach to knowledge representation was the work of Quillian (1967, 1968), who simulated language understanding using a network based on dictionary-like definitions of English words. This system compared the meanings of arbitrary pairs of words by simultaneously searching along all possible paths from each of the nodes corresponding to the original words until a common node was reached. By analogy with the functioning of neural systems, this sort of process was characterized in terms of 'activation' gradually spreading outwards from each concept through the network of associations. Subsequently, Minsky (1975, 1977) developed the notion of a 'frame', a complex set of nodes and relations for representing a stereotyped situation. The higher nodes of a frame were fixed, and these represented features that were always true of the situation in question; the lower nodes were 'slots' which had to be filled by characteristics of specific instances, but which took on default values reflecting prototypical situations. This work has in turn prompted even more complex, object-oriented systems in which structured objects are viewed from the perspective of other (usually prototypical) objects (for example, Bobrow and Winograd, 1977).

Finally, other researchers have turned to the predicate calculus as a formalism for knowledge representation (for example, Kowalski, 1979). Declarative sentences are represented as propositions consisting of a property (that is, a 'predicate' or 'relation') which applies to one or more objects (or 'arguments'). This notation has the advantage that it can be used in a straightforward manner to represent simple statements, general statements involving quantifiers (such as *all*), and complex statements involving multiple predicates, arguments, or quantifiers. Nevertheless, the application of formal logic to knowledge representation in artificial intelligence is still controversial (Newell, 1982).

KNOWLEDGE REPRESENTATION IN COGNITIVE PSYCHOLOGY

In seeking to develop models of knowledge representation in human beings, it was fairly inevitable that cognitive psychologists would try to exploit the formalisms being developed within the field of artificial intelligence. Lachman and Lachman (1979) identified three major requirements that tended to motivate the construction of global models of knowledge representation. First, the system should be sufficient, in the sense of being capable of representing the broad range of things that human beings actually know. Second, given the immense amount of material to be represented, the system should support the efficient search and retrieval of information. This is generally taken to mean that the store of knowledge should be addressed by content rather than by location (for example, Jackson, 1986, p. 29). Third, the system should be capable of efficient, high-speed reasoning and inference.

Associative networks had an obvious attraction for this purpose, since they appeared to offer a formalization of traditional associative views of human memory that also accommodated different categories of associative relationship (Anderson, 1972). In particular, Quillian's (1967, 1968) theory (which had been intended as an exercise in psychological modelling rather than in artificial intelligence *per se*: Oden, 1987) incorporated interesting assumptions about the structural relations among concepts and the process of memory search. As a specific theory of the representation of word meanings, it is known to be empirically false (for example, E.E. Smith *et al.*, 1974). Nevertheless, the general formalism offered by associative networks is both perspicuous and flexible, and it permits the efficient retrieval of relevant information through the mechanism of spreading activation. It is not surprising, therefore, that theorists have been somewhat unwilling to abandon this sort of notation, even within the field of semantic memory (Collins and Loftus, 1975). An associative network is indeed formally equivalent to a structured collection of propositional expressions in which complex concepts are represented as combinations of simple concepts and various operators (Oden, 1987), and in this respect is able to give a reasonable analysis of dictionary-like definitions. However, these networks do not necessarily provide a convenient format in which to make explicit either the constituent structure or the abstract content of the full range of declarative statements.

Such a format is offered by the predicate calculus, which provides a general formalism for articulating the constituent structure of individual propositions. As Lachman and Lachman (1979) observed, the logical concept of a proposition is attractive to researchers in cognitive science because it captures the intuitive notion of the 'gist' of a declarative utterance and it can stand in a type-token relationship to sentences or statements, thus accounting for the linguistic phenomenon of paraphrase. As a result, virtually all contemporary models of knowledge representation incorporate a propositional analysis of stored information in one guise or another. In itself, such an analysis suffers from the limitation that it does not specify the structural relations *between* the resulting representations. As Garnham (1988, p. 124) noted, a bare list of propositions in a uniform notation (such as the predicate calculus) would not promote the efficient retrieval of particular items. In a variety of models that were developed during the early 1970s (for example, Kintsch, 1972, 1974; Rumelhart *et al.*, 1972; Schank, 1972), and especially in Anderson and Bower's (1973) theory of Human Associative Memory (HAM), this problem was handled by embedding the propositional representations of individual statements as subgraphs within an associative network, thus exploiting the advantages of both formalisms.

Anderson and Bower claimed that all knowledge was represented in the form of abstract propositions about properties of objects and relations between objects, and in particular that HAM's representational conventions were sufficient to handle information processing associated with visual imagery (pp. 452–461). This idea contradicted the 'dual coding' theory of Paivio (1971), according to which 'images and verbal processes are viewed as alternative coding systems, or modes of symbolic representation' (p. 8; see also Paivio, 1986). Pylyshyn (1973, 1981) similarly argued that the functional origin of mental imagery lay in a system of knowledge that was essentially conceptual and propositional in nature. Although it would certainly be parsimonious to represent both perceptual and linguistic information in a common propositional base, other theorists have assumed that the representations underlying mental images and verbal information are structurally distinct and functionally independent (for example, Kintsch, 1974; Kosslyn, 1980; Kosslyn and Pomerantz, 1977).

Nevertheless, the predicate calculus only provides a formalism for representing knowledge that is expressed in declarative statements. For instance, the representation of information in the HAM model depended upon the operation of a natural language parser containing syntactic rules that were not in principle amenable to propositional analysis because they did not possess the constituent structure of propositions. This is a specific example of a distinction that is commonly drawn between 'declarative' and 'procedural' knowledge. The former involves propositional information about events and objects that can be consciously retrieved and described; the latter relates to skills and capabilities that can only be manifested in overt performance. Most writers link this distinction with Ryle's (1949) discussion of 'knowing that' versus 'knowing how', although it can be traced back much further (Bergson, 1910, pp. 75–77). It is not clear whether there are functional properties distinguishing the two sorts of knowledge that would demand a theoretical dichotomy between declarative and procedural *representations* (Kintsch, 1979). Possibly the strongest evidence in favour of the latter is the observation that amnesic patients tend to be selectively impaired on tests of declarative memory, whereas their procedural memory may be left relatively intact (Cohen and Squire, 1980; Parkin, 1987, pp. 90–99). However, the main point to be emphasized here is that the representation of *procedural* knowledge seems to demand a *non-declarative* formalism (but cf. Rumelhart and Norman, 1983; M.P. Smith, 1988).

Production rules constitute the obvious alternative format for knowledge representation. These have a natural application to the analysis of procedural knowledge, since they can be used to represent the procedures for achieving specific goals. In principle, however, production systems can just as readily accommodate instances of declarative knowledge: in this case, the action elements of the production rules are those of concluding that particular propositions are true, possibly with a certain degree of confidence (Jackson, 1986, p. 31). Condition-action rules can also be used to represent knowledge at the level of both general categories (such as *dogs*) and specific instances (such as *Rover*: see Gick and Holyoak, 1987, p. 14). Indeed, the earliest applications of production systems to cognitive modelling used production rules as the sole representational format (for example, Newell and Simon, 1972; Winograd, 1972). Within the field of artificial intelligence, this led to disputes between 'proceduralists', who considered that human knowledge was best analysed in terms of production systems, and 'declarativists', who saw intelligence as resting on a set of specific facts or propositions and a general set of procedures for manipulating those facts (Winograd, 1975).

In seeking a synthesis of production-system architecture and the HAM memory system, Anderson (1976) developed a more complex theory concerned with Adaptive Control of Thought (ACT). This employed a production system as an interpreter of the propositional network, and incorporated Quillian's (1967, 1968) notion of spreading activation. The original ACT system was implemented as a computer simulation, ACTE, and then extended to include a theory of production acquisition, ACTF. ACT* (Anderson, 1983), the final version, was presented as a general theory of cognitive architecture and a general model of the acquisition of cognitive skills (such as language, geometry, and programming). The general framework which these models have in common (the ACT production system) consists of three major structural components: declarative memory, production memory, and working memory (see Figure 1).

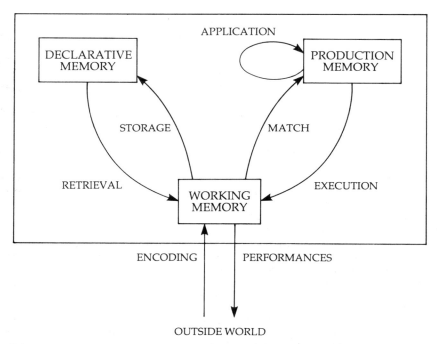

Figure 1. The general framework for the ACT production system, identifying the main structural components and their interlinking processes. (From Anderson, 1983, p. 19.)

Working memory contains active declarative knowledge which has been retrieved from the long-term declarative memory or deposited by encoding processes or the action of productions. New information encoded within working memory may activate associated facts in declarative memory, or it may trigger procedural representations in production memory by matching their conditions. New productions are acquired by the 'compilation' of the declarative information held in working memory (see Anderson, 1987). Although the original ACT system permitted declarative representations expressed only in terms of abstract propositions, ACT* also incorporated at least two other types of cognitive unit: temporal strings and spatial images. These three qualitatively distinct 'representational types' were linked together in network structures referred to as 'tangled hierarchies' (Anderson, 1983, pp. 23–26, 45–48).

MODULAR KNOWLEDGE STRUCTURES

The models that have been discussed so far try to give a perfectly general account of human knowledge representation. They have relatively little to say about the nature of the higher-order structures involved in particular domains of knowledge. Of course, information about pragmatically important concepts will tend to be represented in a contiguous manner, whether the format adopted is based upon abstract propositions (Garnham, 1988) or upon production rules (Gick and Holyoak, 1987). Nevertheless, in order to meet the requirements of an adequate model of knowledge representation (Lachman and Lachman, 1979), it might be desirable to make this sort of organization explicit in the case of certain types of complex molar phenomena; that is, it might be useful to represent knowledge in highly structured 'knowledge packets' (Goldstein and Papert, 1977). Sanford (1985, p. 194) has noted that *how* the information is organized may depend upon how it is used and upon the domain in question. The knowledge structures in question might therefore be expected to be *modular*, in that different types of theoretical entities would be necessary to account for different cognitive processes (Brewer and Nakamura, 1984).

Contemporary psychological accounts of modular knowledge structures are frequently based upon the concept of a *schema* which Bartlett (1932) used to describe 'those masses of organised past experiences and reactions which function in all high-level mental processes' (pp. 197–198). Brewer and Nakamura (1984) provided a detailed exegesis of Bartlett's ideas, and they concluded that for Bartlett schemata were unconscious knowledge structures organized into generic cognitive representations which actively incorporated experienced episodic information. One might characterize schemata as possessing an essentially Janus-like quality: on the one hand, they are a record of past experiences, albeit in a generic form; on the other hand, they are also used in an active manner to make sense of present and future experiences. As Bartlett himself explained the term, ' "Schema" refers to an active organisation of past reactions, or of past experiences, which must always be supposed to be operating in any well-adapted organic response' (1932, p. 201).

Bartlett's ideas had some impact in the UK, but they had virtually none at all elsewhere until the development of research on human knowledge representation during the 1970s. Reflecting upon the revival of interest in the notion of a schema, Rumelhart (1980) considered that for many authors (and not least himself) 'schemata truly are *the building blocks of cognition*. They are the fundamental elements upon which all information processing depends' (p. 33). Rumelhart discussed the general nature and function of schemata in terms of four broad analogies:

1 *Schemata are like plays.* More strictly, the instantiation of a schema corresponds to the enactment of a play:

> The internal structure of a schema corresponds, in many ways, to the script of a play. Just as a play has characters that can be played by different actors at different times without changing the essential nature of the play, so a schema has *variables* that can be associated with (bound to) different aspects of the environment on different instantiations of the schema. (p. 35)

For instance, the generic schema for the concept *buy* contains certain fixed structural relations, and also slots corresponding to the purchaser, the vendor, the merchandise, and the medium of exchange.

2 *Schemata are like theories.* 'Perhaps the central function of schemata is in the construction of an interpretation of an event, object, or situation – that is, in the process of comprehension. . . . The total set of schemata we have available for interpreting our world in a sense constitutes our private theory of the nature of reality' (p. 37). In this analogy, the variables of a generic schema correspond to the parameters of a theory.

3 *Schemata are like procedures.* Unlike both plays and theories, schemata are active processes with a well-defined constituent

structure, and in both these respects they resemble procedures or computer programs: in other words, 'schemata are active computational devices capable of evaluating the quality of their own fit to the available data' (p. 39). Like procedures, schemata can be hierarchically organized, with elements of a more specific nature embedded under more general structures.

4 *Schemata are like parsers.* Schemata are confronted with the task of discovering the constituents and subconstituents of the data currently impinging on the system, in much the same way as a parser is required to determine the constituent structure of a sentence presented in the form of a bare sequence of symbols.

An indication of the potential applicability of modular knowledge structures was given by Minsky (1975) in terms of his concept of a *frame*. As I mentioned earlier, this is a data structure for representing stereotyped situations. It will be recalled that frames are merely structured objects based upon associative networks, and to that extent they are inherently more passive than other sorts of generic knowledge structure (Brewer and Nakamura, 1984). In this regard, Goldstein and Papert (1977) noted that the definition of a frame was based upon 'the traditional *declarative* data structures of objects, properties, and relations' (p. 97). Nevertheless, Minsky's original account (1975, p. 212) implied that certain kinds of procedural knowledge would be associated with individual frames: 'Attached to each frame are several kinds of information. Some of this information is about how to use the frame. Some is about what one can expect to happen next. Some is about what to do if these expectations are not confirmed.' Goldstein and Papert (1977) in turn suggested that procedural knowledge and expertise could be captured by the notion of a 'frame keeper', a procedure whose action was to examine the current context for data that could fill the slots of the relevant frame.

One important application is to the domain of vision. In this case, there are different frames that describe a scene from different viewpoints, and the transformations between one frame and another represent the effect of moving from place to place. Minsky (1977) described in detail the use of frames in recognizing both scenes and objects. In other applications, however, the differences among the frames of a system represent actions, cause–effect relationships, or changes in conceptual viewpoint. Minsky (1975) mentioned five such applications: syntactic frames for noun and verb structures; semantic frames describing the meanings of words in terms of actions, goals, and consequences; thematic frames or scenarios describing social transactions; narrative frames describing the structure of stories, explanations, and arguments; and scientific paradigms.

The idea that there are specific modular knowledge structures involved in the comprehension and retention of stories (as opposed to broad thematic knowledge activated by the mere topic or title of a specific story) has been taken up by several other researchers who have used production systems as the basis of 'story grammars' (for example, J.M. Mandler and Johnson, 1977; Thorndyke, 1977). There may indeed prove to be specific conventions governing the structure of stories that can be employed by hearers or readers to facilitate their understanding. However, many of these story grammars have focused upon the hierarchical structure of plans and goals that is characteristic of all goal-directed behaviour, and not upon the specific conventions of narrative discourse (Wilensky, 1978; Brewer and Lichtenstein, 1981; Garnham, 1988).

Minsky's original discussion (1975) considered the representation of complex stereotyped events (such as a child's birthday party), but also the representation of stereotyped *sequences* of events (such as a typical day). Schank and Abelson (1977) described the notion of a *script*, which was a modular knowledge structure intended specifically to handle stereotypical action sequences. They proposed three major types of script: situational scripts involving stereotypical social interactions (such as visiting a restaurant); personal scripts involving individual stereotypical roles (such as being a pickpocket); and instrumental scripts involving action sequences aimed at particular goals (such as boiling an egg). Once again the representation is a knowledge structure made up of slots or categories of information, such as actions, roles, and props, that are to be filled according to the demands of a specific situation. The original model was designed to simulate the comprehension of narrative text, but a subsequent version was designed to capture the representation of events themselves (Schank, 1982). Scripts are activated when particular cues or keywords are encountered, and are then brought to bear in the subsequent analysis of the situation or discourse in question.

Most typically, a script is a generic sequence of actions appropriate to a particular context and organized around a particular goal. As Nelson (1986) noted, 'An important characteristic of scripts is that their format includes, and indeed is organized around, information about social goals and activities. Thus scripts integrate into one structure knowledge about objects and their relations and knowledge about the world of people and their interactions' (p. 15). That organization takes two different forms. First, scripts exhibit a hierarchical structure in which the superordinate acts or scenes dominate subordinate or optional actions. Second, they exhibit a chronological structure identifying the causal or enabling connections among the constituent events. In this regard, Abelson (1981) distinguished between 'strong' and 'weak' scripts. The former are based upon events that are constrained in terms of the sequence of particular constituent actions: 'visiting a restaurant' is an example of such a script. On the other hand, weak scripts are based upon a loosely structured set of constituent events that lack any inherent sequence: the script of a child's birthday party is relatively weak in this sense.

In short, schemata, frames, and scripts are all examples of modular knowledge structures that underlie the molar aspects of human knowledge and skill. These generic or 'precompiled' representations interact with incoming episodic or contextual information to yield specific instantiated representations of the immediate situation (Brewer, 1987).

EPISODIC KNOWLEDGE STRUCTURES

Although contextualized representations of specific episodes or situations can be produced by the instantiation of schemata, human beings are capable of accommodating a wide variety of complex situations that cannot be dealt with on the basis of generic information retrieved from long-term memory in a modular or 'packeted' form. As Brewer (1987, p. 188) observed, 'We can understand actions that we have never seen carried out before; we can find our way around a town that we have never been in before; and we can understand an argument we have never heard before'. In these situations, Brewer noted, we can only construct non-generic representations based upon broad categories of knowledge concerning space, time, causality, and human intentionality.

To take each of Brewer's examples in turn, the goal-directed quality of human behaviour is especially important when encountering novel social situations. Schank and Abelson (1977) noted that a stereotyped sequence of actions can be interpreted as a mundane instantiation of a generic goal structure or script. However, in the absence of a script, interpretations must be based upon the construction of *plans:* in other words, non-generic structures of actions that might achieve inferred *goals.* To that extent, script-based understanding is a routine problem-solving process, whereas plan-based understanding demands creative problem solving (Sanford, 1985, pp. 214–217). The account given by Schank and Abelson suggested that all intentional human behaviour could be represented in terms of a limited number of primitive types of goal, and these are assembled in different combinations to generate particular plans. Goals, plans, and scripts are organized into higher-order structures or *themes*, which reflect a person's social role, relationships, and aspirations.

The second example was that of finding one's way around an unfamiliar town. It is clear that the generic information that could be used in constructing a representation of the layout of the streets and buildings is extremely limited. An internal representation of such a layout is sometimes described as a 'cognitive map'. This term was introduced by Tolman (1948) in connection with the knowledge of laboratory rats concerning the structure of an experimental maze, but it is commonly used nowadays to describe the representation of spatial knowledge, and of environmental knowledge in particular (see Downs and Stea, 1977). Such a notion has been invoked in considering cognitive representations of the natural environment (for example, Paradice, 1981), the urban environment (for example, Bianchi, 1982), and the work environment (for example, Dobrowolny *et al.*, 1980). These representations have their own constituent structure and are subject to systematic forms of distortion (Lynch, 1960; Byrne, 1982; Golledge *et al.*, 1985). Nevertheless, recent research has suggested that knowledge about the local environment that is obtained by direct personal experience is not represented in a map-like form, in so far as (a) it is represented in an orientation-free format rather than in a standard or conventional orientation, and (b) such representations cannot be mentally rotated as organized wholes (Evans and Pezdek, 1980; M.J.S. Smith, 1982).

With regard to understanding novel arguments, a general account of human reasoning was developed by Johnson-Laird (1980, 1982, 1983), based upon the construction of 'mental models' or represent-ations of particular states of affairs in the real world or in imaginary worlds. Johnson-Laird claimed that reasoning consisted in (a) the construction of mental models on the basis of the specified premises, and (b) the search for alternative models that might render the putative conclusions false. This account was directed against the traditional theory of 'mental logic', which held that human reasoning consisted in the application of formal rules of inference to abstract propositional representations. Johnson-Laird argued that reasoning was based upon the construction and manipulation of mental models rather than upon logical principles such as those contained in the predicate calculus. He also claimed that the syntactic structure of a propositional representation was arbitrary, whereas a mental model was isomorphic or analogous to the situation which it represented: that is, 'its structure mirrors the relevant aspects of the corresponding state of affairs in the world' (1980, p. 98). Nevertheless, it was only because these 'relevant aspects' were initially represented in the form of propositional descriptions that they could then be manifested in a mental model (1983, p. 165).

The theory of mental models was intended to explain the processes of comprehension and inference in general. Indeed, it found an immediate and natural application in the analysis of text comprehension (Garnham, 1981; Johnson-Laird, 1983, ch. 14). In this context, it was clearly assumed that mental models were constructed on the basis of both general knowledge and episodic information. Van Dijk and Kintsch (1983) developed this idea in discussing the notion of a 'situational model', which they described as 'an integrated structure of episodic information, collecting previous episodic information about some situation as well as instantiated general information from semantic memory' (p. 344). Brewer (1987) also noted that Johnson-Laird (1983, p. 11) had used the term 'mental model' in connection with domains such as pure mathematics, where generic knowledge structures would be implicated. In short, mental models can be characterized as cognitive representations integrating contextual and generic knowledge.

In parallel with Johnson-Laird's work on human reasoning, a separate line of inquiry has developed into the cognitive representations involved in the acquisition of expert knowledge (Gentner and Stevens, 1983). Here, also, the term 'mental model' is used to refer to structural analogues of real or imagined situations that are constructed on the basis of both generic and contextual information. The manipulation of these representations permits the vicarious development of expertise, a point that was expressed by Oden (1987, p. 218) in the following manner:

> The appeal to the use of a mental model is based on people's abilities to 'run internal simulations' of what would be expected to happen under various hypothetical situations as a means of evaluating alternative problem solutions and making reliable predictions of outcomes in the world.

The distinctive feature of this research is that it has been predominantly concerned with people's knowledge representations of the causal mechanisms underlying physical systems, both natural and technological. As Brewer (1987, p. 191) commented: 'It seems to me that the crucial aspect of the causal mental model research tradition is that it has focused on physical systems and that the underlying forms of representation for those systems include a domain-specific construct of causality'.

APPLICATIONS IN COGNATE AREAS

Since the latter tradition is concerned with the acquisition of expertise, it is unsurprising that its findings are generally felt to have important implications for educational practice. More generally, researchers in the field of education have for many years recognized the significance of the learner's pre-existing cognitive structures in determining the quality of learning (e.g. Ausubel, 1968; Merrill *et al.*, 1981). For instance, the notion that cognitive development might demand qualitative changes in the learner's knowledge represent-ations or schemata explains why existing knowledge structures might tend to inhibit rather than enhance the rate of learning, especially in scientific disciplines (Champagne *et al.*, 1983; Chaiklin, 1987). The ACT* model developed by Anderson (1983) also has many potential applications in educational settings, and it has already proved useful with regard to the teaching of computing skills (Anderson *et al.*, 1987; Charney and Reder, 1987; Gray and Orasanu, 1987).

A number of other areas of application should be briefly mentioned. First, there is the field of cognitive anthropology, whose programme was described by Tyler (1969, p. 3) in the following manner:

> It is assumed that each people has a unique system for perceiving and organizing material phenomena – things, events, behaviors, and emotions. . . . The object of study is not these material phenomena themselves, but the way they are organized in the minds of men. Cultures then are not material phenomena: they are cognitive organizations of material phenomena.

In seeking ways of representing cultural knowledge, many anthro-pologists have turned to discussions within cognitive psychology concerning generic knowledge structures. The notion of a schema, in particular, has often been exploited to handle culture-specific descriptions of objects, events, and the spatial and causal relation-ships among them; schemata have also been invoked in the interpretation of metaphor and narrative (Casson, 1983). Second, in the field of linguistics, the concept of a frame has been used to explain the way in which abstract conceptual representations are realized in a specific lexical and grammatical form (for example, Fillmore, 1976). Third, the operation of modular knowledge structures in a clinical context can be used to elucidate both the nature of abnormal behaviour and the pattern of therapeutic encounters (Pfeifer and Leuzinger-Bohleber, 1986). Fourth, cognitive maps are of central concern to environmental psychology and behavioural geography (O'Keefe and Nadel, 1978, ch. 2).

Finally, intellectual developments of the sort that I have described in this paper have also influenced the way in which neuroscientists talk about the functioning of the central nervous system. John (1967, p. 2) stated that 'the configuration of external and internal stimuli impinging upon an organism, which constitute an experience, must somehow be coded into a neural representation'. Young (1978, pp. 10–11) proposed 'to use the analogy of the encoding of information by writing to speak about the way in which the brain contains the scripts of the programs that issue in human action. . . . What goes on in the brain must provide a faithful representation of events outside, and the arrangement of the cells in it provides a detailed model of the world'. Similarly, with regard to the nature of visual perception, Frisby (1980, p. 8) claimed that 'it is an inescapable conclusion that there must be a symbolic description in the brain of the outside world, a description cast in symbols which stand for the various aspects of the world of which sight makes us aware'. One especially notable example of this line of thinking is the thesis advanced by O'Keefe and Nadel (1978) that in humans and in many infrahuman species the hippocampus functions as a cognitive mapping system (discussed further in the peer commentary to O'Keefe and Nadel, 1979).

The relationship between these ideas and the accounts of knowledge representation in cognitive psychology can be clarified by considering the recent development of interest in *connectionism*. This is described by Aleksander (1989, p. 48) as 'the study of cellular networks that are in some way like the neural networks of the brain: they are made up of interconnected, adaptable nodes. They possess properties that emerge from the way that such networks are connected and trained'. In these models, individual concepts are represented not by the individual nodes, but by different patterns of activation across the entire system of nodes. Their representations are consequently *distributed* throughout the network and superimposed upon one another rather than associated with any particular location within the system (Oden, 1987). Minsky and Papert (1969) showed that there were intrinsic limitations upon simple models of this sort that involved merely a set of input units mapped directly onto a set of output units. However, this was not the case if such models were augmented by an intermediate layer of 'hidden' units. Nowadays, therefore, connectionist models take the form of multi-layer systems in which the activity of these hidden units is interpreted as an 'internal representation' of the pattern of activation among the input units (for example, Rumelhart, Hinton and Williams, 1986). Some of the resulting coalitions of intermediate units prove to be relatively stable and may be regarded as analogous to schemata (Rumelhart, Smolensky, McClelland and Hinton, 1986).

Hinton (1981; Hinton *et al.*, 1986) emphasized that these distributed representations were not to be seen as alternatives to more conventional accounts such as propositional networks or production systems, since they reflect different levels of analysis. Cognitive representations provide useful and appropriate formalisms for representing human knowledge at a functional level, whereas distributed presentations provide a particular implementation of those abstract formalisms that is motivated by presumed physiological plausibility. (On the latter point, see Crick, 1989.) Whereas the former are regarded as symbolic representations, the latter are 'subsymbolic' representations (Smolensky, 1986). In other words, connectionist theories are directed towards the substrate upon which cognitive representations are built, or the machine language in which they are 'compiled' (Anderson, 1983, p. 35; Oden, 1987).

CONCEPTUAL ISSUES

If these cognitive representations are not themselves to be identified with physical structures at a neural level, then what sort of entity are they supposed to be? The interpretation that is generally encouraged by contemporary writing is that they are *mental* representations invoked to explain human knowledge, skills, and performance (for example, Paivio, 1986), and this raises the question whether they are to be construed as phenomenal experiences directly amenable to conscious introspection. As I mentioned at the beginning of this chapter, traditional philosophical accounts of memory were based upon the idea that acts of recognition and remembering consisted essentially in the occurrence of propositional thoughts which were structurally equivalent to the events being remembered (see Malcolm, 1977, ch. 5). However, current theories are more circumspect as to whether 'mental' representations are to be identified with conscious states. For instance, production rules are sometimes taken to capture the procedural knowledge underlying automatic skills which cannot be readily subjected to conscious scrutiny, although many procedures can be described verbally (such as culinary recipes) while others might be entertained in a pictorial form (Kintsch, 1979). Within Anderson's (1983) ACT framework, working memory seems to reflect the domain of conscious awareness, whether its contents result from the encoding of external events, the retrieval of declarative information, or the execution of production rules (pp. 19–20). Brewer (1987) argued that schemata and other modular knowledge structures were themselves unconscious but were instantiated in the form of episodic knowledge structures which could give rise to phenomenal experience in the course of being 'run' as imaginative anticipations of actual events. To characterize all of these various representations as 'mental' is thus not to equate them with conscious experience, but merely to indicate that they are intended to explain the intellectual capacities of a conscious being.

Classical accounts of memory also claimed that memory representations legitimated knowledge claims by virtue of the fact that they *resembled* the thing or event being remembered. This is just a special case of the idea that a thought has a structure that is isomorphic to the state of affairs that exists if the thought is true (Malcolm, 1977, p. 159). However, this notion of a 'representation' diverges significantly from the everyday use of this expression. A representation is a particular spatial or temporal configuration of symbols that is conventionally regarded as standing in a certain relationship to something else. Representations are things which are created, used, and interpreted by human beings in order to think or to communicate more easily about concepts and ideas that would otherwise be less tractable. It follows that the *object* of a representation (what it is a representation *of*) is determined by how it is intended, not by what it resembles, and that the functional origin of a representation lies in the propositional description that captures the intention of its creator (Richardson, 1980, pp. 39–40).

Fodor (1975, p. 190) sought to draw a distinction between *discursive* representations, in which information was *described*, and non-discursive or *pictorial* representations, in which information was *displayed* in a manner that resembled the original object of the representation in question. He claimed that text and photographs were paradigmatic examples of these two respective categories of representation, while maps and mental images were intermediate cases: 'they convey *some* information discursively and *some* information pictorially, and they resemble their subjects only in respect of those properties that happen to be pictured'. One implication of this is that 'the properties for which the image has to be determinate can have arbitrarily little in common with the visual properties of whatever the image images'. So images need not resemble what they represent. However, this is true not just of images but of all pictorial representations. Malcolm (1977, p. 216) suggested the examples of a cartoon caricature and a work of modern sculpture; moreover, it is perfectly possible to depict entirely abstract concepts. Conversely, even if pictorial representations do resemble what they represent, they can always be interpreted in various ways; for example, a figure of a hexagon together with its major diagonals can be seen either as a plane figure or as a three-dimensional cube viewed from one of its corners (Fodor, 1975, pp. 182–183, 192; see also Malcolm, 1977, pp. 147–153; Richardson, 1980, p. 39).

What all this means is that even a pictorial representation cannot be properly interpreted without knowing what Wittgenstein (1974, pp. 210–214) called the 'method of projection', and that this cannot be conveyed within the representation itself. In this context, it is interesting that Fodor (1975, p. 190) considered the example of maps: he claimed that maps were pictorial in respect of geographical information but discursive in respect of other information (such as population densities or elevations) that had to be interpreted by reference to some key or legend. Nevertheless, with regard to the suggestion that cartography might be said to be a system of representation, Hacker (1987, pp. 497–498) made the following remarks:

> There is . . . no such thing as representing a territory on a map without employing a particular set of conventions of representation involving a specific method of projection, for example, cylindrical (Mercator), conic or azimuthal. . . . Whether a certain array of lines is or is not a map is not an *intrinsic* feature of the lines, nor even a *relational* feature . . . but a *conventional* one.

In general, then, the creation, use, and interpretation of any particular representation depends upon the separate existence of a general *system* of representation consisting of particular *conventions.* This, in turn, means that no 'mental' representation could itself constitute a logically adequate basis for justified knowledge claims (Malcolm, 1977, pp. 157–158). However, Hacker (1987, p. 498) made the fundamental point that 'to *use* a representation correctly one must *know* the conventions of representation, understand them, be able to explain them, recognize mistakes and correct or acknowledge them when they are pointed out'. That is, conventions of representation depend upon the use of a system of representation by some community of 'intelligent, symbol-employing creatures' (p. 497).

In summary, an important logical feature of representations is their *intentionality:* how a representation is to be interpreted depends upon the propositional description under which the representation is intended, together with the conventions that map the former into the latter. This entails that only of a creature which is able to articulate its intentions, and which has a repertoire of behaviour that is broadly comparable to that of human beings themselves, does it make sense to say that it creates, uses, and interprets representations. Both Hacker (1987, p. 492) and Malcolm (1977, pp. 221, 230) drew the conclusion that it is conceptually absurd to apply these intellectual capacities to the *brains* of human or infrahuman species. Hacker noted further (p. 493) that computers are used to record and to store information, and to that extent they might be said to contain knowledge. However, this is not to attribute any cognitive capacities to computers, and 'in the wholly unmysterious sense in which a computer can be said to contain knowledge or information, *brains do not*'. Moreover, in so far as Malcolm directed his argument against both functional and structural accounts of brain function, his conclusions can be taken to apply to the concepts of both 'mental' and 'neural' representations.

It can certainly be acknowledged that recent research in cognitive psychology, like classical philosophical accounts of memory function, has tended to use the concept of 'representation' in a manner that diverges in significant respects from everyday usage (cf. Malcolm, 1977, pp. 131–132). (A similar point was made earlier with regard to the concept of 'coding'.) Contemporary theories in cognitive psychology postulate the existence of knowledge representations as hypothetical causes of intelligent behaviour. These representations are assumed to be created, stored, and retrieved by the mechanism which is responsible for both observable performance and phenomenal experience (namely, the brain). The various formalisms and theories that I have described in this chapter reflect different attempts to characterize the structural properties of that mechanism. However, the force of the criticisms put forward by Malcolm (1977) and by Hacker (1987) is that this technical usage of 'representation' is both muddled and confused. Fodor (1981, p. 29) retorted that to reject the theoretical construct of mental representation on the basis of philosophical arguments, without bothering either to refute or to reconstruct the explanations in which it occurs, is 'simply irresponsible'. Nevertheless, Hacker (1987, p. 501) implied that those researchers who wish to persist in using this construct have a correlative duty to demonstrate that they are not simply offering the mere appearance of explanation by exploiting a misleading analogy with legitimate usage. In short, whether it really makes sense to describe the entities which are postulated by cognitive psychologists as 'representations' will depend upon a thoroughgoing conceptual analysis of their use of that expression, an analysis that has yet to be undertaken.

REFERENCES

Abelson, R.P. (1981) Psychological status of the script concept. *American Psychologist, 36*, 715–729.

Aleksander, I. (1989) Connectionist systems: Information technology goes brain-like (again!). In L.A. Murray and J.T.E. Richardson (eds) *Intelligent Systems in a Human Context*. Oxford: Oxford University Press.

Anderson, J.R. (1972) FRAN: A simulation model of free recall. In G.H. Bower (ed.) *The Psychology of Learning and Motivation: Advances in Research and Theory*, vol. 5. New York: Academic Press.

Anderson, J.R. (1976) *Language, Memory, and Thought*. Hillsdale, NJ: Erlbaum.

Anderson, J.R. (1983) *The Architecture of Cognition*. Cambridge, Ma: Harvard University Press.

Anderson, J.R. (1987) Skill acquisition: Compilation of weak-method problem-solutions. *Psychological Review, 94*, 192–210.

Anderson, J.R. and Bower, G.H. (1973) *Human Associative Memory*. Washington, DC: Winston & Sons.

Anderson, J.R., Boyle, C.F., Farrell, R. and Reiser, B.J. (1987) Cognitive principles in the design of computer tutors. In P. Morris (ed.) *Modelling Cognition*. Chichester: Wiley.

Ausubel, D.P. (1968) *Educational Psychology: A Cognitive View*. New York: Holt, Rinehart & Winston.

Bartlett, F.C. (1932) *Remembering: A Study in Experimental and Social Psychology*. London: Cambridge University Press.

Bergson, H. (1910) *Matière et Mémoire*, 6th ed. Paris: Alcan.

Bianchi, E. (1982) La rappresentazione cognitiva dell'ambiente come problema geografico. *Ricerche di Psicologia, 6*, 269–289.

Bobrow, D.G. and Winograd, T. (1977) An overview of KRL, a knowledge representation language. *Cognitive Science, 1*, 3–46.

Bower, G.H. (1972) Stimulus-sampling theory of encoding variability. In A.W. Melton and E. Martin (eds) *Coding Processes in Human Memory*. Washington, DC: Winston.

Brachman, R.J. and Levesque, H.J. (eds) (1985) *Readings in Knowledge Representation*. Los Altos, Ca: Morgan Kaufmann.

Brewer, W.F. (1987) Schemas versus mental models in human memory. In P. Morris (ed.) *Modelling Cognition*. Chichester: Wiley.

Brewer, W.F. and Lichtenstein, E.H. (1981) Event schemas, story schemas, and story grammars. In J. Long and A. Baddeley (eds) *Attention and Performance IX*. Hillsdale, NJ: Erlbaum.

Brewer, W.F. and Nakamura, G.V. (1984) The nature and functions of schemas. In R.S. Wyer, Jr and T.K. Srull (eds) *Handbook of Social Cognition*, vol. 1. Hillsdale, NJ: Erlbaum.

Byrne, R.W. (1982) Geographical knowledge and orientation. In A.W. Ellis (ed.) *Normality and Pathology in Cognitive Functions*. London: Academic Press.

Casson, R.W. (1983) Schemata in cognitive anthropology. *Annual Review of Anthropology, 12,* 429–462.

Chaiklin, S. (1987) Beyond inferencing: Student reasoning in physical science. In J.T.E. Richardson, M.W. Eysenck and D. Warren Piper (eds) *Student Learning: Research in Education and Cognitive Psychology*. Guildford: SRHE & Open University Press.

Champagne, A.B., Gunstone, R.F. and Klopfer, L.E. (1983) Naive knowledge and science learning. *Research in Science and Technological Education, 1,* 173–183.

Charney, D.H. and Reder, L.M. (1987) Initial skill learning: An analysis of how elaborations facilitate the three components. In P. Morris (ed.) *Modelling Cognition*. Chichester: Wiley.

Cohen, N.J. and Squire, L.R. (1980) Preserved learning and retention of pattern-analyzing skills in amnesia: Dissociation of knowing how from knowing that. *Science, 210,* 207–210.

Collins, A.M. and Loftus, E.F. (1975) A spreading-activation theory of semantic processing. *Psychological Review, 82,* 407–428.

Crick, F. (1989) The recent excitement about neural networks. *Nature, 337,* 129–132.

Davis, R., Buchanan, B. and Shortliffe, E. (1977) Production rules as a representation for a knowledge-based consultation program. *Artificial Intelligence, 8,* 15–45.

Davis, R. and King, J. (1977) An overview of production systems. In E. Elcock and D. Michie (eds) *Machine Intelligence 8*. Chichester: Ellis Horwood.

Dobrowolny, M.B., Misiti, R. and Secchiaroli, G. (1980) Spatial cognitive representation of the working environment and working experience in the factory. *Italian Journal of Psychology, 7,* 1–11.

Downs, R.M. and Stea, D. (1977) *Maps in Minds: Reflections on Cognitive Mapping*. New York: Harper & Row.

Evans, G.W. and Pezdek, K. (1980) Cognitive mapping: Knowledge of real-world distance and location information. *Journal of Experimental Psychology: Human Learning and Memory, 6,* 13–24.

Fillmore, C.J. (1976) Frame semantics and the nature of language. *Annals of the New York Academy of Sciences, 280,* 20–32.

Findler, N.V. (ed.) (1979) *Associative Networks: Representation and Use of Knowledge by Computers*. New York: Academic Press.

Fodor, J.A. (1975) *The Language of Thought*. New York: Crowell.

Fodor, J.A. (1981) *Representations: Philosophical Essays on the Foundations of Cognitive Science*. Brighton: Harvester Press.

Frisby, J.P. (1980) *Seeing: Illusion, Brain and Mind.* Oxford: Oxford University Press.

Garnham, A. (1981) Mental models as representations of text. *Memory and Cognition, 9*, 560–565.

Garnham. A. (1988) Understanding. In G. Claxton (ed.) *Growth Points in Cognition.* London: Routledge.

Gentner, D. and Stevens, A.L. (eds) (1983) *Mental Models.* Hillsdale, NJ: Erlbaum.

Gick, M.L. and Holyoak, K.J. (1987) The cognitive basis of knowledge transfer. In S.M. Cormier and J.D. Hagman (eds) *Transfer of Learning: Contemporary Research and Applications.* New York: Academic Press.

Goldstein, I. and Papert, S. (1977) Artificial intelligence, language, and the study of knowledge. *Cognitive Science, 1,* 84–123.

Golledge, R.G., Smith, T.R., Pellegrino, J.W., Doherty, S. and Marshall, S.P. (1985) A conceptual model and empirical analysis of children's acquisition of spatial knowledge. *Journal of Environmental Psychology, 5,* 125–152.

Gray, W.D. and Orasanu, J.M. (1987) Transfer of cognitive skills. In S.M. Cormier and J.D. Hagman (eds) *Transfer of Learning: Contemporary Research and Applications.* New York: Academic Press.

Hacker, P.M.S. (1987) Languages, minds and brains. In C. Blakemore and S. Greenfield (eds) *Mindwaves: Thoughts on Intelligence, Identity and Consciousness.* Oxford: Blackwell.

Hall, S. (1980) Encoding/decoding. In S. Hall (ed.) *Culture, Media, Language.* London: Hutchinson.

Hinton, G.E. (1981) Implementing semantic networks in parallel hardware. In G.E. Hinton and J.A. Anderson (eds) *Parallel Models of Associative Memory.* Hillsdale, NJ: Erlbaum.

Hinton, G.E., McClelland, J.L. and Rumelhart, D.E. (1986) Distributed representations. In D.E. Rumelhart, J.L. McClelland and the PDP Research Group, *Parallel Distributed Processing: Explorations in the Microstructure of Cognition,* vol. 1: *Foundations.* Cambridge, Ma: MIT Press.

Jackson, P. (1986) *Introduction to Expert Systems.* Wokingham, Berks.: Addison-Wesley.

James, W. (1890) *The Principles of Psychology,* vol. 1. New York: Holt.

John, E.R. (1967) *Mechanisms of Memory.* New York: Academic Press.

Johnson, N.F. (1972) Organization and the concept of a memory code. In A.W. Melton and E. Martin (eds) *Coding Processes in Human Memory.* Washington, DC: Winston.

Johnson-Laird, P.N. (1980) Mental models in cognitive science. *Cognitive Science, 4,* 71–115.

Johnson-Laird, P.N. (1982) Thinking as a skill. *Quarterly Journal of Experimental Psychology, 34A,* 1–29. Revised version (1983) in J. St B.T. Evans (ed.) *Thinking and Reasoning: Psychological Approaches.* London: Routledge & Kegan Paul.

Johnson-Laird, P.N. (1983) *Mental Models: Towards a Cognitive Science of Language, Inference, and Consciousness.* Cambridge: Cambridge University Press.

Kintsch, W. (1972) Notes on the structure of semantic memory. In E. Tulving and W. Donaldson (eds) *Organization of Memory.* New York: Academic Press.

Kintsch, W. (1974) *The Representation of Meaning in Memory.* Hillsdale, NJ: Erlbaum.
Kintsch, W. (1979) Levels of processing language material: Discussion of the papers by Lachman and Lachman and Perfetti. In L.S. Cermak and F.I.M. Craik (eds) *Levels of Processing in Human Memory.* Hillsdale, NJ: Erlbaum.
Kohlberg, L. (1969) Stage and sequence: The cognitive-developmental approach to socialization. In D.A. Goslin (ed.) *Handbook of Socialization Theory and Research.* Chicago, Il: Rand McNally.
Kosslyn, S.M. (1980) *Image and Mind.* Cambridge, Ma: Harvard University Press.
Kosslyn, S.M. and Pomerantz, J.R. (1977) Imagery, propositions, and the form of internal representations. *Cognitive Psychology, 9,* 52–76.
Kowalski, R. (1979) *Logic for Problem Solving.* Amsterdam: North-Holland.
Lachman, J.L. and Lachman, R. (1979) Comprehension and cognition: A state of the art inquiry. In L.S. Cermak and F.I.M. Craik (eds) *Levels of Processing in Human Memory.* Hillsdale, NJ: Erlbaum.
Lynch, K. (1960) *The Image of the City.* Cambridge, Ma: MIT Press.
Malcolm, N. (1977) *Memory and Mind.* Ithaca, NY: Cornell University Press.
Mandler, G. (1967) Organization and memory. In K.W. Spence and J.T. Spence (eds) *The Psychology of Learning and Motivation: Advances in Research and Theory,* vol. 1. New York: Academic Press.
Mandler, J.M. and Johnson, N.S. (1977) Remembrance of things parsed: Story structure and recall. *Cognitive Psychology, 9,* 111–151.
Melton, A.W. and Martin, E. (1972) Preface to A.W. Melton and E. Martin (eds) *Coding Processes in Human Memory.* Washington, DC: Winston.
Merrill, M.D., Kelety, J.C. and Wilson, B. (1981) Elaboration theory and cognitive psychology. *Instructional Science, 10,* 217–235.
Miller, G.A. (1956a) The magical number seven, plus or minus two: Some limits on our capacity for processing information. *Psychological Review, 63,* 81–97.
Miller, G.A. (1956b) Information and memory. *Scientific American, 195* (2), 42–46.
Minsky, M. (1975) A framework for representing knowledge. In P.H. Winston (ed.) *The Psychology of Computer Vision.* New York: McGraw-Hill. Revised version (1981) in J. Haugeland (ed.) *Mind Design.* Cambridge, Ma: MIT Press.
Minsky, M. (1977) Frame-system theory. In P.N. Johnson-Laird and P.C. Wason (eds) *Thinking: Readings in Cognitive Science.* Cambridge: Cambridge University Press.
Minsky, M. and Papert, S. (1969) *Perceptrons.* Cambridge, Ma: MIT Press.
Nelson, K. (1986) Event knowledge and cognitive development. In K. Nelson (ed.) *Event Knowledge: Structure and Function in Development.* Hillsdale, NJ: Erlbaum.
Newell, A. (1972) A theoretical exploration of mechanisms for coding the stimulus. In A.W. Melton and E. Martin (eds) *Coding Processes in Human Memory.* Washington, DC: Winston.
Newell, A. (1982) The knowledge level. *Artificial Intelligence, 18,* 87–127.
Newell, A. and Simon, H.A. (1972) *Human Problem Solving.* Englewood Cliffs, NJ: Prentice-Hall.
Oden, G.C. (1987) Concept, knowledge, and thought. *Annual Review of*

Psychology, 38, 203–227.

O'Keefe, J. and Nadel, L. (1978) *The Hippocampus as a Cognitive Map.* Oxford: Oxford University Press.

O'Keefe, J. and Nadel, L. (1979) Précis of O'Keefe & Nadel's *The Hippocampus as a Cognitive Map. Behavioral and Brain Sciences, 2,* 487–533.

Paivio, A. (1971) *Imagery and Verbal Processes.* New York: Holt, Rinehart & Winston. (Reprinted 1979, Hillsdale, NJ: Erlbaum.)

Paivio, A. (1986) *Mental Representations: A Dual Coding Approach.* New York: Oxford University Press.

Paradice, W.E.J. (1981) Cognitive representations of the natural environment. *Dissertation Abstracts International, 42B,* 849.

Parkin, A.J. (1987) *Memory and Amnesia: An Introduction.* Oxford: Blackwell.

Pfeifer, R. and Leuzinger-Bohleber, M. (1986) Applications of cognitive science methods to psychoanalysis: A case study and some theory. *International Review of Psycho-Analysis, 13,* 221–240.

Pylyshyn, Z.W. (1973) What the mind's eye tells the mind's brain: A critique of mental imagery. *Psychological Bulletin, 80,* 1–24.

Pylyshyn, Z.W. (1981) The imagery debate: Analogue media versus tacit knowledge. *Psychological Review, 88,* 16–45.

Quillian, M.R. (1967) Word concepts: A theory and simulation of some basic semantic capabilities. *Behavioral Science, 12,* 410–430.

Quillian, M.R. (1968) Semantic memory. In M. Minsky (ed.) *Semantic Information Processing.* Cambridge, Ma: MIT Press.

Richardson, J.T.E. (1980) *Mental Imagery and Human Memory.* London: Macmillan.

Rumelhart, D.E. (1980) Schemata: The building blocks of cognition. In R.J. Spiro, B.C. Bruce and W.F. Brewer (eds) *Theoretical Issues in Reading Comprehension: Perspectives from Cognitive Psychology, Linguistics, Artificial Intelligence, and Education.* Hillsdale, NJ: Erlbaum. Revised version (1984) in R.S. Wyer, Jr and T.K. Srull (eds) *Handbook of Social Cognition,* vol. 1. Hillsdale, NJ: Erlbaum.

Rumelhart, D.E., Hinton, G.E. and Williams, R.J. (1986) Learning internal representations by error propagation. In D.E. Rumelhart, J.L. McClelland and the PDP Research Group, *Parallel Distributed Processing: Explorations in the Microstructure of Cognition,* vol. 1: *Foundations.* Cambridge, Ma: MIT Press.

Rumelhart, D.E., Lindsay, P.H. and Norman, D.A. (1972) A process model for long-term memory. In E. Tulving and W. Donaldson (eds) *Organization of Memory.* New York: Academic Press.

Rumelhart, D.E. and Norman, D.A. (1983) *Representation in Memory.* Center for Human Information Processing Technical Report No. 116. La Jolla, Ca: University of California, San Diego. Abridged version (1985) in A.M. Aitkenhead and J.M. Slack (eds) *Issues in Cognitive Modeling.* London: Erlbaum. Original version (1988) in R.C. Atkinson, R.J. Herrnstein, G. Lindzey and R.D. Luce (eds) *Stevens' Handbook of Experimental Psychology, Second Edition,* vol. 2: *Learning and Cognition.* New York: Wiley.

Rumelhart, D.E., Smolensky, P., McClelland, J.L. and Hinton, G.E. (1986) Schemata and sequential thought processes in PDP models. In J.L. McClelland, D.E. Rumelhart and the PDP Research Group, *Parallel Distributed Processing: Explorations in the Microstructure of Cognition,* vol. 2:

Psychological and Biological Models. Cambridge, Ma: MIT Press.

Ryle, G. (1949) *The Concept of Mind*. London: Hutchinson.

Sanford, A.J. (1985) *Cognition and Cognitive Psychology*. London: Weidenfeld & Nicolson.

Schank, R.C. (1972) Conceptual dependency: A theory of natural language understanding. *Cognitive Psychology, 3*, 552–631.

Schank, R.C. (1982) *Dynamic Memory: A Theory of Reminding and Learning in Computers and People*. New York: Cambridge University Press.

Schank, R.C. and Abelson, R.P. (1977) *Scripts, Plans, Goals, and Understanding*. Hillsdale, NJ: Erlbaum.

Smith, B.C. (1985) Prologue to 'Reflection and semantics in a procedural language'. In R.J. Brachman and H.J. Levesque (eds) *Readings in Knowledge Representation*. Los Altos, Ca: Morgan Kaufmann.

Smith, E.E., Shoben, E.J. and Rips, L.J. (1974) Structure and process in semantic memory: A featural model for semantic decisions. *Psychological Review, 81*, 214–241.

Smith, M.J.S. (1982) Are cognitive maps like real maps? *Dissertation Abstracts International, 43B*, 1286.

Smith, M.P. (1988) Styles of computational representation. *Behavioral and Brain Sciences, 11*, 530–531.

Smolensky, P. (1986) Information processing in dynamical systems: Foundations of harmony theory. In D.E. Rumelhart, J.L. McClelland and the PDP Research Group, *Parallel Distributed Processing: Explorations in the Microstructure of Cognition*, vol. 1: *Foundations*. Cambridge, Ma: MIT Press.

Thorndyke, P.W. (1977) Cognitive structures in comprehension and memory of narrative discourse. *Cognitive Psychology, 9*, 77–110.

Tolman, E.C. (1948) Cognitive maps in rats and men. *Psychological Review, 55*, 189–208.

Tulving, E. (1962) Subjective organization in free recall of 'unrelated' words. *Psychological Review, 69*, 344–354.

Tulving, E. (1964) Intratrial and intertrial retention: Notes towards a theory of free recall verbal learning. *Psychological Review, 71*, 219–237.

Tulving, E. and Donaldson, W. (eds) (1972) *Organization of Memory*. New York: Academic Press.

Tyler, S.A. (ed.) (1969) *Cognitive Anthropology*. New York: Holt, Rinehart & Winston.

Underwood, B.J. (1972) Are we overloading memory? In A.W. Melton and E. Martin (eds) *Coding Processes in Human Memory*. Washington, DC: Winston.

Van Dijk, T.A. and Kintsch, W. (1983) *Strategies of Discourse Comprehension*. New York: Academic Press.

Wilensky, R. (1978) Why John married Mary: Understanding stories involving recurring goals. *Cognitive Science, 2*, 235–266.

Winograd, T. (1972) *Understanding Natural Language*. New York: Academic Press.

Winograd, T. (1975) Frame representations and the declarative/procedural controversy. In D.G. Bobrow and A.M. Collins (eds) *Representation and Understanding: Studies in Cognitive Science*. New York: Academic Press.

Wittgenstein, L. (1974) *Philosophical Grammar* (trans. A.J.P. Kenny). Oxford: Blackwell.

Young, J.Z. (1978) *Programs of the Brain*. Oxford: Oxford University Press.

OBJECTIVE TESTS OF FREUD'S THEORIES
Paul Kline

Despite the claims of Eysenck (Eysenck and Wilson, 1973) that Freudian theory is scientifically valueless, its faults having been revealed by the advances of academic psychology, in recent years there has been a spate of new and impressive books on Freudian theory. Grünbaum (1984) has examined the philosophical foundations of psycholanalysis and found them wanting, a claim that has been rebutted by Edelson (1984). Gellner (1985) has attempted to explain the attraction of Freudian theory by likening it to religion and he also pours scorn on its scientific pretensions. Eysenck (1985) has reiterated his attacks on the scientific veracity of Freudian hypotheses, while Masson (1984) has impugned the truthfulness of Freud, arguing that his claim that the Oedipus complex was fantasy arose from an attempt to avoid the facts of incest in well-known families. As if this attack on Freud's character were not enough, Thornton (1983) has attempted to demonstrate that psychoanalytic theory is nothing but a fantasy of cocaine addiction, a quasi-scientific Kubla Khan; although, surely, the provenance of a theory is not important. More balanced accounts of Freud have also appeared in studies of his life (Clark, 1980) and of the background to his scientific ideas by Sulloway (1979). But this is not all. Some psychologists have fought back against this tide of anti-Freudianism. Kline (1984) has summarized a considerable amount of empirical evidence in support of Freudian theory and demonstrated that the psychoanalytic unconscious can be laid open for scientific verification (Kline, 1987b). Masling, too, is attempting to provide empirical support for psychoanalysis, in a series of volumes (for example, 1983). Finally it should be mentioned that Freudian theory is receiving continued attention in philosophy, as evinced in the recent volume by Clark and Wright (1988) where efforts have been made to examine it in the tradition of hermeneutics rather than science. All these important arguments are raised because they demonstrate that Freudian theory is still a powerful intellectual force. To claim that it is dead, as do many experimental psychologists – at least by implication for it rarely influences their thinking – must be either ignorance or wishful thinking.

From all this work a number of issues emerge as salient for psychology. One most important point concerns the hermeneutic analysis of Freudian theory. Many modern psychoanalysts are increasingly defending their theory on hermeneutic grounds (for example, Stolorow et al., 1987). The question here is whether such hermeneutics are compatible with a scientific psychology. Another vital issue is the simple question of whether psychoanalytic theory has empirical support or is subject to empirical verification, in any important sense. The third issue to be discussed is the value of Freudian theory: why it is worth examining at all given that it is close to one hundred years old and is open to many valid objections.

HERMENEUTICS

First, I shall examine the value of the hermeneutic analysis of Freudian theory. Hermeneutics dispenses with causal explanations, which are the aim and virtue of the scientific method, in favour of interpretations, of which no single one is true. This is certainly the approach to psychoanalysis that is favoured by Schafer (1980). In hermeneutics, therefore, psychoanalytic claims are regarded not as true or false but as possible interpretations. Since there can be many interpretations of the same phenomena, various criteria are used to decide which is the best interpretation. These include aesthetic beauty, comprehensiveness of explanation, internal coherence and consistency with other psychological knowledge (Stolorow et al., 1987). There can be little doubt that these hermeneutic criteria were developed as a counterweight to the Popperian emphasis on the falsifiability of hypotheses in the scientific method.

There are several points here which require discussion. First, hermeneutic analysis is unquestionably appropriate for the arts or for subjects which form closed systems and do not impinge on other systems in the world. A good example of this was drawn by Sharpe (1988) who argued that there are several interpretations of a Beethoven sonata some of which, in the hands of maestri, will be of equal value. Note that if an interpretation is regarded as inferior it is often in terms of the coherence of the whole piece and in terms of aesthetic beauty. Music is a closed system and thus hermeneutic analysis makes excellent sense. It is almost nonsense to talk of a correct or incorrect interpretation, providing the player has not violated the instructions of the composer. Classical composers expected the player to interpret the score of which, quite deliberately, only the essentials were made explicit.

Unfortunately for the hermeneutic position psychoanalysis is not a closed system. We ought to take the theory separately from the therapy since the former is more like a closed system than the latter, but even so it does impinge on the real world. For example, the Oedipus complex is seen as the kernel of neurosis. Now, this is elegant and it has considerable explanatory power, to take the first two of the hermeneutic criteria. However, it also impinges on the real world since it implies that children love one parent and wish to kill the other. These are real events in the real world and are therefore (in principle at least) verifiable. In the sense that these claims are either true or not, it matters not a whit whether hermeneutic criteria are fulfilled. What use is coherence if the theory is simply wrong? This is even more true of psychoanalytic therapy. There can be the most brilliant interpretations of the analytic sessions, coherent, aesthetically beautiful and of great explanatory power. Patients, however, at the end of the analytic hour, leave the therapeutic couch and step into the world of reality. It is difficult to see how hermeneutics could ever be appropriate for what, ultimately, is an empirically-based theory which refers back to the experiences of patients.

Actually it is interesting to note that Stolorow and his colleagues, who have long advocated the hermeneutic approach to the understanding of psychoanalysis, themselves offend the criterion of coherence, as has been pointed out in a detailed analysis of their work (Kline, in press). Thus one of their hermeneutic criteria is accordance with psychological knowledge. However, this is to relate the interpretation to something beyond the system and, in effect, to the real world. Indeed it is also noteworthy that in their excellent studies of psychoanalytic therapy they do cite clinical studies as support for their claims. This recourse to evidence is not hermeneutical but stems from a different tradition – that of the scientific approach to theory which attempts to provide evidence for hypotheses. This leads on to the second issue: namely, the scientific, objective support for Freudian theory. At this juncture, however, I draw the conclusion that psychoanalysis, both the theory and the therapy, is not suited to hermeneutic analysis.

THE SCIENTIFIC STATUS OF PSYCHOANALYSIS

The second major issue and the one that is of the greatest importance to modern psychology (which is an essentially empirical science, hence its enthusiastic adoption in America), concerns the scientific status of psychoanalysis. Ever since the 1950s, culminating in his recent book, *The Decline and Fall of The Freudian Empire*, Eysenck has attacked the scientific incompetence of Freudian theory. He has adopted the Popperian position that the theory is unscientific because it is not falsifiable. In addition, he has pointed out other severe weaknesses of psychoanalytic theory, namely that the samples on which the observations are made are small and unrepresentative, that the observations are rarely recorded but are inextricably bound up with interpretations, and that theory is so constructed that prediction is impossible but *post hoc* explanation is always effortless. Its complete lack of quantification renders it impossible to put to any precise test and – the *coup de grâce* – the psychotherapy derived from it is certainly ineffective and probably harmful. In brief psychoanalysis is scientifically valueless.

In general, this Eysenckian view that Freudian theory is of nothing more than historical interest has been generally accepted in scientific departments of psychology, although a small number of psychologists have attempted to meet Eysenck on his own ground and argue that there is objective support for some aspects of Freudian theory. Kline (1972, 1981) and Fisher and Greenberg (1977) have collated large numbers of experiments relevant to psychoanalytic theory and have shown that a blanket rejection of Freud's work is too extreme. Kragh and Smith (1970) in Scandinavia, have developed percept-genetic analysis both as a theory and a technique and have provided support for psychoanalytic notions, as I shall discuss later in this chapter. A number of other workers have also provided interesting evidence, both cross-culturally, as in the hologeistic school (Whiting and Child, 1953), and experimentally. Silverman (1983) would be a good example of the latter. Before I discuss this experimental evidence, however, I want to make a few points about Eysenck's objections, which have been too readily accepted simply because *some* of them are indisputably well taken.

Falsifiability

First, as Grünbaum (1984) has pointed out, there is a powerful objection to the Popperian notion of falsifiability which, ultimately, means little more than that the writer can think of some way to falsify the statement. Second, many of the objections raised by Eysenck can be raised against experimental psychology in general. For example, although it is true that Freud's samples were unrepresentative, to object is to maintain a double standard. Many psychological experiments use white American undergraduates, press-ganged by the desire for grades, while others use the Norwegian hooded rat. However, even if the Eysenckian objections are taken at face value, there is still no need to reject Freudian theory out of hand.

Farrell (1961) has argued that it is an error to regard Freudian theory as a unified theory which may be rejected or accepted. Rather it should be considered as a collection of hypotheses, some of which may turn out to be true, others false, when put to the Popperian test. Certainly some are more critical than others. Thus it would alter considerably the nature of psychoanalysis, thus refined by empirical testing, if it turned out that no process resembling repression could be verified. However, if it was demonstrated that the Oedipus complex was more pronounced in small than in large families, then this would not radically affect the theory. This view of psychoanalysis, as a collection of hypotheses, is the one adopted by almost all empirical psychologists involved in its investigation.

In a chapter of this length it is not possible to review in detail all the objective, experimental work which has been carried out in the investigation of Freudian hypotheses. Kline (1981) discussed more than a thousand studies and Fisher and Greenberg (1977) included even more. Instead, I shall make a few general points about these investigations and concentrate upon what appears to be the most significant work.

There are a number of problems in the adoption of the procedure advocated by Farrell for the verification of Freudian theory and these have rendered the research less effective than might be hoped by its advocates. The first difficulty concerns the formulation of the hypothesis to be tested. Unless it is an actual statement from the Master, logically it is always possible to argue that it is not Freudian and hence irrelevant to the theory. Another difficulty lies in the instantiation of the theory in the hypothesis. For example, it is implicit in repression that painful words will be remembered less well than pleasant controls. However, to test this hypothesis with words like sugar and quinine, for example, is absurd; and this constitutes an actual case. A similar error was perpetrated by Valentine, in his day a respected British psychologist. Sceptical of the Oedipus complex he naively questioned boys and girls as to which parent they liked the better. Of course, it is a matter of subjective judgement as to whether a given procedure does or does not test the theory but it is a judgement which has to be made. Such an example, incidentally, strongly indicates why meta-studies of topics, such as the efficacy of psychotherapy, should be regarded with extreme caution. The summation of bad studies in no way robs them of their badness.

There is another point concerning the testing of hypotheses which is probably of greater importance. It can be easily shown that experimental psychology, in its relentless search for rigour, has preferred to tackle trivial problems with scientific precision and *élan* rather than difficult, complex questions which may force us to use less than perfect methods (Kline, in press). This is particularly pertinent to the study of psychoanalysis which is, essentially, concerned with a subjective and unconscious world of feeling. Such a field is particularly resistant to elegant, quantitative analysis so that it is little wonder that many researchers into psychoanalytic theory have plumped for easier topics, which are hardly of central importance. Thus, for example, there are a considerable number of researches into psychosexual personality syndromes such as the anal or oral character because these can be tackled with standard psychometric techniques. (Incidentally, I have studied both these syndromes and do not excuse myself from this criticism.) There are far fewer attempts to investigate the unconscious processes under-lying the castration complex, for obvious reasons. However, this does mean that many of the central questions concerning the scientific validity of Freudian concepts have no reliable answers.

CROSS-CULTURAL STUDIES

It is well known that one of the distinctive things about Freudian theory is that it makes universal statements about humankind in general, a peculiarly irritating trait given that middle-aged, Viennese, Jewish women comprised a majority of the sample. For this reason cross-cultural psychology has always been of interest to psychologists concerned with the validation of Freudian theory. This is particularly true for investigating those aspects of Freudian theory which make claims concerning the impact of the environment. However, there are a number of problems in cross-cultural psychology which mean that all findings must be treated with considerable caution. First, tests developed in one culture are not necessarily valid in another culture; validity in the new culture must always be demonstrated. Even if the test is valid, direct comparison of means across cultures can be misleading. Careful standardization is always necessary but, of course, this can obscure real differences. Some cross-cultural psychologists (for example, Berry, 1983) would deny the value of comparing cultures at all on common variables and argue that it is more meaningful to use the variables most salient to each particular culture. What is of interest here is the nature of the variables which are salient. This is what is somewhat inelegantly called the emic–etic dilemma. In addition to this there are other, more practical, difficulties in cross-cultural psychology which further compound the problems. For instance, many cultures which have unusual or distinctive child-rearing practices and which are, therefore, of considerable interest in testing psychoanalytic theory, are also under-developed and have largely illiterate populations. This makes testing difficult because any literate samples are not representative. Furthermore, test *naïveté* and experimental demands which are totally foreign to the culture can distort results. For all these reasons, attractive as cross-cultural psychology is, few clear results relevant to Freudian theory have emerged from it.

There is another cross-cultural approach which is far more powerful and which has provided some support for certain psycho-analytic hypotheses. This is the hologeistic method which was first brought into prominence by Whiting and Child (1953) with their studies of child rearing. This method involves rating ethnographic and antropological reports of a large sample of societies for psycho-logical variables and submitting these ratings to some form of statistical analysis, usually correlations or chi-squares depending on the particular variables and the questions asked. For example, if we are interested in the oral character then we can rate all the reports for emphasis on orality in childhood and adulthood. Typical variables might be: length of breast feeding, age of weaning, severity of weaning, importance of finishing meals, place of food in rituals, amount of drinking, place of food and drink in stories, dependence of adults and so on. When all these variables are correlated across societies it should be possible to see whether or not child-rearing practices are related to adult orality. Most aspects of Freudian theory can be put to the test in this way, as can other theories of child development. This method has the obvious advantage that it tests the universality of the claims and is a powerful antidote to the original sampling defects.

However, there are a number of objections which have been raised against the hologeistic method which have been well summarized by

Campbell and Naroll (1972). The two most important of these require some discussion. The most obvious one concerns the accuracy of the original anthropological material. Some anthropologists use reports rather than observations as their sources. In one study of ego development in Africa, the reports of a colonial planter, with no anthropological training, were used. In another study, also to be found in Münsterberger (1969), a sample of 17 Chinese waiters from San Francisco was used as a basis for a discussion of gambling among the Chinese, of whom, on the mainland alone, there are more than one billion. Furthermore, even the most respected studies in anthropology have been called into question. For example, Freeman (1984) has cast considerable doubt on the work of Margaret Mead in Samoa (Mead, 1928). Fortunately, this particular objection is not as devastating as might be thought. All these inaccuracies add in error. Thus they simply reduce the level of all observed correlations. If, therefore, in these noisy conditions, any correlations can be observed we can feel confident that these are under- rather than over-estimates.

The second and related point asserts that these inaccuracies add in systematic error and can, therefore, mislead the investigator. Such errors, the argument runs, reflect the biases of the anthropologists and any correlations would simply reflect the implicit theories of the original observers. For example, Freudian anthropologists might well emphasize the importance of the child-rearing procedures which are critical to Freudian theory. However, in most hologeistic studies there are a large number of reports from a wide range of anthropologists and, since there is no agreed theory among them, the possibility of systematic error is small.

For all these reasons, hologeistic studies, when properly conducted (using a large number of societies and raters who are unacquainted with the theory being tested), do seem capable of putting psycho-analytic theory to the test. One such investigation was that of Stephens (1961) into menstrual taboo, which formed part of a larger cross-cultural study of the Oedipus complex (Stephens, 1962). Stephens argued that the length of menstrual taboo on intercourse in a society reflected the degree of castration anxiety in that society, reasoning that the notion of blood on the female genitalia elicited the normally repressed castration anxiety. Since, in this hologeistic investigation, Stephens used the data from 72 societies, this constitutes an excellent test of the universality of the castration complex. There were no direct measures of castration anxiety in the anthropological reports, so Stephens examined the child-rearing procedures which, in Freudian theory, are likely to cause it. In addition he looked for castration-like incidents in myths and customs – male circumcision might be one such – and, finally, he measured the extent of menstrual taboo in each society. If Freudian theory is correct, then there should be a positive relationship between the length of menstrual taboo and the incidence of the relevant child-rearing procedures. These include post-partum sex taboo, severity of punishment for masturbation, severity of sex training, severity of aggression training, pressure for obedience, and whether or not father is the main disciplinarian. In all, ten such measures were used.

Five of these measures were significantly related to length of menstrual taboo and all except the general pressure for obedience were in the predicted direction. Furthermore, a total score for castration anxiety which was based upon all ten scores was related to the menstrual taboo scale at a highly significant level, a result that could have occurred by chance only 1 in 100,000 times. This means that measures of castration anxiety are related to the length of menstrual taboo within a spectrum of societies that embraces virtually all types. In turn this supports the universality of both the Oedipus and the castration complexes (for the latter is dependent on the former), and also the psychoanalytic claim that negative feelings about menstruation are related to castration fears. This study, therefore, provides prima facie support for some of the most fundamental concepts in psychoanalysis.

In discussing this research it has been argued by those opposed to Freudian theory that there is a far simpler explanation of the findings and that, like Occam's razor, this is to be preferred. This argument claims that severe child-training leads to inhibited and restrained behaviour of which the taboo on sexual intercourse at the time of menstruation is an example. This argument, however, will not do. The point of psychoanalytic theory is to explain menstrual taboo, not to accept it as a given, as if it were obvious that it should be a basis for restraint. Psychoanalysis accounts for the fact that it is considered, in some societies, dirty or unhygienic or whatever the rationalization is.

Indeed more detailed analysis of the findings precludes the simpler explanation because the individual variables most highly associated with menstrual taboo are those which, in Freudian theory, are most closely related to the Oedipus and castration conflicts: post-partum sexual taboo, which allows the child to sleep with its mother; severity of masturbation punishment, which is certainly the most salient (for castration is talion revenge); and finally, father as the main disciplinarian. In summary this study by Stephens must be considered as good evidence for the widespread applicability of the Oedipus and castration complexes and for the power of the hologeistic method to put psychoanalytic theory to the objective test.

Studies of the unconscious

As was argued earlier, one of the difficulties with studies examining the validity of Freudian theory is that, in the interests of scientific respectability and rigour, some relatively unimportant topics have been investigated. In recent years, however, a few workers have begun the experimental investigation of the unconscious – the core of psychoanalytic theory – and I shall now scrutinize this research.

PERCEPT-GENETICS

First, percept-genetics, a Scandinavian development of psycho-analytic and Gestalt notions of perception (Kragh and Smith, 1970) must be examined. In percept-genetic methods a stimulus picture, which includes a peripheral threat, is presented tachistoscopically to subjects in a series of exposures, at gradually increasing levels of illumination. At each exposure subjects have to draw and describe what they see. In percept-genetic theory perception is a process between individual and stimulus which is normally automatic and instantaneous; a process, however, which the serial presentation fragments and lays open to scrutiny. In percept-genetic methods the searchlight of consciousness is directed on to what is normally automatic and preconscious (Westerlundh, 1976). Investigation of these processes reveals information concerning defence mechanisms, drives, complexes and repressed conflicts and life events, according to percept-genetic theory. One set of stimuli has been fully developed into a test, the Defence Mechanism Test (Kragh, 1969). And in Scandinavia, there is a considerable volume of research, mainly with clinical groups, using percept-genetic techniques, much of it summarized in Kragh and Smith (1970) and Kragh (1985). Thus, if these claims are supported, percept-genetic methods would appear to offer a method of investigating the unconscious.

The problem lies in the validity of these methods, especially the Defence Mechanism Test – the Scandinavians tend to accept the findings as valid and to use them in clinical diagnosis and treatment and even in selection (Kragh, 1962). I shall now describe a series of studies into the validity of the DMT by Kline and Cooper (1977) and

Cooper and Kline (1986) because to establish the validity of the test variables would *ipso facto* support the Freudian theory. Furthermore if the test is valid it immediately suggests how percept-genetic methods could be extended into the investigation of other Freudian concepts.

If percept-genetic theory is correct it should be possible to use a variety of stimuli in the study of defences, in fact virtually anything against which there are supposed to be defences. Kline and Cooper (1977), therefore, presented tachistoscopically an oral stimulus, a suckling pig, and a neutral pig control in percept-genetic presentations. A comparison of the two sets of responses indicated clearly that there were no apparent defences elicited to the neutral pig but to the suckling pig there were a number of examples. For instance, denial was evinced when, at one exposure, a subject claimed that some animal was feeding but, at the next exposure, rejected this hypothesis. In their paper responses were simply set out in order that readers might judge for themselves whether defences had been elicited. However, as Kline (1987a) has argued, a word of caution is necessary. Data such as these do not prove the validity of percept-genetic methods; rather they present for public scrutiny observations, made under controlled conditions, which are similar to the observations made by analysts in their sessions. As in psychoanalytic theory the same act of interpretation has to be made in order to label them as defences. Nevertheless they are impressive in that they do resemble what analysts have described as defences. To prove their validity, however, it would be necessary to predict which subjects would show which defences to which stimuli. This relatively simply experiment has never been carried out.

Cooper and Kline (1986) investigated the validity of the DMT by relating its scores to a number of other well-known measures of personality. It was established in this study that the DMT was not simply a measure of neuroticism – one of the two most persuasive personality factors. The modest correlations of the DMT with the Cattell 16PF (Cattell *et al.*, 1970) also supported the validity of the scales. For example, Cattell's 'M', imagination, correlated -0.39 with the defence of isolation. In addition to this, a general factor obtained from the DMT scales correlated 0.52 with a measure of repression derived from a study of perceptual defence. Dixon (1981) has demonstrated that perceptual defence is a real phenomenon, rather than an experimental artefact, if proper methods of measuring the threshold are used. One such is the dark adaptation method of Wallace and Worthington (1970) which was utilized in this investigation. There was a huge difference in the thresholds to 'VD' and 'TV'.

Since, as Kline has argued (Kline, in press), perceptual defence is an example of Freudian repression, where something is excluded from consciousness, this correlation seems good support for the validity of the DMT as related to defences, all of which have a similar purpose.

Cooper (1982) showed that this general factor of defence was negatively correlated with success on a high-speed jet fighter course, a result which is in accord with work in Scandinavia (Neumann, 1971) and with research reported by Kragh (1985) into stressful occupations. The argument here is that defensive individuals defend against frightening indices of things going wrong and thus have more accidents. As a final test of the DMT, Cooper and Kline (1986) used a percept-genetic stimulus with a smiling face instead of the standard horrible face in the periphery of the picture. To this there were no defensive responses, which supports the notion that the DMT responses are defensive.

If these results are considered alongside the clinical data accumulated over the years by Kragh, Smith and their colleagues in Sweden and Scandinavia the following conclusions can be drawn. The Defence Mechanism Test does seem able to reveal and lay open for scrutiny aspects of perception which are usually unconscious. Other percept-genetic techniques, which are more specialized and which cannot be described in this chapter, have this same capability. Whether the responses are defences or not is more difficult to decide but the distortions clearly resemble the defence described in psychoanalysis. It must be stressed again, however, that these data require the same interpretative act as clinical data to label them as defences. Nevertheless it seems apparent that percept-genetic methods are capable of allowing experimental analysis of the unconscious and it remains only for ingenious experimenters to put them to good use.

THE WORK OF SILVERMAN

Another method of investigating unconscious mental processes is the drive-activation method developed by Silverman and his colleagues in New York, much of which has been summarized by Silverman (1983). In this method, as the name suggests, unconscious drives and their derivatives, which in psychoanalysis are held to be the basis of psychopathology, are activated or soothed by the exposure of relevant subliminal stimuli. The stimuli must be subliminal to activate the drives. If they were conscious they would have no effect since defences would be brought into operation. Typical verbal stimuli are: beating Dad is wrong; beating Dad is OK; Mommy and I are one. The former is, of course, relevant to the Oedipus complex, the latter to regression in schizophrenia.

Silverman, in his 1983 survey, reports the findings from about eighty investigations almost all of which support the validity of the method. What is particularly impressive is the pattern of results. Thus subliminal activating stimuli increase pathology while subliminal drive-reducing stimuli decrease it. Control subliminal stimuli have no effect and neither do activating and reducing stimuli exposed above threshold. An example will clarify the work and enable some possible objections to be discussed.

Schizophrenics, after the subliminal exposure of a drive-activating stimulus, a snarling man with a dagger, show increases in pathology, as measured by thought disorder (using a test of recall), and non-verbal indices, such as finger-tapping or giggling. A clever test of psychoanalytic theory and the validity of the method is to use stimuli which are relevant to each of several groups. Thus anal stimuli were used with stutterers, oral stimuli with depressives and incest stimuli with homosexuals. As was hypothesized, these stimuli produced increased pathology only with the appropriate groups.

On these grounds Silverman and his colleagues have claimed that the drive-activation method allows the experimental study of Freudian drive theory. However, a variety of objections have been raised to this work. It is alarming that most of the research stems from Silverman and his associates. This is not to imply fraud; rather there may be some artefact of their methods accounting for the results. Recently, however, Westerlundh (1986) has compared Silverman's method with his own percept-genetic approach. He demonstrated that the findings were replicable in other laboratories although the cognitive processing involved in the messages was far too complex such that the general affect of the words rather than the semantics was the important feature.

A further objection to the work was made by Watson (1975) who pointed out that the measures of psychopathology were exceedingly feeble and show little evidence of validity. This is certainly a well taken point especially where Rorschach indices and simple rating scales are used. Nevertheless, if this is so and the tests are invalid the impressive and hypothesized pattern of results, which fit psycho-analytic hypotheses, cannot be explained. Clearly, however, better measures of psychopathology are required.

In conclusion, I think it can be maintained that the Silverman method offers a good opportunity for the experimental study of Freud's unconscious drives although there is no doubt that the methodology can be improved in detail.

PROJECTIVE TESTS

There is one further method which deserves a brief discussion although it has never been put into practice. This concerns the use of objectively-scored projective tests in the study of the unconscious. First it must be made clear that all the objections to projective tests – that they are not reliable, have little evidence of validity and, ultimately, have no underlying rationale – are fully accepted. Their psychometric qualities are weak, as Eysenck (1959) asserts. Furthermore, their claims to measure deep layers of the personality seem undermined by the fact that relatively trivial variables, such as test condition and the age, sex, or race, of the tester, can affect the results (Vernon, 1964).

Nevertheless, projective tests can be useful. First, the studies of validity usually necessitate the test protocols to be scored blind. This is, in fact, absurd. Responses can only be correctly interpreted in the light of our knowledge of the individual who made them. A preoccupation with, say, cricket balls, is surely of different significance for a professional cricketer compared with any other person. Thus academic, blind studies need to be interpreted with caution. The reliability of projective tests can be improved by scoring, where the presence or absence of a variable in test protocols is scored 1 or 0. Thus, if in the House, Tree, Person (HTP) test (Buck, 1948) a subject has drawn an acorn, he scores one on the variable 'acorn' as do all others who drew one. Subjects who do not draw an acorn score 0. In this way, projective tests can be scored with perfect reliability (Holley, 1973; Hampson and Kline, 1977). In addition to this, some projective test users appear to obtain powerful psychological insights from them – Carstairs (1957) is a good example of this with his work on the Rajputs of Southern India – and it seems senseless to abandon them.

Thus, objectively scored projective tests are valuable. The following example illustrates how they may be used in the study of the unconscious. According to the manual to the HTP (Buck, 1980) the description of a tree as a 'soft maple' indicates impotence, while the maple itself represents a female. Now the response of drawing a maple tree has conscious determinants, for it is a sensible and rational response, and also unconscious determinants, namely (if Buck be correct) impotence and femininity. Thus, if the objective scores on the HTP were factored we would expect the response 'soft maple' to load on two factors, one conscious the other unconscious. If we included percept-genetic and drive-activation measures in the analysis we would have clear markers for the unconscious factor or factors. This procedure certainly allows projective tests to be used in the study of the unconscious and it would put to severe test the claim that projective tests measure deeper and unconscious layers of the personality. If they do, then they become valuable in the objective study of psychoanalytic theory.

So far, in this chapter, it has been shown that Freudian theory is still a topic which is of considerable interest both to psychology and other fields, despite the well-founded doubts as to its scientific merits. One approach to overcome these, the treatment of psycho-analysis as hermeneutics, was found to be incoherent but it was demonstrated that the scientific study of Freudian theory is possible if the theory is regarded as a collection of hypotheses each of which could be separately verified. This was the method which was generally adopted but it had the drawback that it led, often, to the testing of relatively trivial aspects of the theory. However, in addition to the valuable hologeistic, cross-cultural research, three methods have been discussed: percept-genetics, the drive-activation method and the objective analysis of projective tests, all of which are capable of subjecting unconscious processes, the core of the theory, to experimental study. These methods have yielded evidence in support of such important concepts as the defence mechanisms and the Oedipus and castration complexes, distinctively Freudian notions which are not well dealt with by other theories.

PSYCHOANALYSIS AND MODERN PSYCHOLOGY

I now turn to the final issue of this chapter in which the reasons for continuing to study psychoanalytic theory are discussed. This is an important topic, since, with the modern explosion of science, in most subjects, theories which were developed one hundred years ago are outmoded by more recent discoveries. This is without doubt the viewpoint of orthodox, academic psychology. However, as is so often the case, this orthodoxy is strangling rather than resuscitating the subject.

First it is not argued here that psychoanalytic theory is correct and that it must be believed. Far from it. That is why its objective, scientific validation has been advocated. However, psychoanalytic theory has much to offer academic, scientific psychology which in some respects is profoundly lacking. Psychoanalysis is concerned with the inner mental world of individuals. Although this is difficult to study scientifically, this is no reason to ignore it as, essentially – influenced by ideas of scientific method and behaviourism – psychology has done. In its emphasis on mental processes psycho-analysis ensures that these are not abandoned in the interests of rigour and precision. This leads on to the second point. As I have argued (Kline, 1988) academic psychology has largely concerned itself with topics trivial to the human condition. Love, death, evil and human destiny, these have been the concerns of people, universally, and they receive short shrift in current academic psychology. Models of working memory, computer recognition of origami ducks, prisoners' dilemmas – who in all honesty really cares about the findings from these experiments, whose subjects, in the main, are students desperate for grades? Thus academic psychology, following the chimera of science, has trivialized itself. Psychoanalytic theory, in contrast, is concerned with the profundities of human life, as conceived by poets, philosophers, sages and divinities.

There is a further, perhaps even more important, aspect of psychoanalysis which is of great value for psychology. This is its model or concept of humanity. Different models of humanity have profound implications for society. Modern, scientific psychology has adopted a model which essentially regards people as machines. If they are ill then replace or repair the parts, just as an example, and there are similar implications for education and the organization of society. With such a model, because machines are always designed for some purpose, people become objects to be used. No wonder that the model underpins totalitarian states where human beings are valued for what they can produce. Thus scientific psychology, by its adoption of this model, denigrates the humanity of people, those aspects which are not useful or valuable to the state or to industry. People are not valued for themselves. This, again, is in complete contrast to psychoanalysis where each person is valued, and where the aim of therapy is to free the patient from the bondage of the unconscious that he or she may make rational choices in everyday life. Psychoanalysis is a radical philosophy that values freedom, hence its proscription by fascism, communism and catholicism. There can be few greater tributes. In brief, psychoanalysis has human values which psychology, perhaps in the guise of science, seems not to possess but which are essential in the study of people. The point is that scientific psychology has values but these are implicit rather than explicit and, on examination, turn out to be inhumane.

There is one final point. The scientific method relies on simplification, the law of parsimony, and in the natural sciences, that has proved useful. Psychoanalysis, on the other hand, has tried to embrace the full richness of human behaviour and has not eschewed complexity. This is yet another reason why scientific psychology has failed to come to terms with what is really human.

That is why, in the final analysis, it is essential that we do not abandon psychoanalysis, as Eysenck would have us do. What is necessary is to combine the richness and the humanity of psychoanalysis with the rigour of scientific psychology. This is a much harder task than the blind adherence to one of these systems and the consequent denigration of the other. If it is not done, psychoanalysis will retreat into a mediaeval hermeneutics and scientific psychology will become yet more rigorous and trivial. For these reasons the objective study of psychoanalytic theory must continue. Fortunately, as has been shown in this chapter, there are methods available which make this a viable possibility.

REFERENCES

Berry, J.W. (1983) Textured contexts: Systems and situations in cross-cultural psychology. In S.H. Irvine and J.W. Berry (eds) *Human Assessment and Cultural Factors*. New York: Plenum.

Buck, J.N. (1948) The HTP test. *Journal of Clinical Psychology, 4*, 151–159.

Buck, J.N. (1980) *The House Tree Person Technique: Revised Manual*. Los Angeles: Western Psychological Services.

Campbell, D.T. and Naroll, R. (1972) The hologeistic method. In F.L.K. Hsu, *Psychological Anthropology*. Cambridge, Mass.: Schenkman.

Carstairs, G.M. (1957) *The Twice-Born*. Hogarth Press: London.

Cattell, R.B., Eber, H.W. and Tatsuoka, M.M. (1970) *The Sixteen Personality Factor Questionnaire*. Champaign: Institute for Personality and Ability Testing.

Clark, P. and Wright, C. (eds) (1988) *Mind, Psychoanalysis and Science*. Blackwell: Oxford.

Clark, R.W. (1980) *Freud: The Man and The Cause*. London: Cape.

Cooper, C. (1982) *An Experimental Study of Freudian Defence Mechanisms*. Unpublished doctoral thesis, University of Exeter.

Cooper, C. and Kline, P. (1986) An evaluation of the Defence Mechanism Test. *British Journal of Psychology, 77*, 19–31.

Dixon, N.F. (1981) *Preconscious Processing*. Chichester: Wiley.

Edelson, M. (1984) *Hypothesis and Evidence in Psychoanalysis*. Chicago: University of Chicago Press.

Eysenck, H.J. (1959) The Rorschach Test. In O.K. Buros (ed.) *The Fifth Mental Measurement Yearbook*. New Jersey: Gryphon Press.

Eysenck, H.J. (1985) *The Decline and Fall of the Freudian Empire*. Harmondsworth: Penguin Books.

Eysenck, H.J. and Wilson, G.D. (1973) *The Experimental Study of Freudian Theories*. London: Methuen.

Farrell, B.A. (1961) Can psychoanalysis be refuted? *Inquiry*, 4, 16–36.

Fisher, S. and Greenberg, P.R. (1977) *The Scientific Credibility of Freud's Theory and Therapy*. Brighton: Harvester Press.

Freeman, D. (1984) *Margaret Mead and Samoa: The Making and Unmaking of the Paradise Island Myth*. Harmondsworth: Penguin.

Gellner, E. (1985) *The Psychoanalytic Movement*. London: Paladin Books.

Grünbaum, A. (1984) *The Foundations of Psychoanalysis*. Berkeley: University of California Press.

Hampson, S. and Kline, P. (1977) Personality dimensions differentiating certain groups of abnormal offenders from non-offenders. *British Journal of Criminology*, 17, 310–331.

Holley, J. (1973) Rorschach Analysis. In P. Kline (ed.) *New Approaches in Psychological Measurement*. Chichester: Wiley.

Kline, P. (1972) *Fact and Fantasy in Freudian Theory*. London: Methuen.

Kline, P. (1981) *Fact and Fantasy in Freudian Theory* (2nd ed). London: Methuen.

Kline, P. (1984) *Psychology and Freudian Theory*. London: Methuen.

Kline, P. (1987a) The scientific status of the DMT. *British Journal of Medical Psychology*, 60, 53–9.

Kline, P. (1987b) The experimental study of the psychoanalytic unconscious. *Personality and Social Psychology Bulletin*, 13, 363–378.

Kline, P. (1988) *Psychology Exposed: The Emperor's New Clothes*. London: Routledge.

Kline, P. (in press) Hermeneutics, science and psychoanalysis. *Journal of Psychoanalytic Studies*.

Kline, P. and Cooper, C. (1977) A percept-genetic study of some defence mechanisms in the test PN. *Scandinavian Journal of Psychology*, 18, 148–152.

Kragh, U. (1962) Prediction of success by Danish attack divers by the Defence Mechanism Test. *Perceptual and Motor Skills*, 15, 103–106.

Kragh, U. (1969) *The Defence Mechanism Test*. Copenhagen: Testforlaget.

Kragh, U. (1985) *DMT (Defence Mechanism Test) Manual*. Stockholm: Persona.

Kragh, U. and Smith, G.S. (1970) *Percept-Genetic Analysis*. Lund: Gleerups.

Masling, J. (ed.) (1983) *Empirical Studies of Psychoanalytic Theories*. Hillsdale: Analytic Press.

Masson, J.M. (1984) *The Assault on the Truth*. London: Faber.

Mead, M. (1928) *Coming of Age in Samoa*. New York: New American Library.

Münsterberger, W. (ed.) (1969) *Man and Culture*. London: Rapp & Whiting.

Neuman, T. (1971) Perceptual defence organisation as a predictor of the pilot's adaptive behaviour in military flying. In *Reports of the 9th conference for aviation psychology*. Cambridge: Ministry of Defence.

Schafer, R. (1980) Action and narrative in psychoanalysis. *New Literary History*, 12.

Sharpe, R. (1988) Mirrors, lamps, organisms and texts. In P. Clarke and C. Wright (eds) (1988). (See above.)

Silverman, L.H. (1983) The subliminal psychodynamic activation method: overview and comprehensive listing of studies. In J. Masling (ed.) (1983). (See above.)

Stephens, W.N. (1961) A cross-cultural study of menstrual taboos. *Genetic Psychology Monograph, 64,* 385–416.

Stephens, W.N. (1962) *The Oedipus Complex Hypothesis: Cross-Cultural Evidence.* Glencoe: Free Press.

Stolorow, R.D., Brandchaft, B. and Atwood, G.E. (1987) *Psychoanalytic Treatment: An Intersubjective Approach.* Hillsdale: Analytic Press.

Sulloway, F.J. (1979) *Freud, Biologist of the Mind.* London: Deutsch.

Thornton, E.N. (1983) *Freud and Cocaine: The Freudian Fallacy.* London: Blond & Briggs.

Vernon, P.E. (1964) *Personality Assessment.* London: Methuen.

Wallace, G. and Worthington, A.G. (1970) The dark adaptation index of perceptual defence: A procedural improvement. *Australian Journal of Psychology, 22,* 41–46.

Watson, J.P. (1975) An experimental method for the study of unconscious conflict. *British Journal of Medical Psychology, 48,* 301–302.

Westerlundh, B. (1976) *Aggression, Anxiety and Defence.* Lund: Gleerups.

Westerlundh, B. (1986) On reading subliminal sentences. A psychodynamic activation study. *Psychological Research Bulletin, 26, No 10.* Lund: University of Lund.

Whiting, J.W.M. and Child, I.L. (1953) *Child Training and Personality.* New Haven: Yale University Press.

CRIMINOLOGICAL AND LEGAL PSYCHOLOGY

Clive R. Hollin

In a previous edition of *Psychology Survey*, Borrill (1983) addressed the topic of 'Psychology and Crime'; while I wish to address the same area, I have elected to employ the title 'Criminological and Legal Psychology'. This latter term, I believe, serves better to emphasize the distinctive quality of a discrete field of study emerging from the blending of various independent disciplines, most notably criminology and psychology. While it would be overstating the case to maintain a strict division, criminological psychology can be seen as concerned with the study of criminal behaviour and its management; legal psychology as concerned with the law and legal procedures. The subject matter of criminological psychology is vast, ranging from juvenile delinquents to murderers, from policing to clinical intervention with offenders. Legal psychology is concerned with statutes such as the Police and Criminal Evidence Act, and with courtroom processes such as jury studies and judicial decision making. The field is recognized as being of concern to psychologists, as testified by The British Psychological Society's Division of Criminological and Legal Psychology, by a similar division in the American Psychological Association, and by recent reviews (for example, Hollin, 1989; Lloyd-Bostock, 1988; Weiner and Hess, 1987).

In this chapter my aim is to offer a sequel to Borrill (1983) by providing a summary of three topics not covered in detail previously. These are the measurement of crime, eyewitness memory, and clinical approaches to criminal behaviour.

MEASURING CRIME

In England the practice of gathering court statistics to gauge the country's moral health dates back to the late 1700s – well before

146

psychologists began to measure behaviour. In 1856 the *Judicial Statistics* was for the first time compiled using 'crimes known to the police', rather than court convictions or numbers imprisoned, as the standard measure of crime. This measure is still favoured, and reported annually in the Home Office publication *Criminal Statistics*, which presents a record of the number and types of crimes recorded by the police in England and Wales. In America the Uniform Crime Reports, collected annually by the FBI, serve a similar function. The official statistics have a number of uses: to record the total volume of crime; to assess the effectiveness of preventative measures; to detect changes in rates of crime; and to provide data for policy decisions.

From crimes recorded in *Criminal Statistics* an ominous trend is apparent: the annual figure for recorded crime has risen from approximately 500,000 in the 1950s to about 1,000,000 in the mid-1960s, around 2,000,000 by the mid-1970s, and 3,000,000 in the early 1980s. The crime rate, as the media continually report, is rising rapidly. The logical implication is that the present methods of crime control are not working, and that policy changes are urgently needed. However, before making this leap from statistics to policy, the reliability of the figures must be questioned. How accurate is the official figure as a measure of the real amount of crime in society? In attempting to answer this question, researchers have turned to the three agents involved in crime – the police, the offender, and the victim.

Police recording of crime

If an offence is reported to the police, is it guaranteed to appear in the official statistics? An American study noted by Hood and Sparks (1970) suggests not: only about two-thirds of serious crimes which victims claimed to have reported to the police were actually recorded in police files. A British survey similarly found that there were discrepancies between reported crime and the police-recorded crime: the percentage shortfall – crimes reported but not recorded – ranged from 75 per cent for robbery to 27 per cent for bicycle theft (Hough and Mayhew, 1985). However, some offence categories, for example sexual offences and thefts of motor vehicles, showed no shortfall. While human error may play a part in misrecording or 'losing' crimes, and the exact figures involved may be open to question, it is also true that the police have considerable discretion over the recording of reported crime.

As Hough and Mayhew (1985) note, the police may, with

justification, feel that a reported 'crime' is a mistake in that no offence has actually been committed, or that there is a lack of evidence to uphold the report. In other instances an informal caution may be given, in which case the offence will not appear in the official figures. In a similar vein, the criminal incident may be satisfactorily resolved by the appearance of a police officer: family disputes and arguments in public houses are examples of incidents in which a crime might be reported but go unrecorded. Alternatively, after reporting a crime the injured party may ask for charges to be dropped, and so the incident is written off as 'no crime' – again failing to appear in the statistics. In a survey of three London areas, Sparks *et al.* (1977) found that 'no crime' cases accounted for between 18 and 28 per cent of all initially recorded crimes. The time lapse between the committing of the crime and the reporting of it to the police is also important; those judged as being too 'stale' to merit investigation may fail to be recorded (Farrington and Bennett, 1981). Thus, for a variety of reasons the discrepancy between the number of crimes actually committed and the number recorded by the police suggests that the official statistics are not telling the full story – at least for some types of crime. Crimes are committed, some serious, which fail to appear in the statistics. The amount of this 'unknown' crime is traditionally referred to as the *Dark Figure*. In attempting to shed light on the magnitude of the Dark Figure, research has turned away from the police towards the other two parties involved in crime – the offender and the victim.

Offender surveys

In the 1960s a number of offender surveys were carried out for which the most commonly employed methodology was to select a sample on the basis of age or geographical location, then to ask them whether they had committed any crimes, either detected or undetected (Hood and Sparks, 1970). This information was gathered by questionnaire or interview, conducted with the target group themselves or people who knew them well. A British study of theft reported by Belson (1975) illustrates a typical survey. A sample of 1,445 boys, aged from 13 to 16 years, was randomly selected from a large sample of London households. Interviews with the boys revealed that approximately 70 per cent of the sample had stolen from a shop, and about 17 per cent had stolen from private premises. Thus the majority of boys had committed an offence for which, had they been caught, they would have been liable to prosecution.

The general picture which emerges from the self-report studies is that the official figures underestimate the true extent of crime, especially amongst the young. Indeed, Hood and Sparks (1970) suggest that these figures represent on average only one-quarter of those who actually commit offences: in other words, they estimate that the Dark Figure is about four times greater than the official figure.

Critics of self-report studies have pointed to several methodological shortcomings, the principal one being confidence in the veracity of the data. Does the respondent always tell the truth? Are some crimes withheld, others invented or exaggerated? It has been shown that a number of interviewer and interviewee characteristics – age, sex, socioeconomic status, and race – can influence the quality of information. There may also be sampling problems: if a survey is carried out at a school, for example, it will fail to include those absent or playing truant – who may be engaged in committing serious crimes.

Such criticisms led a number of investigators to refine the self-report methodology to include reliabilty checks on the data. The most frequently used verification technique is to compare self-report with police records. Studies using this check have found high correlations between the two measures of offending (Blackmore, 1974). Other verification methods include using peer informants to ensure that reports match; testing respondents twice to determine if their answers remain constant; and including lie scale questions in the schedule as a general check on honesty. Hindelang *et al.* (1981), following a comprehensive review of self-report methodology, conclude that there is a good match between self-report data and official recording, although Huizinga and Elliott (1986) caution that reservations about self-report data should not be entirely dismissed. However, despite the assurances of researchers such as Hindelang *et al.*, the trend in recent times has moved away from offender surveys to victim surveys. One reason for this is that not only can victim surveys reveal information about crime, they can also be used to gather data on other issues such as public attitudes towards crime and public fear of crime.

Victim surveys

The first contemporary victim surveys were carried out in the United States in the late 1960s, followed by the first American national survey in 1972. Similar national surveys were subsequently carried out in other parts of the world, including Australia and the Scandinavian countries. Smaller-scale victim surveys have been conducted to examine crime in specific parts of a country – in England, for example, surveys have been conducted in the Midlands (Farrington and Dowds, 1985) and on Merseyside (Kinsey, 1984) – or in different areas of the same city, such as London (Sparks *et al.*, 1977).

Victim research has a range of available methodologies (Sparks, 1981), but *household surveys* offer perhaps the most important means of data collection. This methodology is typified by the first British Crime Survey (Hough and Mayhew, 1983), which selected 16,000 households from the electoral register, with the aim of interviewing one person aged 16 years or older from each household, and achieved an 80 per cent success rate. In interviews, respondents answered

Table 1. Offences in England and Wales: British Crime Survey (1983) estimates

HOUSEHOLD OFFENCES	Best estimate	Rate per 10,000 households
Vandalism	2,650,000	1,494 ± 182
Theft from motor vehicle	1,240,000	700 ± 88
Burglary	726,000	410 ± 70
Theft of motor vehicle	277,000	156 ± 34
Bicycle theft	209,000	118 ± 24
Theft in a dwelling	139,000	78 ± 36
Other household theft	1,480,000	835 ± 114
PERSONAL OFFENCES		Rate per 10,000 people aged 16+
Common assault	1,490,000	396 ± 94
Theft from the person	422,000	112 ± 32
Wounding	368,000	98 ± 34
Robbery	160,000	42 ± 28
Sexual offences	30,000	16 ± 10
Other personal theft	1,560,000	413 ± 64

Source: Hough and Mayhew (1983)

questions about crimes of which they had been the victim, and about their attitudes towards crime.

The extent of crime. Crime surveys produce vast amounts of data, but across studies a consistent pattern emerges. The most striking finding is the extent of crime, as Sparks (1981) notes: 'Criminal victimization is an extremely rare event . . . crimes of violence are extremely uncommon' (p. 17). The first British Crime Survey was in agreement with Sparks's observations. As is shown in Table 1, although trivial crimes such as theft from a motor vehicle are relatively common, serious offences such as assault and robbery occur very infrequently. Indeed, Hough and Mayhew (1983) estimate that the 'statistically average' person over the age of 16 years can expect to be burgled once every 40 years, and to be robbed once every 500 years.

Crime is not, however, a random event, and the surveys illustrate this point. The majority of respondents – Sparks (1981) estimates about 90 per cent – report no experience of crime. On the other hand, some people report having been the victims of two, three, four, or even more crimes. This leads to the important distinction between the *incidence* of victimization and the *prevalence* of victimization. The incidence is the average crime rate over the whole population; the prevalence is that percentage of the population who actually

Table 2. Offences in England and Wales: percentage change in British Crime Survey estimates (1983 and 1985) and offences recorded by the police in the same period

	% CHANGE	
	Survey estimates	*Recorded offences*
Vandalism	+ 9	+15
Theft from a motor vehicle	+ 7	+12
Burglary in a dwelling	+21	+24
Theft of motor vehicle	0	− 2
Bicycle theft	+34	+13
Theft in a dwelling	+ 2	+13
Theft from a person or robbery	+ 9	− 1
TOTAL	+10	+12

Source: Hough and Mayhew (1985)

experience crime. Thus, surveys reveal that burglaries are most prevalent in inner-city areas; that cars parked on the street at night are more likely to be stolen; and that the most likely victims of assault are not the elderly but young males, who typically have assaulted others themselves.

If surveys are repeated over regular periods, trends in crime rates can be described. Sparks (1981) discusses some figures from the American National Crime Survey over the period 1973–1979: rates for burglary and robbery dropped, while rates for household and personal larceny (without contact) fluctuated. In Britain such trends cannot be calculated, as only two national crime surveys have been completed (Hough and Mayhew, 1983, 1985). The second of these showed rises in almost all categories of offence as detailed in Table 2. It can also be seen that these rises closely parallel changes in the amount of crime recorded by the police. This is not always the case: McClintock *et al.* (1963) found that while violent crime as measured by victim surveys was decreasing, higher levels of reporting caused an increase in official figures.

Victim decision-making. As well as the extent of crime, victim surveys can also gather information on some of the psychological processes

Table 3. Percentage of offences in the 1983 British Crime Survey reported to the police

	% Reported to the police
HOUSEHOLD OFFENCES	
Vandalism	22
Theft from motor vehicle	30
Burglary	66
Theft of motor vehicle	95
Bicycle theft	64
Theft in a dwelling	18
PERSONAL OFFENCES	
Theft from the person	31
Wounding	39
Robbery	47
Sexual offences	28

Source: Hough and Mayhew (1983)

associated with victimization. The first British Crime Survey showed that victims were selective in the crimes they reported to the police. Table 3 shows a very high rate of reporting for theft of a motor vehicle but a low rate for theft in a dwelling (theft inside a home by someone who is there legitimately, such as a workman or a party guest, for example).

The two British surveys also examined the reasons behind the decision of whether to report or not. A sample of the most popular reasons is shown in Table 4.

Table 4. Reasons for notifying/not notifying the police following victimization

Notifying	*Not notifying*
'You should' A serious crime Stops repeats of crime Satisfy insurance conditions Punish and catch the offender	Too trivial; no loss or damage Police could do nothing Inappropriate for police; dealt with matter personally Fear/dislike of the police Inconvenient

Source: Hough and Mayhew (1985)

In summary, victim surveys provide a good picture of the type and amount of crime, but they are not without drawbacks. The figures they produce will always underestimate the amount of crime: they focus on offences against the person and against property, omitting the whole area of 'white collar crime' such as fraud and embezzlement. They do not include 'victimless crimes' such as drug offences; nor can they include instances in which the victims are unaware that crimes have been committed against them. The problems of respondent accuracy, as with offender surveys, also apply to victim surveys. Factors such as the type of interview (by telephone or in person), interviewer and interviewee characteristics (such as age and sex), and the use of multiple interviews can all influence the quality of information gained. Nevertheless, the figures produced by crime surveys are an important source of information, with great potential for shaping theories of crime and influencing political and social policies towards managing and controlling it.

EYEWITNESS MEMORY

What causes wrongful conviction? Huff and Rattner (1988) have little doubt: 'The single most important factor contributing to wrongful conviction is eyewitness misidentification' (p. 135). The study of eyewitness memory has since the turn of the century (for example, Whipple, 1909) been a matter of legal importance which has attracted the interest of psychologists. (As such it is one of the three topics which have dominated 'psychology in the courtroom': the others are the jury, and the psychologist as expert witness – see Kerr and Bray, 1982; Sales and Hafemeister, 1985.)

In reviewing studies of eyewitness memory, a number of writers have drawn upon the three stages of *acquisition, retention,* and *retrieval* traditionally identified in human memory research (for example, Goodman and Hahn, 1987; Loftus, 1981). In the case of the eyewitness these stages correspond to the sequence: witnessing the incident, the waiting period prior to giving evidence, and finally giving evidence. Overlaying this sequence are a number of factors which may influence eyewitness memory: some of these factors are taken from the facial memory research literature; others are suggested by the eyewitness situation itself. A summary of these factors is shown in Table 5.

Table 5. Variables in the study of eyewitness memory

Social	Situational	Individual	Interrogational
Attitudes	Complexity of event	Age	Artists' sketches
Conformity	Duration of event	Cognitive style	ID parades
Prejudice	Illumination	Personality	Mugshot
Status of	Time delay	Race	Photofit
interrogator	Type of crime	Sex	Computer systems
Stereotyping		Training	

The study of eyewitness memory has been concerned with the effects of these variables at the stages of acquisition, retention, and retrieval. This endeavour has generated a vast body of research, summarized in several books (Clifford and Bull, 1978; Lloyd-Bostock and Clifford, 1983; Loftus, 1979; Shepherd *et al.,* 1982; Wells and

Loftus, 1984; Yarmey, 1979). I have attempted here to give a flavour of this research and what it tells us of the reliability of eyewitness memory.

Acquisition

The length of time given to observation appears to influence memory; Clifford and Richards (1977) found better person recall from policemen after 30 seconds' rather than after 15 seconds' exposure to the target person. The illumination at the scene of the crime is also important. Kuehn (1974) found that witnesses made less complete statements when the incident took place at twilight as opposed to day or night. Yarmey (1986) reported that both recall of the details of the incident and recognition of the people involved was more accurate in daytime and at the start of twilight than at the end of twilight or at night.

The nature of the witnessed incident has been the concern of a number of studies. Clifford and Scott (1978) showed subjects one of two short filmed incidents. While both incidents involved the same people, in one the content was violent, with scenes of physical assault. It was found that recall was significantly better for the non-violent incident. Clifford and Hollin (1981) reported a study which looked at both the nature and the complexity of the witnessed incident. Subjects were shown one of six different videotaped crime scenes: three showed a violent incident in which a woman was attacked and her bag stolen, three a non-violent incident involving the same people; for each scene the male target was seen either alone, with two companions, or with four companions. It was found that recall of the appearance of the target was significantly less accurate in the violent scenes. In the non-violent scenes recall was not affected by the number of people, but in the violent scenes became progressively less accurate as the number of people increased. Loftus and Burns (1982) showed subjects a filmed bank robbery: in one version, shots were fired but no injury occurred; in another, a small boy was hit in the face and collapsed bleeding from the head. Witnesses to the violent scene gave less accurate recollections.

In seeking a theoretical basis for these findings, Deffenbacher (1983) suggested that the level of witness arousal may be an important factor in considering the impact of different types of crime. Moderately arousing incidents may lead to accurate memory performance; crimes associated with high arousal, perhaps because of violence, lead to poorer performance. This theory has been expanded further with the suggestion, taken from the mainstream psychological

156 / Clive R. Hollin

literature (Easterbrook, 1959), that high arousal causes a narrowing of the range of factors to which the witness attends (Clifford and Hollin, 1981). Indeed, attention may be influenced by dominant aspects of the crime: the notion of 'weapon focus' refers to a witness's concentration on a weapon to the exclusion of other details (Loftus *et al.*, 1987). While there is some evidence in favour of an arousal hypothesis (Brigham *et al.*, 1983), a thorough investigation of eyewitness arousal and memory performance remains to be carried out.

Retention

The common-sense view is that memory becomes less accurate with the passage of time between acquisition and retrieval. However, it seems that faces constitute a special class of stimuli, more resistant to decline in accuracy with time, so that long delays do not automatically reduce recognition accuracy. This is not to say that eyewitness identification is unaffected by long delays: Shepherd (1983) concluded from his review of the evidence that the results 'seem to suggest that the lapse of time reduces the chances of errorless identification. If this is so, we should expect criminal cases in which there was a long delay between the offence and the identification parade to show more disagreement among witnesses and lower rates of identification than those in which the delay was much shorter' (p. 177).

While the length of delay is important, events which occur in the retention interval can also be crucial. Two which have proved particularly important are discussion among witnesses prior to giving testimony and the viewing of 'mugshots' before making an identification.

Alper *et al.* (1976) reported a study in which witnesses to a staged incident first gave individual recall and then, following a group discussion, contributed to an averaged group response. The group consensus descriptions were more complete than the individual descriptions, but at the cost of an increase in errors of commission (reporting items not seen in the incident). In a similar study, Warnick and Sanders (1980) found that witnesses who had discussed the incident gave more accurate recall than those who had not. Warnick and Sanders suggested that 'group discussion prior to the delivery of testimony is probably an advantageous procedure' (p. 235). Hollin and Clifford (1983) expressed concern at this suggestion, arguing that group dynamics could equally well produce systematic errors in testimony. To test this concern, Hollin and Clifford carried out a study in which witnesses to an incident first gave recall without discussion, then took part in a group discussion, then gave individual recall once again. Immediately before the group discussion two individuals were surreptitiously established as likely sources of correct answers: these two individuals were confederates of the experimenters, with a number of prepared incorrect answers. Analysis of the real witnesses' recall revealed that after discussion a significant number of them changed their original responses to bring their answers into line with the (incorrect) responses of the confederates. The group discussion did produce a consensus – by changing correct responses to incorrect responses. A second study, reported in the same paper, showed that witnesses were selective in changing their recall, in that changes were most likely to occur for items which were difficult to remember. Hollin and Clifford concluded that: 'It would seem prudent to amend Warnick and Sanders' suggestion. We suggest it would be preferable to try to obtain uncontaminated testimony from each witness before he or she is allowed, or has had the opportunity to communicate with other witnesses. Where this is impossible, extreme caution should prevail; agreement, unanimous or otherwise, is not always an index of accuracy' (p. 242).

The effects of hearing or reading verbal descriptions and seeing photographs prior to making an identification have been examined in a number of studies. Loftus and Greene (1980) staged an incident in which witnesses viewed a central target: afterwards, the witnesses read an account of the incident which contained erroneous details of the target's appearance. When later asked to recall the appearance of the target, some witnesses incorporated the misleading information into their descriptions: straight hair became curly, a moustache was reported when none existed. If verbal descriptions can have a misleading effect, does the same apply when witnesses assist in making photofits, artists' impressions, and the like? It would seem not; several studies have found that these activities have little effect on later recognition performance (Davies *et al.*, 1978).

Attempts to reconstruct a face, either verbally or by artificial means, appear not to influence testimony; but if 'mugshots' are viewed between acquisition and retrieval, then testimony may be affected. Davies *et al.* (1979) found that the act of looking at photographs of faces prior to a recognition task lowered memory performance. Although if subjects were told after viewing these mugshots that the target had not been seen among them, this impairment was not found. The likely explanation, therefore, is that viewing the mugshots increases levels of caution and so leads to fewer identifications being made. However, if the same face is present in both the mugshots and the identification parade, matters change. Brown *et al.* (1977) found that witnesses most readily identified a person seen previously in both the incident and in mugshots; unfortunately, witnesses were as ready to identify a face seen in mugshots but not in the incident, as to identify a target who had not been seen in mugshots. It appears that a face may be correctly identified as having been previously seen, but in the wrong *context*. What, then, might happen if a witness selected a mugshot of an innocent person, and that innocent person was later seen in an identification parade? Gorenstein and Ellsworth (1980) experimentally tested such a situation and found that, despite the presence of the real target, almost half the witnesses identified an innocent person they had previously picked out from a set of mugshots. It appears that once a choice is made, it tends to be maintained despite all else. In summarizing the evidence, Shepherd *et al.* (1982) note: 'The use of mugshots presents hazards . . . the showing of photographs to prospective witnesses should be limited to what is necessary to make a search effective' (p. 69).

Retrieval

At this stage the emphasis is on the witness's ability to gain access to and retrieve information from memory. In many cases retrieval takes place through the process of questioning: a number of studies have investigated the effects of different types of question on eyewitness memory. It has been shown that even the most subtle changes in question wording can influence testimony (Harris, 1973; Loftus *et al.*, 1975; Loftus and Palmer, 1974; Loftus and Zanni, 1975). The study by Loftus and Palmer illustrates the general principle. Witnesses to a filmed road accident were asked to estimate the speed of the cars when 'they . . . into each other'; for different groups of witnesses the blank contained one of the following verbs: 'contacted', 'hit', 'bumped', or 'smashed'. It was found that the witnesses' estimates of the speed increased with the severity of the verbs (in the order given above) from 31.8 to 40.8 m.p.h. Further, in later questioning those subjects who had been asked about the 'smash' were most likely to say, mistakenly, that they had seen broken glass at the scene of the accident. Two studies have, however, failed to replicate some of these leading-question effects (Read *et al.*, 1978; Zanni and Offerman, 1978).

The process of questioning may also be a source of misleading information that can produce later effects on the accuracy of testimony (Loftus, 1975; Loftus *et al.*, 1978; Miller and Loftus, 1976). In a typical study, Loftus (1975) showed subjects a film in which, among other events, a car was seen on a country road. When questioned, half the subjects were asked to judge the speed of the car 'as it passed the barn'; the others were also asked about the speed of the car, but without reference to the fictitious barn. One week later, subjects were asked, along with other questions, if they had seen a barn: over 17 per cent of the 'primed' subjects wrongly said that they had, compared to less than 3 per cent of the unprimed subjects. Further work has established that misleading information is most likely to be accepted if the source is of high status (Bregman and McAllister, 1982; Dodd and Bradshaw, 1980); that peripheral details rather than central events are more likely to be influenced (Read and Bruce, 1984); and that if the witness is warned in advance about the possibility of misleading information, the effects are much reduced (Christiaansen and Ochalek,1983).

Loftus (1981) has proposed that misleading information causes permanent memory changes, so that the original material is lost. This theoretical position has sparked a fierce debate, with a number of studies presenting evidence in support of the proposal that the effects found by Loftus are products of the questioning procedures themselves, rather than of permanent changes in memory (for example, Bekerian and Bowers, 1983; Zaragoza *et al.*, 1987). Counter-arguments and experimental data have been presented by proponents of the 'reconstructive hypothesis' (for example, Schooler *et al.*, 1986). In summary, while the theoretical position is unclear, from a practical point of view it would seem prudent to acknowledge that misleading information may result in distortions and errors in eyewitness testimony.

Along with questioning-effects, a body of psychological research has also been concerned with the design and use of face-recall systems such as the photofit and identikit procedures for constructing likenesses of faces (Davies, 1983), the line-up or identity parade (Shepherd *et al.*, 1982), or artist sketches (Laughery and Fowler, 1980), and with the development of computer-based systems to aid face recognition (Lenorovitz and Laughery, 1984).

Much of the research discussed above has pointed to the limitations and shortcomings of eyewitness memory, which is an outcome to be welcomed should it alert the legal profession to possible miscarriages of justice. Recently, psychologists have turned to a more constructive task, seeking to develop ways of improving the quality of testimony. Training programmes in face recognition have been developed (Malpass, 1981), along with interviewing techniques which use various memory-retrieval mnemonics to enhance recall (Geiselman *et al.*, 1985). Hypnosis has also been used, although recent experimental evidence suggests that this is not of great benefit in aiding witness memory (Yuille and McEwan, 1985). The polygraph or lie detector has also generated considerable debate, especially over its ethical and practical limitations as an aid in assessing the validity of testimony (Iacono and Patrick, 1987).

The legal-psychology debate

If it is accepted that there is a discrete body of empirical knowledge labelled 'psychological', should that knowledge be made known in open court? The sticking point here is the notion of *generalizability*: the degree to which findings from psychological studies, mainly laboratory-based, can be applied to the 'real world'. While critics (for example, Konečni and Ebbesen, 1986) are concerned with experimental limitations – the use of staged crimes, filmed sequences, students as subjects, and so on – it is not clear exactly why generalization might not be expected. Indeed, two studies have found that eyewitnesses perform at similar levels in laboratory and real-life conditions (Brigham *et al.*, 1982; Sanders and Warnick, 1981). Yuille and Cutshall (1986) adopted a different methodology, with a case study of eyewitness memory in which 13 of 21 witnesses to a real-life shooting incident were re-interviewed four to five months after the event. Several of the results were contrary to what might have been predicted on the basis of laboratory findings. While this is interesting, this type of field study falls prey to criticisms which are less applicable to laboratory research, notably concerning the degree of control the investigator has over the study. Thus, in the Yuille and Cutshall study, it is not known how much witnesses talked with each other, how accurate the missing 38 per cent of witnesses would be, and how much influence newspaper and television coverage had. While it is easy to be enthusiastic about real-life studies, considerable caution is required. As Bray and Kerr (1982) note: 'Social scientists should not, in their zeal for realism, dismiss the utility of closely controlled experimental simulations, nor be unmindful of the practical and methodological drawbacks of more realistic methods' (p. 318). The strongest approach may well be one which gathers evidence from an amalgam of methodologies, including case studies, field studies, laboratory and archival studies.

A further issue is the lack of predictive power of psychological research: it is a fact that psychological research cannot predict whether a given witness, offering a particular piece of evidence in a given case, is correct or incorrect in his or her testimony. The position is therefore one in which some psychologists argue that the court can be informed by probabilistic statements based on empirical research (Loftus, 1986), while others maintain that this is not adequate for legal purposes and that it reduces psychologists to offering nothing beyond common sense (Pachella, 1986). Loftus (1986) cuts through this debate with the pragmatic suggestion that 'we take a Darwinian approach. Let the fittest expert evolve and survive' (p. 259). While Loftus clearly feels able to support her position in open court, it is debatable whether a 'battle of experts' would be desirable (although it would undoubtedly be entertaining) from either a professional or a legal perspective.

At another level, Konečni and Ebbesen (1986) suggest that psychologists investigating eyewitness memory are wasting too much energy, as the small number of wrongful convictions on the basis of witness testimony is an 'acceptable risk' (p. 119). While the findings of Huff and Rattner (1988) might call into question the 'small number' of wrongful convictions, what is being debated is not an exercise in risk but in ethics and morals: as Wells (1986) notes, 'we must consider the potential effects of not giving expert testimony' (p. 83) – potential effects which became reality for James Hanratty, Peter Hain, George Ince, Patrick Meehan, and all the others who have been imprisoned or even executed because of mistaken eyewitness testimony (Hain, 1976).

CLINICAL CRIMINOLOGY

A clinical approach to criminal behaviour is not intended to invoke a 'medical' model, in which deviant behaviour is seen as pathological, but rather to focus to a greater extent on the individual and on psychological methods of producing change (Hollin and Howells, 1986; Howells and Hollin, 1988). In seeking to affirm the potential of clinical criminology, West (1980) suggested that 'the crucial importance of economic, social and political factors in the definition and incidence of crime is undeniable, as is the need for socio-political change, but the part played by individual characteristics in determining who becomes labelled a criminal should not be neglected' (p. 619). The inherent danger, as West acknowledges, is that in concentrating upon the individual, environmental factors may be forgotten. Indeed, the criticism can be made that a clinical approach colludes with the system, placing responsibility and blame solely on the individual, to the exclusion of environmental factors (Goff, 1986). However, such a criticism applies more to dated psychoanalytic theories than to contemporary cognitive-behavioural explanations which emphasize the importance of environmental factors in understanding behaviour. Overall, there is a strong case both for reform of the system and for intervention at an individual level: there is no reason why social and clinical change should be incompatible.

Even the most cursory glance at the literature reveals that vast numbers of clinically orientated programmes have been conducted with offenders of all descriptions. The treatments used can be categorized in a variety of ways: the focus may be on a treatment which follows a particular psychological theory such as behavioural approaches in general (Morris and Braukmann, 1987) or social learning theory in particular (Nietzel, 1979); the treatment may be aimed at a particular age group, such as juvenile delinquents (Burchard and Burchard, 1987), or it may be aimed at a particular type of offence, such as violent crime (Stuart, 1981). A further consideration is the *setting* in which the intervention takes place, and it is by reference to this that I have structured the present discussion. The weight of studies is too great for a complete review, but a selection will give an overall picture of the field. In an ideal world, prevention programmes (Johnson, 1987) would be the main focus. Unfortunately, the clinician most often comes into contact with the offender after legal intervention; this bias is reflected in the majority of studies discussed below. (There is a further bias in the predominance of behavioural studies cited, reflecting both my own preference and the trend in recent years. The conclusions regarding the efficacy of intervention would, however, be the same regardless of theoretical and clinical style.)

Secure institutions

Prisons. The advent of behaviour modification techniques – especially the token economy, a system in which 'good behaviour' earns points or tokens which can later be exchanged for rewards such as cigarettes, watching television, and so on (Kazdin, 1982) – provided the means to design programmes which could operate on a large scale. Prison token economies to increase compliance with institutional rules have been used principally in the United States (Nietzel, 1979). This use of behaviour modification attracted a great deal of hostile criticism on both legal and ethical grounds, culminating in lawsuits and hearings in Congress, and eventual withdrawal of funding. In Britain, behaviour modification has been used for more clinically orientated purposes. For example, Cullen and Seddon (1981) designed a behavioural programme based on a token economy for disturbed young offenders serving a borstal sentence. The programme was successful, in that the offenders acquired new, socially acceptable behaviours.

In a similar vein, the use of social skills training (SST) has proved popular in institutions for both young (Henderson and Hollin, 1986) and adult offenders (Howells, 1986). While skills training programmes are generally successful in modifying social behaviour, there is little evidence that they reduce offending after discharge from custody. Howells (1986) suggested a number of explanations for this: the difficulties of maintaining and generalizing changes in skills; the poor motivation for change found in some prisoners; the inadequate theoretical integration of SST into analyses of offending; and institutional constraints, such as staff resistance, which pose problems for the implementation of treatment.

More broad-based treatments have been designed for violent (W. Davies, 1982) and sexual offenders (Perkins, 1987). The work of Perkins with sex offenders, at a prison in Birmingham, England, provides a model for effective treatment within a penal setting. The justification for the programme was carefully described in clinical, ethical, preventative, and economic terms. Reliable assessment methods were used to select offenders suitable for treatment; and a range of treatment techniques were employed, drawn mainly from a cognitive-behavioural model of sex offending. Community links were established to ensure that treatment does not stop when the offender leaves prison. Finally, meticulous follow-up research has shown the effectiveness of the programme in reducing sexual offences. In stark economic terms, Perkins estimates that the cost of the programme 'amounted to £192 per reconviction prevented' (p. 215). Its value in terms of preventing the distress of potential future victims is incalculable.

Special hospitals. The special hospitals, of which there are five in England and Scotland, are secure institutions for mentally disordered offenders. The treatment offered in them is similar to that in any other psychiatric hospital – medication as appropriate, education, occupational therapy, psychotherapy, and behaviour therapy. As in prisons, SST has been a feature of clinical work in special hospitals, particularly with violent and sexual offenders (Crawford and Allen, 1979). As Howells (1987) notes, other clinical techniques have been used with such offenders, including cognitive-behaviour therapy for violent offenders, and multimodal assessment and treatment programmes for sex offenders. In a review of the structure and management of special hospitals, Hamilton (1985) suggested that 'there is probably a need for a modest expansion of clinical psychology departments' (p. 99). The newly formed Regional Secure Units are generating a substantial amount of research, although at this early stage in their history no outcome studies are available (Berry, 1985).

Residential settings

There are many criticisms of closed institutions: that they reinforce criminal behaviour; that they label individuals; that they are, by their very nature, unsuitable for rehabilitation. An alternative may be found in a setting which is residential but in which the emphasis is transferred from security to treatment. The majority of such residential programmes have been for young offenders.

Therapeutic communities. As Sinclair and Clarke (1982) note, a variety of therapeutic communities have been used in the treatment of offending. One typical study by Cornish and Clarke (1975) compares two regimes in an Approved School for 13- to 15-year-old boys. One was a traditional training and control regime, the other a liberal therapeutic community. At a two-year follow-up, the recidivism rate was 70 per cent for the boys from the therapeutic community and 69 per cent for the boys from the traditional regime. In a similar American study, almost one thousand convicted delinquents were randomly assigned to residential establishments based on the therapeutic techniques of either transactional analysis or behaviour modification (Jesness, 1975). At two-year follow-up, 77 per cent of the sample had been arrested for further offences; there was no difference in recidivism between the two regimes. The picture is broadly similar across all studies of this type: one of therapeutic gains in the treatment setting which fail to be translated into a reduction in recidivism.

Achievement Place. A new model for residential provision, with a much greater 'community' emphasis, was developed in Kansas at Achievement Place (Phillips, 1968). The residential care at Achievement Place has two distinct points of emphasis: the consistent use of behavioural theory and associated clinical methods, giving the flexibility to conduct individual treatment programmes, and the maintaining of close community links.

The principal means of intervention is via 'teaching-parents': the young offender lives in residential accommodation, usually a house, with two adults who assume the joint roles of parent and teacher. Thus, the teaching-parents not only provide a caring family environment, they are also responsible for administering individual treatment programmes. As the offender makes progress, both in terms of satisfactory residential behaviour and achieving therapeutic targets (mainly through skills training), various rewards become available, including time at home with the natural parents. When this stage is reached, the (natural) parents are helped to maintain the gains made at Achievement Place. The success of Achievement Place as a residential establishment led to a number of similar programmes (Weber and Burke, 1986). Unfortunately, this success is not reflected in reduced offending: Kirigin *et al.* (1982) found that during their residential placement, the offenders in the teaching-parent homes had fewer contacts with the authorities; but at follow-up this advantage had disappeared, and there was no difference in re-offending between the teaching-parent group and a control.

In total, the picture is not unlike that with treatment in institutions: the intervention is initially successful but fails, in the main, to generalize beyond the treatment setting to prevent re-offending. With this in mind, a number of British programmes have modified the Achievement Place plan to attempt to capitalize upon its strengths and amend the lack of generalization. While the work of Glenthorne Youth Treatment Centre in Birmingham is perhaps best documented (Reid, 1982), the Shape Project, also in Birmingham, is of particular interest. Shape provides living accommodation, work training in preparation for employment (more recently, preparing for unemployment), offence counselling, and individual life and social skills training. In the first instance, the offender, generally referred by probation and social service departments, lives in a hostel with a structured daily routine; the next step is to semi-independent shared accommodation; then, finally, to full independence in non-shared accommodation. Training and counselling takes place at all stages. The project is selective in that it does not accept offenders with serious drug or alcohol problems, nor those with a history of severe violence. The most recently published re-offending statistics show a 78 per cent *success* rate, measured in terms of non-reconviction over a 6- to 18-month follow-up period (Ostapiuk, 1982). Given this, it is ironic that, at the time of writing, Shape is in extreme financial difficulties and unable to accept referrals.

Community programmes

If institutional and residential programmes generally lack the power to reduce recidivism, then perhaps the best option lies in treatment which takes place in the 'natural environment' – the community in which the offending occurs. Community intervention may take the form of individual or group treatment on an out-patient basis at a hospital or regional secure unit, or can take place within an organized project.

Individual and group therapy. A multitude of community-based treatments for offenders have been reported, ranging from projects to cater for large groups of clients to individual case studies (Ostapiuk, 1982). In an innovative project, Fo and O'Donnell (1974, 1975) set up a 'buddy system' in which young offenders were paired with friendly adults in their own community. The aim was to increase the offender's socially acceptable behaviour by making both social and material rewards contingent upon good behaviour. The results were mixed: those young people with previous offences showed improvement; those without previous offences became worse. The full range of behavioural techniques has been used on a community basis, particularly with young offenders: token economies, reinforcement programmes, and contracts have been successful in changing the target behaviour; instruction and modelling less so (Blakely and Davidson, 1984). A number of studies have incorporated techniques from cognitive therapy into programmes for offenders, although there are few outcome studies that have measured recidivism (Ross and Fabiano, 1985). However, while successful in modifying targets such as academic skills and social behaviour, the impact of most interventions on recidivism is, at best, inconclusive.

As in prisons and residential establishments, SST has proved popular in community programmes with offenders (Hudson, 1986). The outcome data do not lend themselves to the conclusion that SST is an effective intervention for offending. Spence and Marzillier (1981) reported that six months after training, the SST group, compared with control groups, showed the lowest level of police convictions (although not statistically significant). On a self-report measure of offending, however, the SST group showed a *higher* level of offending than the controls. Another approach lies in the use of family therapy to attempt to change delinquent behaviour. In a typical study, Alexander and Parsons (1973) found lower recidivism at 18-month follow-up with a family therapy group than with a control group. There are, of course, other community-based interventions, including parole and diversionary projects, but psychologists are not well represented here – in the literature, at least.

In total, the evidence regarding the effectiveness of psychological treatment is mixed: while there are undoubted successes (Garrett, 1985; Gendreau and Ross, 1979), the pooled data, as the major reviews conclude with monotonous regularity, show no *consistent* effectiveness of treatment in reducing criminal behaviour. This should not be interpreted as 'nothing works' – a position effectively opposed by Thornton (1987); rather, that there are unanswered questions about research and practice. The problem remains that some interventions do work for some offenders; specifically what works, for whom, and why, remains to be discovered. As Sechrest and Rosenblatt (1987) suggest, there are three ways of interpreting the evidence: '(1) there really is no good way to rehabilitate juvenile offenders; (2) there may be good ways to rehabilitate juvenile offenders, they have just not been found; or (3) owing to methodo-logical problems in earlier research, we really don't know much of anything about which approaches to rehabilitation work or don't work. We believe that this last option best describes the true state of affairs' (p. 417). I agree; I also think the point holds for all offenders, not just juveniles. Elsewhere, I have offered a series of pointers to guide the practice of clinical criminology (Hollin, 1989). They include a greater emphasis on criminological targets; the use of multi-component, individually tailored programmes; a sense of realism, and acknowledgement of forces other than just the psychological in crime; an awareness of the potential harm of labelling, and therefore a willingness to discriminate in offering treatment; organization of effective institutional systems; a reappraisal of research metho-dologies; and a greater emphasis on criminology in the training of psychologists who work with offenders.

CONCLUSION

This short excursion into the field of criminological and legal psychology has, I hope, illustrated the range of application of psychological methods and theories. However, as I hope has also become evident, one of the challenges of this field is the breadth of knowledge that it demands. The criminological and legal psychologist must not only be competent as a psychologist, but also familiar with theories and findings from other disciplines such as sociology, criminology, law, and politics. From the material covered in this chapter alone, it should be evident that the formulation of psychological theories of crime must be informed by data from crime surveys; that the psychologist in the courtroom must not only know the research evidence but must also be sensitive to legal issues; that the clinician must be aware of criminological theories of crime and, of course, the relevant legislation for their specific client.

At present, there appears to be a growth of interest in criminological and legal psychology, in terms of both research and practice, which should expand the field still further. Indeed, the advent of Britain's first academic course leading to a higher degree in applied criminological psychology suggests that professionalism in this field is about to enter a new era. While there is a substantial knowledge base, much remains to be done.

REFERENCES

Alexander, J.F. and Parsons, B.V. (1973) Short-term behavioral intervention with delinquent families. *Journal of Abnormal Psychology, 81*, 219–225.

Alper, A., Buckhout, B., Chern, S., Harwood, R. and Slomovits, M. (1976) Eyewitness identification: Accuracy of individual vs. composite recollection of a crime. *Bulletin of the Psychonomic Society, 8*, 147–149.

Bekerian, D.A. and Bowers, J.M. (1983) Eyewitness testimony: Were we misled? *Journal of Experimental Psychology: Learning, Memory, and Cognition, 9*, 139–145.

Belson, W. (1975) *Juvenile Theft: The Causal Factors.* New York: Harper & Row.

Berry, M.J. (1985) Secure units: A bibliography. *Special Hospitals Research Report, No. 18.* London: Special Hospitals Research Unit.

Blackmore, J. (1974) The relationship between self-reported delinquency and official convictions amongst adolescent boys. *British Journal of Criminology, 14*, 172–176.

Blakely, C.H. and Davidson, W.S. (1984) Behavioral approaches to delinquency: A review. In P. Karoly and J.J. Steffan (eds) *Adolescent Behavior Disorders: Foundations and Contemporary Concerns.* Lexington, Ma: Lexington Books.

Borrill, J. (1983) Psychology and crime. In J. Nicholson and B. Foss (eds) *Psychology Survey 4*. Leicester: The British Psychological Society.

Bray, R.M. and Kerr, N.L. (1982) Methodological considerations in the study of the psychology of the courtroom. In N.L. Kerr and R.M. Bray (eds) *The Psychology of the Courtroom*. New York: Academic Press.

Bregman, N.J. and McAllister, H.A. (1982) Eyewitness testimony: The role of commitment in increasing reliability. *Social Psychology Quarterly, 45*, 181–184.

Brigham, J.C., Maass, A., Martinez, D. and Whittenberger, G. (1983) The effect of arousal on facial recognition. *Basic and Applied Social Psychology, 4*, 279–293.

Brigham, J.C., Maass, A., Snyder, L.D. and Spaulding, K. (1982) Accuracy of eyewitness identifications in a field setting. *Journal of Personality and Social Psychology, 42*, 673–681.

Brown, E., Deffenbacher, K.A. and Sturgill, W. (1977) Memory for faces and the circumstances of the encounter. *Journal of Applied Psychology, 62*, 311–318.

Burchard, J.D. and Burchard, S.N. (eds) (1987) *Prevention of Delinquent Behavior*. Beverly Hills, Ca: Sage Publications.

Christiaansen, R.E. and Ochalek, K. (1983) Editing misleading information from memory: Evidence for the coexistence of original and postevent information. *Memory and Cognition, 11*, 467–475.

Clifford, B.R. and Bull, R. (1978) *The Psychology of Person Identification*. London: Routledge & Kegan Paul.

Clifford, B.R. and Hollin, C.R. (1981) Effects of the type of incident and the number of perpetrators on eyewitness memory. *Journal of Applied Psychology, 66*, 364–370.

Clifford, B.R. and Richards, V.J. (1977) Comparison of recall of policemen and civilians under conditions of long and short durations of exposure. *Perceptual and Motor Skills, 45*, 503–512.

Clifford, B.R. and Scott, J. (1978) Individual and situational factors in eyewitness testimony. *Journal of Applied Psychology, 63*, 352–359.

Cornish, D.B. and Clarke, R.V.G. (1975) *Residential Treatment and its Effects on Delinquency*. Home Office Research Study, No. 32. London: HMSO.

Crawford, D.A. and Allen, J.V. (1979) A social skills training programme with sex offenders. In M. Cook and G. Wilson (eds) *Love and Attraction*. Oxford: Pergamon Press.

Cullen, J.E. and Seddon, J.W. (1981) The application of a behavioural regime to disturbed young offenders. *Personality and Individual Differences, 2*, 285–292.

Davies, G.M. (1983) Forensic face recall: The role of visual and verbal information. In S. M. A. Lloyd-Bostock and B. R. Clifford (eds) *Evaluating Witness Evidence: Recent Psychological Research and New Perspectives*. Chichester: Wiley.

Davies, G.M., Ellis, H.D. and Shepherd, J.W. (1978) Face recognition accuracy as a function of mode of representation. *Journal of Applied Psychology, 63*, 180–187.

Davies, G.M., Shepherd, J.W. and Ellis, H.D. (1979) Effects of interpolated mugshot exposure on accuracy of eyewitness identification. *Journal of Applied Psychology, 64*, 232–237.

170 / *Clive R. Hollin*

Davies, W. (1982) Violence in prisons. In P. Feldman (ed.) *Developments in the Study of Criminal Behaviour, Volume 2: Violence.* Chichester: Wiley.
Deffenbacher, K.A. (1983) The influence of arousal on the reliability of testimony. In S.M.A. Lloyd-Bostock and B.R. Clifford (eds) *Evaluating Witness Evidence: Recent Psychological Research and New Perspectives.* Chichester: Wiley.
Dodd, D.H. and Bradshaw, J.M. (1980) Leading questions and memory: Pragmatic constraints. *Journal of Verbal Learning and Verbal Behaviour, 21,* 207–219.
Easterbrook, J.A. (1959) The effect of emotion on cue utilization and the organization of behavior. *Psychological Review, 66,* 183–201.
Farrington, D.P. and Bennett, T. (1981) Police cautioning of juveniles in London. *British Journal of Criminology, 21,* 123–135.
Farrington, D.P. and Dowds, E.A. (1985) Disentangling criminal behaviour and police reaction. In D.P. Farrington and J. Gunn (eds) *Reactions to Crime: The Police, Courts and Prisons.* Chichester: Wiley.
Fo, W.S.O. and O'Donnell, C.R. (1974) The buddy system: Relationship and contingency conditions in a community intervention program for youth and non-professionals as behavior change agents. *Journal of Consulting and Clinical Psychology, 42,* 163–168.
Fo, W.S.O. and O'Donnell, C.R. (1975) The buddy system: Effect of community intervention on delinquent offences. *Behavior Therapy, 6,* 522–524.
Garrett, C.J. (1985) Effects of residential treatment on adjudicated delinquents: A meta-analysis. *Journal of Research in Crime and Delinquency, 22,* 287–308.
Geiselman, R.E., Fisher, R.P., MacKinnon, D.P. and Holland, H.L. (1985) Eyewitness memory enhancement in the police interview: Cognitive retrieval mnemonics versus hypnosis. *Journal of Applied Psychology, 70,* 401–412.
Gendreau, P. and Ross, R. (1979) Effective correctional treatment: Bibliotherapy for cynics. *Crime and Delinquency, 25,* 463–489.
Goff, C. (1986) Criminological appraisals of psychiatric explanations of crime: 1936–1950. *International Journal of Law and Psychiatry, 9,* 245–260.
Goodman, G.S. and Hahn, A. (1987) Evaluating eyewitness testimony. In I.B. Weiner and A.K. Hess (eds) *Handbook of Forensic Psychology.* New York: Wiley.
Gorenstein, G.W. and Ellsworth, P.C. (1980) Effect of choosing an incorrect photograph on a later identification by an eyewitness. *Journal of Applied Psychology, 65,* 616–622.
Hain, P. (1976) *Mistaken Identity: The Wrong Face of the Law.* London: Quartet Books.
Hamilton, J.R. (1985) The special hospitals. In L. Gostin (ed.) *Secure Provision.* London: Tavistock.
Harris, R. (1973) Answering questions containing marked and unmarked adjectives and verbs. *Journal of Experimental Psychology, 97,* 399–401.
Henderson, M. and Hollin, C.R. (1986) Social skills training and delinquency. In C. R. Hollin and P. Trower (eds) *Handbook of Social Skills Training, Volume 1: Applications Across the Life Span.* Oxford: Pergamon Press.

Hindelang, M.J., Hirschi, T. and Weis, J. (1981) *Measuring Delinquency.* Beverly Hills, Ca: Sage Publications.

Hollin, C.R. (1989) *Psychology and Crime: An Introduction to Criminological Psychology.* London: Routledge.

Hollin, C.R. and Clifford, B.R. (1983) Eyewitness testimony: The effects of discussion on recall accuracy and agreement. *Journal of Applied Social Psychology, 13,* 234–244.

Hollin, C.R. and Howells, K. (eds) (1986) *Clinical Approaches to Criminal Behaviour. Issues in Criminological and Legal Psychology, No. 9.* Leicester: The British Psychological Society.

Hood, R. and Sparks, R. (1970) *Key Issues in Criminology.* London: Weidenfeld & Jackson.

Hough, M. and Mayhew, P. (1983) *The British Crime Survey: First Report.* London: HMSO.

Hough, M. and Mayhew, P. (1985) *Taking Account of Crime: Key Findings from the Second British Crime Survey.* London: HMSO.

Howells, K. (1986) Social skills training and criminal and antisocial behaviour in adults. In C.R. Hollin and P. Trower (eds) *Handbook of Social Skills Training, Volume 1: Applications Across the Life Span.* Oxford: Pergamon Press.

Howells, K. (1987) Forensic problems: Treatment. In S.J.E. Lindsay and G.E. Powell (eds) *Handbook of Clinical Psychology.* Aldershot, Hants: Gower.

Howells, K. and Hollin, C.R. (1988) *Clinical Approaches to Aggression and Violence. Issues in Criminological and Legal Psychology, No. 12.* Leicester: The British Psychological Society.

Hudson, B.L. (1986) Community applications of social skills training. In C.R. Hollin and P. Trower (eds) *Handbook of Social Skills Training, Volume 1: Applications Across the Life Span.* Oxford: Pergamon Press.

Huff, C.R. and Rattner, A. (1988) Convicted but innocent: False positives and the criminal justice process. In E. Scott and T. Hirschi (eds) *Controversial Issues in Crime and Justice.* Beverly Hills, Ca: Sage Publications.

Huizinga, D. and Elliott, D.S. (1986) Reassessing the reliability and validity of self-report delinquency measures. *Journal of Quantitative Criminology, 2,* 293–327.

Iacono, W.G. and Patrick, C.J. (1987) What psychologists should know about lie detection. In I.B. Weiner and A.K. Hess (eds) *Handbook of Forensic Psychology.* New York: Wiley.

Jesness, C.F. (1975) Comparative effectiveness of behavior modification and transactional analysis programs for delinquents. *Journal of Consulting and Clinical Psychology, 43,* 758–779.

Johnson, E.H. (ed.) (1987) *Handbook of Crime and Delinquency Prevention.* New York: Greenwood Press.

Kazdin, A.E. (1982) The token economy: A decade later. *Journal of Applied Behavior Analysis, 15,* 431–445.

Kerr, N.L. and Bray, R.M. (1982) *The Psychology of the Courtroom.* New York: Academic Press.

Kinsey, R. (1984) *Merseyside Crime Survey: First Report.* Liverpool: Merseyside County Council.

172 / *Clive R. Hollin*

Kirigin, K.A., Braukmann, C.J., Atwater, J.D. and Wolf, M.M. (1982) An evaluation of teaching-family (Achievement Place) group homes for juvenile offenders. *Journal of Applied Behavior Analysis, 15*, 1–16.
Konečni, V.J. and Ebbesen, E.B. (1986) Courtroom testimony by psychologists on eyewitness identification issues. *Law and Human Behavior, 10*, 117–126.
Kuehn, L. (1974) Looking down a gun barrel: Person perception and violent crime. *Perceptual and Motor Skills, 39*, 1159–1164.
Laughery, K.R. and Fowler, R.F. (1980) Sketch artist and identi-kit procedures for recalling faces. *Journal of Applied Psychology, 65*, 307–316.
Lenorovitz, D.R. and Laughery, K.R. (1984) A witness–computer interactive system for searching mug files. In G.L. Wells and E.F. Loftus (eds) *Eyewitness Testimony: Psychological Perspectives*. Cambridge: Cambridge University Press.
Lloyd-Bostock, S.M.A. (1988) *Law in Practice*. Leicester: The British Psychological Society; London: Routledge.
Lloyd-Bostock, S.M.A. and Clifford, B.R. (eds) (1983) *Evaluating Witness Evidence: Recent Psychological Research and New Perspectives*. Chichester: Wiley.
Loftus, E.F. (1975) Leading questions and the eyewitness report. *Cognitive Psychology, 7*, 560–572.
Loftus, E.F. (1979) *Eyewitness Testimony*. Cambridge, Ma: Harvard University Press.
Loftus, E.F. (1981) Eyewitness testimony: Psychological research and legal thought. In M. Tonry and N. Morris (eds) *Crime and Justice: An Annual Review of Research*, Vol. 3. Chicago: University of Chicago Press.
Loftus, E.F. (1986) Ten years in the life of an expert witness. *Law and Human Behavior, 10*, 241–263.
Loftus, E.F., Altman, D. and Geballe, R. (1975) Effects of questioning upon a witness's later recollections. *Journal of Police Science and Administration, 3*, 162–165.
Loftus, E.F. and Burns, T.E. (1982) Mental shock can produce retrograde amnesia. *Memory and Cognition, 10*, 318–323.
Loftus, E.F. and Greene, E. (1980) Warning: Even memory for faces can be contagious. *Law and Human Behavior, 4*, 323–334.
Loftus, E.F., Loftus, G.R. and Messo, J. (1987) Some facts about 'weapon focus'. *Law and Human Behavior, 11*, 55–62.
Loftus, E.F., Miller, D.G. and Burns, H.J. (1978) Semantic integration of verbal information into visual memory. *Journal of Experimental Psychology: Human Learning and Memory, 4*, 19–31.
Loftus, E.F. and Palmer, J.C. (1974) Reconstruction of automobile destruction: An example of the interaction between language and memory. *Journal of Verbal Learning and Verbal Behavior, 13*, 585–589.
Loftus, E.F. and Zanni, G.R. (1975) Eyewitness testimony: The influence of the wording of the question. *Bulletin of the Psychonomic Society, 5*, 86–88.
Malpass, R.S. (1981) Training in face recognition. In G.M. Davies, H.D. Ellis and J.W. Shepherd (eds) *Perceiving and Remembering Faces*. London: Academic Press.
McClintock, F.H., Avison, N.H., Savill, N.C. and Worthington, V.L. (1963) *Crimes of Violence*. London: Macmillan.

Miller, D.G. and Loftus, E.F. (1976) Influencing memory for people and their actions. *Bulletin of the Psychonomic Society, 7,* 9–11.

Morris, E.K. and Braukmann, C.J. (1987) *Behavioral Approaches to Crime and Delinquency: A Handbook of Application, Research, and Concepts.* New York: Plenum Press.

Nietzel, M.T. (1979) *Crime and its Modification: A Social Learning Perspective.* Oxford: Pergamon Press.

Ostapiuk, E.B. (1982) Strategies for community intervention in offender rehabilitation: An overview. In P. Feldman (ed.) *Developments in the Study of Criminal Behaviour, Volume 1: The Prevention and Control of Offending.* Chichester: Wiley.

Pachella, R.G. (1986) Personal values and the value of expert testimony. *Law and Human Behavior, 10,* 145–150.

Perkins, D.E. (1987) A psychological treatment programme for sex offenders. In B.J. McGurk, D.M. Thornton and M. Williams (eds) *Applying Psychology to Imprisonment: Theory & Practice.* London: HMSO.

Phillips, E.L. (1968) Achievement Place: Token reinforcement procedures in a homestyle rehabilitation setting for 'pre-delinquent' boys. *Journal of Applied Behavior Analysis, 1,* 213–233.

Read, J.D., Barnsley, R.H., Ankers, K. and Whisham, I.Q. (1978) Variations in severity of verbs and eyewitnesses' testimony: An alternative explanation. *Perceptual and Motor Skills, 46,* 795–800.

Read, J.D. and Bruce, D. (1984) On the external validity of questioning effects in eyewitness testimony. *International Review of Applied Psychology, 33,* 33–49.

Reid, I. (1982) The development and maintenance of a behavioural regime in a secure Youth Treatment Centre. In P. Feldman (ed.) *Developments in the Study of Criminal Behaviour, Volume 1: The Prevention and Control of Offending.* Chichester: Wiley.

Ross, R.R. and Fabiano, E.A. (1985) *Time to Think: A Cognitive Model of Delinquency Prevention and Offender Rehabilitation.* Johnson City, Tn: Institute of Social Sciences and Arts.

Sales, B.D. and Hafemeister, T.L. (1985) Law and psychology. In E.M. Altmaier and M.E. Meyer (eds) *Applied Specialities in Psychology.* London: Lawrence Erlbaum.

Sanders, G.S. and Warnick, D.H. (1981) Truth and consequences: The effect of responsibility on eyewitness behavior. *Basic and Applied Social Psychology, 2,* 67–79.

Sechrest, L. and Rosenblatt, A. (1987) Research methods. In H.C. Quay (ed.) *Handbook of Juvenile Delinquency.* New York: Wiley.

Schooler, J.W., Gerhard, D. and Loftus, E.F. (1986) Qualities of the unreal. *Journal of Experimental Psychology: Learning, Memory, and Cognition, 12,* 171–181.

Shepherd, J.W (1983) Identification after long delays. In S.M.A. Lloyd-Bostock and B.R. Clifford (eds) *Evaluating Witness Evidence: Recent Psychological Research and New Perspectives.* Chichester: Wiley.

Shepherd, J.W., Ellis, H.D. and Davies, G.M. (1982) *Identification Evidence: A Psychological Evaluation.* Aberdeen: Aberdeen University Press.

Sinclair, I. and Clarke, R. (1982) Predicting, treating, and explaining delinquency: The lessons from research on institutions. In P. Feldman (ed.) *Developments in the Study of Criminal Behaviour, Volume 1: The Prevention and Control of Offending*. Chichester: Wiley.

Sparks, R.F. (1981) Surveys of victimization – an optimistic assessment. In M. Tonry and N. Morris (eds) *Crime and Justice: An Annual Review of Research*, Vol. 3. Chicago: University of Chicago Press.

Sparks, R.F., Genn, H.G. and Dodd, D.J. (1977) *Surveying Victims: A Study of Criminal Victimization, Perceptions of Crime, and Attitudes to Criminal Justice*. Chichester: Wiley.

Spence, S.H. and Marzillier, J.S. (1981) Social skills training with adolescent male offenders: II. Short-term, long-term and generalized effects. *Behaviour Research and Therapy, 19,* 349–368.

Stuart, R.B. (ed.) (1981) *Violent Behavior: Social Learning Approaches to Prediction, Management and Treatment*. New York: Brunner Mazel.

Thornton, D.M. (1987) Treatment effects on recidivism: A reappraisal of the 'nothing works' doctrine. In B.J. McGurk, D.M. Thornton, and M. Williams (eds) *Applying Psychology to Imprisonment: Theory & Practice*. London: HMSO.

Warnick, D.H. and Sanders, G.S. (1980) The effects of group discussion on eyewitness accuracy. *Journal of Applied Social Psychology, 10,* 249–259.

Weber, D.E. and Burke, W.H. (1986) An alternative approach to treating delinquent youths. *Residential Group Care & Treatment, 3,* 65–85.

Weiner, I.B. and Hess, A.K. (eds) (1987) *Handbook of Forensic Psychology*. New York: Wiley.

Wells, G.L. (1986) Expert psychological testimony: Empirical and conceptual analyses of effects. *Law and Human Behavior, 10,* 83–95.

Wells, G.L. and Loftus E.F. (eds) (1984) *Eyewitness Testimony: Psychological Perspectives*. Cambridge: Cambridge University Press.

West, D.J. (1980) The clinical approach to criminology. *Psychological Medicine, 10,* 619–631.

Whipple, G.M. (1909) The observer as reporter: A survey of 'the psychology of testimony'. *Psychological Bulletin, 6,* 153–170.

Yarmey, A.D. (1979) *The Psychology of Eyewitness Testimony*. New York: Free Press.

Yarmey, A.D. (1986) Verbal, visual, and voice identification of a rape suspect under different levels of illumination. *Journal of Applied Psychology, 71,* 363–370.

Yuille, J.C. and Cutshall, J.L. (1986) A case study of eyewitness memory of a crime. *Journal of Applied Psychology, 71,* 291–301.

Yuille, J.C. and McEwan, N.H. (1985) Use of hypnosis as an aid to eyewitness memory. *Journal of Applied Psychology, 70,* 389–400.

Zanni, G.R. and Offerman, J.T. (1978) Eyewitness testimony: An exploration of question wording upon recall as a function of neuroticism. *Perceptual and Motor Skills, 46,* 163–166.

Zaragoza, M.S., McCloskey, M. and Jamis M. (1987) Misleading postevent information and recall of the original event: Further evidence against the memory impairment hypothesis. *Journal of Experimental Psychology: Learning, Memory, and Cognition, 13,* 36–44.

CHILDREN AS WITNESSES
Graham Davies

In 1983, a three-year-old child called Susie was abducted from outside her house by a man in a car. According to her four-year-old brother who raised the alarm, the man had simply told her to get into the car and this she had done. Some 70 hours later Susie was discovered by a pair of hikers in an abandoned house in the mountains many miles from her home. She was trapped six feet down in the base of an earth closet into which she had been thrust by her attacker. Normally, the child would have drowned in the chemical sediment at the bottom of the privy but, fortunately, it leaked, and the child had gathered some sticks together which allowed her to perch precariously above the ooze.

Susie took about six days to recover from her ordeal but the doctors could find no evidence of sexual abuse, apart from some bruising on the buttocks which could have been caused by her fall down the pit. She was interviewed by the police and was able to provide a description of her abductor and her ordeal in the outhouse. On the basis of this information, the police felt sufficently confident to show her photographs of six men with previous convictions for sexual offences against minors. From this group, she identified one man as the 'bad man'. Five days later, sitting on her mother's knee, she viewed a videotape of a 'lineup' (identification parade) while her behaviour was recorded on film. When the camera panned to the suspect, Susie said aloud: 'That's him. That's the bad man who put me in the hole'.

At this point, the psychiatrist, Dr David Jones, was brought into the case, both to assist in interviewing the child and to offer therapy. He was able to establish through questioning that the man had fondled Susie and made her reciprocate. Armed with this testimony, which fitted the known *modus operandi* of the suspect, the man was detained and brought before a judge at a preliminary hearing. Here it was ruled that there was sufficient evidence to justify an indictment. The suspect continued to maintain his innocence as the case moved towards a full hearing. Meanwhile, the child's psychological condition continued to give cause for concern, with persistent nightmares, apathy and weight loss. At the hearing, Dr Jones petitioned that the child should be allowed to testify using a videotaped interview to protect what was left of her emotional well-being, a motion to which both the prosecution and the defence agreed.

Accordingly, the little girl was interviewed on camera by the psychiatrist, with parents, judge, defence and prosecuting counsel viewing the proceedings from behind a one-way screen. The psychiatrist was able to communicate with the lawyers via an earpiece micro-receiver so that he could ask any question they wished to ask, subject only to a veto on those he considered too emotionally harmful or inappropriate. Not surprisingly, her testimony in this rather stark and alien setting was more stilted than before, but provided enough information to confirm the gist of her previous statement. The case was then adjourned. Fifteen months after the original incident and one month before trial, the accused's lawyer entered into plea bargaining on behalf of his client. The accused agreed to plead guilty to a lesser charge and made a full confession which corroborated the child's story and added new detail. He was given a ten-year sentence for sexual assault and attempted murder (Jones and Krugman, 1987).

Susie's case took place in the United States. Such a scenario would not have been possible in a British court. In England and Wales, legal precedent rarely permits a child below eight years of age, let alone a three-year-old, to testify in criminal cases. The introduction of video evidence and the interrogation of the accused by a third party are procedures which are alien to the British criminal justice system. Sadly, the new legislation embodied in the Criminal Justice Bill (1988) would have made no substantial impact on the kinds of problem embodied in Susie's case. To understand the position of the British courts, it is necessary to say a little about the philosophy underlying the adversarial legal system.

LAW AND THE CHILD WITNESS

The adversarial principle makes it the duty of the Crown to prove a case against the accused. It is the right of the defendant to refute that case by disproving or undermining the evidence offered by the prosecution. The forensic tool by which proof is established is examination and cross-examination in open court with the judge playing the role of referee and arbiter. Whatever its merits for adults, such a system presents formidable obstacles for the child, who appears as victim, witness or, more typically, combining both these roles. Traditionally, the law has made no special provision for those of tender years. Children had to stand in the alien atmosphere of the courtroom to be questioned and cross-examined by counsel, one side intent upon eliciting from the child the strongest possible case against the accused, the other intent upon discrediting whatever he or she has said. 'The right of confrontation' between accuser and accused, enshrined in law, was interpreted to mean that victim and accuser must share the same room and be visible to each other. On occasion, where the accused has elected to represent him or herself, this has meant that children have been cross-examined by the very person(s) who they maintain abused them.

While children have been treated as no different from adults, from the point of view of examination in court, the standards of proof demanded in cases involving children have always been high. There is, first, the competency requirement: witnesses are expected to take the oath and understand the special duty to speak the truth that the oath implies. Prior to July 1988, only such sworn testimony could convict an accused. The oath is administered as a matter of course to those over 14 years, but youngsters below this age must be questioned by the judge to decide if they fully understand the nature of the oath. If the judge decides that they do, they may give evidence in the usual way. If, however, the judge on the basis of questioning decides that, to quote the 1933 Children and Young Persons Act, 'he [*sic*] is possessed of sufficient intelligence to justify the reception of the evidence and he understands the duty of speaking the truth' then unsworn evidence can be tendered. However, prior to the new Act, such evidence could not itself convict the accused. To do so, the evidence would have to be corroborated, either by the word of an adult or by direct material evidence. Moreover, one unsworn child's evidence was not allowed to be used to corroborate that of another, even in cases of sexual abuse, where one child has been assaulted in the presence of another, or a series of separate assaults displayed marked similarities of approach and behaviour. In addition, courts in England and Wales do not normally admit the evidence of any child less than 5 years of age. Such children were considered to have no useful information to convey to the court (Spencer, 1987a).

Thus, prior to the 1988 Criminal Justice Bill, the law had created three leagues of child witness: an élite division who were allowed to testify as adults; a second division whose evidence could wound but not kill; and a third mute division who failed the test of appearance in open courtroom and whose allegations, even when made to a responsible adult, would be treated as hearsay and would never be answered in the courts. All three leagues, however, were covered by a blanket admonition, administered by judges in their summing up, which cautioned juries of the dangers of convicting on the basis of the evidence of a minor, even when that evidence was given under oath. Clearly, in the eyes of the law, all sworn witnesses were equal, but some were more equal than others.

Psychological assumptions concerning competency

The special status traditionally accorded by our legal system to child witnesses stems from an implicit psychological conception of the cognitive abilities of the developing child to perceive, memorize and recall. Children are assumed to be untrustworthy and unreliable witnesses whose evidence is quantitatively and qualitatively inferior to that of adults. The social consequences of this position and the injustices it perpetuates have come under widespread and sustained attack from social workers, psychiatrists, children's interest groups and some lawyers. The media too have highlighted as never before the plight of the child victim of sexual abuse, the most serious, if not the only, role in which a young child may be called before the court. However, it is the psychologist who must answer the fundamental questions regarding the competence, or incompetence, of the child to tell the truth before God and the judge. It is an applied problem to which increasing numbers of psychologists steeped in laboratory research in social, developmental and cognitive psychology have found themselves drawn.

PSYCHOLOGICAL RESEARCH ON CHILD EYEWITNESSES

Allegations against using children as witnesses may be subsumed under four major headings. These are:

1. inaccuracy of memory
2. proneness to fantasy and invention
3. deliberate lying
4. receptivity to suggestion.

These issues were all ones which also preoccupied the pioneers of forensic psychology like Binet and Stern, who conducted some of the earliest research on children as witnesses at the turn of the century (Sporer, 1982). They developed two techniques for assessing children's competency in the laboratory. In picture tests, the child would be shown a picture and subsequently asked to report on detail from the picture and be questioned about its content. In event tests, the child would be the unwitting witness to a staged incident in a classroom and subsequently would be questioned about his or her reactions to the incident, and the accuracy of what was reported would be assessed objectively. Such event tests are still used in modern research although picture tests have long since given way to the use of short films or video sequences as tests of a child's witnessing ability. Not surprisingly, perhaps, the results of more recent research have not always confirmed, and have sometimes challenged, the conclusions of the pioneers regarding these four points of contention.

1. Inaccuracy of memory

The German psychologist William Stern pioneered the study of the 'psychology of Aussage' (testimony), first in his native country and later in the United States. He was among the first researchers to test systematically groups of subjects aged from 7 to 18 years, using memory for the contents of a picture. Stern (1939) observed that the amount of spontaneous information offered by his young witnesses increased steadily with age. While these initial spontaneous accounts were often fragmentary and incomplete, they were generally accurate. Moreover, the proportion of inaccurate statements stayed remarkably stable over age; there was no evidence that errors were disproportionately greater among the younger subjects. This finding of Stern's has been sustained by later research which has used altogether more realistic scenarios, such as an argument between two adults (Marin *et al.*, 1979) or an interruption during a school lesson (Dent and Stephenson, 1979).

However, the amount of information spontaneously volunteered about an event, particularly by younger children, is relatively small and in practice must be extended by systematic questioning. Here again, Stern's research provided the first systematic data on the accuracy of juveniles under questioning. He reported that while accounts arising from such interrogation contained more information than spontaneous statements, the accuracy was also lower. Further, his younger subjects were less accurate under questioning than their elders. This lowered accuracy was particularly marked when so-called 'leading questions' were employed – questions which invite only one answer ('Don't you recall the man had a stick in his hand?').

Subsequent research has supported Stern's general finding of a trade-off between accuracy and completeness under questioning, but has not always found that younger witnesses are more vulnerable. It is notable that the clearest relationship between age and vulnerability to leading questions has emerged in studies which have used relatively passive and non-involving procedures such as observation of a short film of a bag snatch (Cohen and Harnick, 1980) or events from a child's illustrated story (Ceci *et al.*, 1986). Rather more encouraging results from the standpoint of children's general reliability have emerged from a new strain of research which has sought to capitalize on naturally occurring stresses in the child's life, such as a visit to a doctor or dentist. A pioneer of such work is the American psychologist Gail Goodman.

Goodman *et al.* (1987) describe one study which examined the memory of children for a visit to a clinic for a blood test, a painful and stressful experience for any child, especially for the 3- and 7-year-olds studied. The recall performance of this group was compared to a second group of control children who visited the same clinic to have a transfer smoothed onto their arm by the technician. Recall of the central events was high for both groups of children and the performance of the stressed group was not worse than that of the controls. The children were also asked a number of leading questions ('The person didn't touch you, did she?') and questions of the kind asked in abuse cases ('Did the person put anything in your mouth?'). Goodman *et al.* (1987) reported that while the readiness to resist such leading questions improved with age (a finding also reported by Stern), subjects of all ages resisted answering positively the so-called abuse questions.

Similar findings emerged from a later study of the testimony of children aged 3 years or 6 years who received a programme of inoculations involving needles being put into each arm, a painful process for which some children had to be held down. Recall of the central events of the incident was high in all groups and once again abuse questions were answered negatively by children of both ages. Thus, no child gave a positive answer to the question 'Did the nurse hit you?', and only one answered affirmatively to, 'Did the nurse kiss you?' Initial questioning took place up to nine days after the event, but Goodman *et al.* (1987) questioned the children again a year later and showed that resistance to abuse questions remained high.

Gail Goodman's research illustrates a theme which differentiates modern research from that of the pioneers: a quest for realistic and relevant experimentation. Rhona Flin and I, in our Aberdeen studies, also attempted to invest our experiments with a degree of realism. All involved a live interaction between a child and a stranger, and the kind of information we asked about was that which is typically requested in the course of police investigations.

In one study, for instance, groups of five children assisted a stranger in setting up equipment supposedly for a slide show. The task was undertaken by children ranging in age from 7 to 11. A fortnight afterwards, we invited the children to provide information on the height, weight and age of the stranger and subsequently to try to select him from an array of photographs. The proportion of children ready to venture estimates rose from 81 per cent at seven years of age to 94 per cent amongst the oldest children. There was some small improvement in accuracy with age on all measures, but overall accuracy was still low. One target was variously estimated to be between 20 and 45 years of age (actual age 20 years), to weigh between 70 and 252 lbs (189 lbs), and to be between 50 and 74 inches tall (74 inches). Clearly, children have poorly internalized tables of such measures. However, if we asked them the same questions in a slightly different way, which bypassed the knowledge problem, for example by asking for judgements relative to the height, weight or age of the experimenter, then the accuracy of these relative judgements appeared higher and could have provided the police with useful and usable information on these critical parameters for the oldest group in around 70 per cent of cases (Davies *et al.*, 1988).

On the identification task, we asked our children to try to select the man they had seen from an array of 12 photographs. Such tasks require recognition rather than recall and thus make fewer demands on immature retrieval strategies. Previous researchers had reported that younger subjects were remarkably precocious on such tasks and performed as well as adults at selecting the 'guilty' person (see Davies and Flin, in press, for a review). Our own results indeed confirmed that around 65 per cent of our sample at each age recognized the confederate; a further 25 per cent selected another photograph while the remainder refused to make a choice.

However, the convenience of having the suspect in the array cannot realistically be assumed in real-life criminal investigation and it was essential to test a second group of subjects on a photo array from which our confederate was absent. Here our results confirmed findings of North American researchers (King and Yuille, 1987;

Peters, 1987) in showing a strong and significant tendency among the youngest subjects to choose someone from the array. Approximately 87 per cent of the 7- to 8-year-olds made such a choice compared with less than 50 per cent of the older two groups.

It appeared that these younger children were responding to the demand characteristics of the situation: 'the suspect must be present so I must choose someone'. In an effort to eliminate this tendency, we included an experimental condition in which children had the opportunity to select the experimenter's own photograph from among three others and then to repeat the process with the experimenter's photograph now absent. To our surprise, this training had absolutely no effect on the behaviour of our young witnesses: they went ahead and chose from the main array with the same misplaced enthusiasm as their untutored colleagues.

We have examined this problem of inhibiting choice in a more recent study conducted with Mandy Tarrant (Davies *et al.*, in press). Given the prevalence of child abuse cases, we felt the need to use more directly confrontational procedures between stranger and child than hitherto. After much anguish, we came up with the idea of a simulated medical inspection. A stranger in a white coat introduced himself to individual children and interviewed them noting the colour of their eyes, the condition of their teeth, and then weighed and measured them. For this, it was necessary for the children to remove their shoes to stand on the scales and for the experimenter at some point to touch each child with his hand. He also mentioned his name. The children were aged 6 to 7 years or 10 to 11 years and were interviewed after a week's delay.

We expected the recall of items to be more sensitive to increases in age than those involving recognition and this indeed proved to be the case. For instance, on the question of the stranger's name, only 20 per cent of the younger group remembered it correctly, compared to 52 per cent of the older group; but, as with earlier research, the proportion of erroneous responses was much the same for both groups (around 27 per cent of all responses). A similar pattern of increasing recall with age also applied to the question of touching. The proportion of children correctly recalling when and where they were touched rose from 20 per cent at 7 to 8 years of age to 38 per cent in the older age group. Interestingly, no difference emerged between boys and girls: bodily boundaries, it seems, are equally rigid for both sexes at this age. Virtually all the children mentioned their shoes when asked the question: 'Did the man ask you to take any of your clothes off?', and there were no wild flights of imagination.

On this occasion, identification performance showed a rather different pattern, with no significant difference between the age groups, not only on photographic arrays where the stranger was present, but also on arrays where he was absent. It appeared that the greater element of interaction inherent in a personal confrontation between stranger and child led to an increase in accuracy with the younger children, a result encouraging to those who must evaluate the identification competency of younger children who are involved in prolonged face-to-face contact with a stranger during criminal activity.

One final area we have explored is the ability to construct the appearance of a stranger's face with the police Photofit kit. Roz Markham and I (Flin *et al.*, in press) asked individual children aged either 8 to 9 years or 11 to 12 years to observe a photograph of one of six male faces which they subsequently described verbally and then cooperated with a technician to reproduce as a Photofit picture. Later, we assessed the quality of both the descriptions and the Photofit composites by asking a group of adults to try to decide which composite or description went with which of the six faces. Judged by this criterion, performance improved steadily with age and descriptions proved consistently to be a better guide to likeness than did the Photofits. Of course, the conditions of the test were very much those of the laboratory, but a subsequent study, in a more realistic setting, showed the same trend of increased performance in older children in making up the face of a stranger seen for the first time (Davies *et al.*, in press).

In sum, on the question of accuracy, it appears that there is a steady improvement with age in the amount of information provided by children. Such age-related differences are minimized on tasks which make least demands on retrieval skills and involve tasks which are most familiar to the child like identification. They are maximized on those tasks which make heaviest demands on recall skills and draw on specialized knowledge, like composing a Photofit picture, making a detailed verbal description or estimating height, weight and age. Error as a proportion of total recall seems remarkably constant across age: there is no evidence from any of these studies that a young child's spontaneous recall is accompanied by excessive amounts of spontaneously-produced error.

2. Fact and fantasy

What of the question of fantasizing? Children frequently report having imaginary friends, conducting conversations with them or even reserving a chair for them at meal times. Can a child distinguish reality from fantasy when he or she enters the witness box? This question is raised in its most acute form by the use of so-called anatomically correct dolls as aids to assist children to demonstrate the behaviour inflicted upon them in sexual abuse cases. One opponent has likened their use in abuse cases to the provision of model houses, a fire engine, matches and a can of petrol to a child suspected of arson (Family Law Reports, 1987, pp. 316–317) and no less a figure than the former Lord Chancellor deplored the use of so-called 'explicit models and suggestive questions' by investigators attempting to substantiate cases of child abuse in Cleveland. Sadly, Lord Hailsham seemed unaware that the initial diagnoses in all these cases were based primarily on medical inspections of the children's bottoms: anal rather than oral examinations.

Be that as it may, what evidence is there that children are prone to fantasizing during the use of such aids? Two American studies suggest that fears over the anatomically correct dolls may have been exaggerated. White *et al.* (1986) compared the play of abused and non-abused children with such dolls and found marked differences in the ratings of independent judges regarding the sexual content of such play. Gail Goodman too (Goodman and Aman, 1987) has reported that non-abused children aged 3 to 5 years show no higher likelihood of responding positively to leading questions concerning abuse when playing with explicit, as opposed to conventional, dolls. A similar picture emerges from research conducted at Guy's Hospital by Glaser and Collins (1988). They observed the spontaneous play of 86 children aged from 3 to 6 with anatomically correct dolls. Only five children showed spontaneously sexualized play with such dolls and, in virtually all of these instances, this could be explained by previous sexual experience or observation. From such research in Britain and the United States, there seems little evidence to support the widespread anxieties over the use of dolls as such as aids to the interrogation of young children.

What happens if we deliberately encourage children to fantasize about an event? Will such children then be unable to distinguish fact from fantasy? Jim Baxter and I explored this issue with groups of 7- and 11-year-old children (Davies and Baxter, 1988). We first showed them a film of a theft from a parked car where the thief opened the door by slipping his arm through the quarterlight of the window. Two days later, half the children were encouraged to construct a story about a car theft using a series of props which included a chisel, a toy police car and a brown handbag, none of which had figured in the film. A further two days later the same children answered a series of questions relating to the film. One question referred to the method of entry to the car: would the children who had invented the story confuse this with the content of the film? A significant proportion of them did so although this was not significantly greater in the younger as opposed to the older group.

This confusion effect is not unique to children: similar confusion of so-called 'post event information' with the original incident has been repeatedly demonstrated by Loftus (1979) among university students. Moreover, as with the impact of leading questions, it was easier to alter the memory for a peripheral detail than for a central action. Thus, while we were able to demonstrate confusion as to the method of entry, only five of the 28 children could be persuaded that they had seen a policeman in the original film. In sum, while it is occasionally possible to provoke children under these rather special circumstances into confusing fact with fantasy, there is as yet no evidence for gross distortions of the kind likely to lead to miscarriages of justice.

3. Lying

What of the tendency of children to lie in the witness box? It appears that only a small minority of children produce spontaneously untruthful accounts of events to which they have been a party whether as witness or participant. This is the main finding to emerge from the study in Denver, Colorado, by Jones and McGraw (1987). They examined 576 cases of alleged sexual abuse reported in 1983 in the Denver area and concluded that only eight appeared to have been fabricated by the child. In four of these cases the children involved had been previously abused and had transferred the allegation of sexual abuse from one adult to another. The criterion used in evaluating the truth or falsity of the children's statement was the development of a technique which is routinely employed in West Germany for evaluating children's statements. Since 1954, all statements of children alleging adult sexual abuse are routinely evaluated by a psychologist using various criteria for truthfulness based on an examination of features of the statement (Undeutsch, 1984). A refinement of this procedure appears to offer a promising method of identifying that small minority of children's statements which should be treated with caution (Stellar *et al.*, in press).

4. *Suggestibility of children*

Can children be persuaded to say whatever an adult wants them to say? This was certainly the view of the Belgian psychologist Varendonck writing in 1911: 'those who have the habit of living with children do not attach the least value to their testimony because children cannot observe and because their suggestiveness is inexhaustible'. Varendonck was responsible for some of the earliest demonstrations of suggestibility in children. As part of a court case, he had asked a class of 7-year-olds the colour of the beard of a particular teacher. A total of 16 members of the class had answered black and two had not replied. The teacher had no beard, needless to say.

As a demonstration of the infinite suggestibility of young children, Varendonck's pioneering work falls well short of the definitive. The classroom setting he employed confuses three quite different effects. The first might be termed true *malleability* of memory in the sense of an adult's suggestion materially altering the memory of the child. A second is *compliance*, the tendency of a younger person to go along with the views of a more powerful adult without necessarily internalizing these views as their own. A third is *conformity*, the tendency to submit to peer group pressure. This pressure would be very evident in the classroom setting which Varendonck employed. From the point of view of evaluating the testimony of young children, true malleability is much the most serious charge to consider: both compliance and conformity offer the possibility of later reversal, given appropriate context and delicate questioning procedures.

Subsequent research has provided little evidence for true malleability, at least as regards the significant central features of events. For instance, in the 'helping a stranger' study referred to earlier, we had three instances in our script where the visitor said he was going to do something, but then did not do so. At one point, the stranger dropped a box of slides which fell to the floor with a realistic splintering crash. He exclaimed, 'Oh, I've broken my slides'. However, the box remained sealed and no evidence of breakage was ever seen by the children. Would they later remember having seen broken slides? The answer is no. There was little evidence that the youngsters readily mixed up observation and inference at any age (only six out of 96 made this error). There was no significant trend on any of the probed items for younger children to be more suggestible than their elder brethren, a finding consistent with much American work, which implies that true suggestibility, in the sense of confabulation concerning the central thread of a witnessed event, is very rare. Such distortions can occur in real cases as in the English witch trials of the 17th century; but it is often forgotten that adults as well as children testified to miscegenation between women and bats, foxes and other assorted wild life (Seth, 1969).

While compliance remains a relatively under-researched area, Jim Baxter and I have readily been able to demonstrate conformity effects in child witnesses (Baxter and Davies, 1987). On this occasion, we showed a video of a children's game which ended in a scuffle between two of the participants. Subsequently the children, aged 7 and 13 years, answered a series of questions concerning aspects of the incident. Prior to giving their own answers, we showed some of the children film of one or four other children giving answers which, on the critical questions, were wrong. The tendency for the 7-year-olds to go along with their filmed counterparts was as much as four times greater than that for the 13-year-olds. Moreover, the impact of four wrong answers was rather less than one wrong answer. Conformity, then, can be a problem, but even here there is hope of salvation. In a more recent study, Baxter has been able to show that such effects can be reduced if the child gives an answer prior to exposure of the panel's opinion (Baxter, 1988).

It is apparent from this representative review of the literature, that differences in competence between younger and older witnesses appear to have been grossly exaggerated. I have chosen to highlight work with which I have been associated, but rather similar conclusions could have been reached by a more comprehensive overview of the literature (see for instance Davies *et al.*, 1986a; Davies *et al.*, 1986b). Younger witnesses differ from their older counterparts in terms of the quantity of their testimony rather than in terms of quality. They take in less information and consequently report fewer incidents, but seem no more likely than their older counterparts to confabulate or confuse surmise with facts. There are conditions when younger witnesses may be disproportionately poorer: I have instanced the offender-absent parade and the impact of conformity as two examples, but in each instance, techniques for ameliorating the problem may be possible. Despite the inevitable limitations on criminal realism of many of the experiments which have been described, there is no indication of infinite suggestibility, sometimes supposed to be a characteristic of the young witness. Children, like adults, can be misled on detail, but seem just as immovable on the central events of incidents to which they have been a party.

LEGAL REFORM

In July 1988, the new Criminal Justice Act came into law in England and Wales. This Act seeks, in some respects, to ameliorate the difficulties faced by the child witness and reflects a degree of consideration for the psychological issues discussed in this chapter. The greatest impact of such research is probably on the decision to modify the corroboration rule. In May 1987, David Mellor, the then Home Office Minister, commissioned an in-house review of the psychological research on the competency of child witnesses. This covered much of the experimental evidence and rehearsed many of the same arguments which have been propounded here. Not surprisingly, perhaps, it came to rather similar conclusions, namely that the special provisions attached to children's evidence could not be justified by empirical research (Hedderman, 1987). The result of this report was the introduction of a clause into the Act to abolish the legal requirement of corroboration for child witnesses. For the first time, under the new Act, the uncorroborated evidence of the child can, on its own, be sufficient to convict. In addition, the caution routinely administered by judges regarding the evidence of a child has been abolished, although it will be retained in cases involving sexual offences; a matter of giving with one hand and taking with the other, given the prevalence of sexual abuse among the categories of cases in which children are likely to be called as witnesses. For the first time, one unsworn child's evidence can corroborate another. This is, to quote the legal expert John Spencer, 'a major step toward rationality' in the treatment of child witnesses (Spencer, 1987b).

A second major change in judicial procedure is designed to facilitate children giving evidence in the courtroom. This is the introduction of the so-called 'video link' or 'live link': essentially closed circuit television designed to allow the child to testify from outside the courtroom. The idea is a laudable one: to protect the child from the intimidating atmosphere of the dock and the sight of the accused. A Government consultative paper which examined its use suggested some ambiguity and imprecision over the details of its operation (Home Office Consultative Paper, 1987). The original proposal did not specify whether the child would see the questioner and the questioner the child, that is, whether the video was to be one-way or two-way; it now appears it will be two-way. As yet, no research has been commissioned to assess the impact of such procedural details. Nor do we know, for instance, what the impact on the quality of testimony is likely to be from being questioned at a distance as opposed to being questioned directly. We may be able to make some educated guesses from research on tele-conferencing for adults, but no research has yet been carried out specifically with children (Davies, 1988).

Likewise, the impact on the jury of seeing evidence presented on the small screen as opposed to live is again unknown. Are witnesses perceived as more or less or equally plausible? There is also the matter of the particular form of camera shot employed. Is it to be a medium shot, a close-up or a mixture of shots? And how will this influence the perceived plausibility of the child? This is not known, but ought to be, before the introduction of such a major reform.

It is apparent that the proposed scheme will not address a major source of a child's problems, namely the form of examination and cross-examination employed by counsel. The British Psychological Society, along with a number of other organizations, put forward proposals that all examinations should be by a child advocate, who would be someone who knew the witness, had been assigned to the case at an early stage, and would be able to relay the questions of the defence and prosecution counsel to the child in their presence via an earpiece micro-receiver. This procedure is already in use in a number of countries including some American states and seems to work effectively, as in the case of Susie cited earlier. Sadly, the arguments of the legal lobby on the need to directly confront witnesses were successful in persuading the Home Office not to pursue this particular reform and children in England and Wales are likely to continue to be faced with cross-examination by a stranger, albeit at a distance. Happily, the Scottish Law Commission has taken this idea very seriously and has canvassed legal opinion as to whether it is proper that it should be introduced in Scotland (Scottish Law Commission, 1988).

The live link was introduced in 14 regional centres in England in January 1989, and it is proposed that all cases involving child witnesses will be channelled through these courts. The progress of this experiment is to be monitored by the Home Office and the Law Commission. It must be fervently hoped that this experiment will be crowned with success, but the haste with which these reforms have been introduced combined with the lack of prior experimentation does not augur well.

No reforms are to be implemented in the competency rule. This means, effectively, that the law will continue to deal on a regular basis only with witnesses of 8 years or over and to deny access to the law for those of 5 years of age or below. For them, only the facility to testify via a prior tape-recorded interview can offer a possible way into the legal system. This avenue has been consistently denied to young witnesses in criminal cases, but continues to be available in civil cases, where the rules of evidence and the standards of proof are less demanding (Spencer, 1988). Attempts to introduce a clause into the Criminal Justice Bill to allow the admission of tape-recorded testimony were consistently refused even when this was attached to a provision that the child should be available to testify in open court when required.

The matter is now to be considered by a Home Office Commission of Enquiry under Lord Justice Piggot. It is to be hoped that this will not be yet another report which is buried in the Home Office archives. The advantages of video testimony, particularly for very young witnesses, have been well rehearsed. These include the reduction in the number of times the child has to give the same evidence and be examined upon it and the advantage of securing an early account of an event, given the sometimes lengthy delays between a complaint being made and an appearance before the court. Finally, there is the possibility of securing a conviction on the basis of an admission by the accused following the viewing of a taped interview and so eliminating the need for a court appearance by the child altogether.

The problem that advocates of taped evidence have had to confront has been how to produce tapes which meet the exacting demands of the criminal law. Taped interviews with children often start life as psychiatric enquiries: abuse is suspected but not proven. The child may initially give ambiguous answers or deny outright that anything is wrong. Such denials might co-exist with physical evidence consistent with abuse or with allegations from within the family. In order to try to secure an admission from the child, the questioner might apply a measure of pressure, as much if not more than was applied by the offending adult to make the child 'keep their secret'. The range of questions may include the hypothetical ('If Daddy was to touch you there, would it be nice or yucky?'), or even leading ('It was Uncle John who touched your willy wasn't it?').

It is not surprising that taped evidence gathered for a therapeutic purpose may be treated harshly by the courts (Family Law Reports, 1987). If tapes are to be used in the criminal court, it will be necessary to evolve entirely new ways of interrogating children, building on research of the kind recently conducted at Great Ormond Street (Bentovim and Tranter, 1988) and by Bexley Social Services (1988). Such interviews should have the stamp of judicial acceptability, while at the same time being sufficiently sympathetic to the needs of the child to elicit effectively the necessary information. If these twin goals can be achieved then the introduction of videotape into the criminal as well as the civil courts can be advocated with confidence. The present hiatus engendered by the Committee of Enquiry should also enable psychologists, doctors and social workers to collaborate in improving and perfecting interview techniques. It will also enable a cadre of trained personnel to be assembled and prepared when and if the Home Office decides in favour of the introduction of videotape into the criminal courtroom. Only when this reform is in place, and changes are introduced into the competency rule, can British justice be said to cater for the full spectrum of the population under the law.

REFERENCES

Baxter, J.S. (1988) Children as eyewitnesses: A developmental study. Unpublished doctoral thesis. University of Aberdeen.

Baxter, J.S. and Davies, G.M. (1987) Conformity and the child witness. Unpublished paper presented at the Society for Research in Child Development Convention, Baltimore, Maryland, USA.

Bentovim, A. and Tranter, M. (1988) The sexual abuse of children and the courts. In G.M. Davies and J. Drinkwater (eds) *The Child Witness: Do the Courts Abuse Children?* Division of Legal and Criminological Psychology Monograph Series No. 13. Leicester: The British Psychological Society.

Bexley Social Services and Metropolitan Police (1988) Child sexual abuse joint investigative programme: Bexley experiment. Information package available from Bexley Social Services and the Metropolitan Police.

Ceci, S.J., Ross, D.F. and Toglia, M.P. (1986) Suggestibility of children's memory: Psycholegal implications. *Journal of Experimental Psychology, 116*, 38–49.

Cohen, R.L. and Harnick, M.A. (1980) The susceptibility of child witnesses to suggestion. *Law and Human Behavior, 4*, 201–210.

Davies, G.M. (1988) Use of video in child abuse trials. *The Psychologist, 1*, 20–22.

Davies, G.M. and Baxter, J. (1988) Children's ability to distinguish fact from fantasy. In M. Steller (Chair) *Children's statements and credibility.* Unpublished paper presented at NATO Advanced Study Institute, Maratea, Italy.

Davies, G.M. and Flin, R. (in press) Children's identification evidence. In G. Kohnken and S.L. Sporer (eds) *Identifizierung von Tatverdachtinger: Psychologische Erkenntrisse, Probleme und Perspektiven.* Gottinger: C.J. Hogrefe.

Davies, G.M., Flin, R. and Baxter, J. (1986a) The child witness. *The Howard Journal, 25*, 81–99.

Davies, G.M., Stevenson-Robb, Y. and Flin, R. (1986b) The reliability of children's testimony. *International Legal Practitioner, 11,* 81–108.

Davies, G. M., Stevenson-Robb, Y. and Flin, R. (1988) Tales out of school: Children's memory of an unexpected event. In M.M. Gruneberg, P.E. Morris and R.N. Sykes (eds) *Practical Aspects of Memory: Current Research and Issues.* Chichester: Wiley.

Davies, G.M., Tarrant, A. and Flin, R. (in press) Close encounters of the witness kind – children's memory for a simulated health inspection. *British Journal of Psychology.*

Dent, H.R. and Stephenson, G. (1979) An experimental study of the effectiveness of different techniques of questioning child witnesses. *British Journal of Social and Clinical Psychology, 18,* 41–51.

Family Law Reports (1987) Special Issue, Number 4.

Flin, R.H., Markham, R. and Davies, G.M. (in press) Making faces: Developmental trends in the construction and recognition of photofit faces. *Applied Developmental Psychology.*

Glaser, D. and Collins, C. (1988) The response of young, non-sexually abused children to anatomically correct dolls. Unpublished paper.

Goodman, G.S. and Aman, C. (1987) Childen's use of anatomically correct dolls to report an event. In M. Steward (Chair) *Evaluation of suspected child abuse: Developmental, clinical and legal perspectives on the use of anatomically correct dolls.* Symposium presented at the Society for Research in Child Development Convention, Baltimore, Maryland, USA. Unpublished.

Goodman, G.S., Aman, C. and Hirschman, J. (1987) Child sexual and physical abuse: Children's testimony. In S.J. Ceci, M.P. Toglia and D.F. Ross (eds) *Children's Eyewitness Memory.* New York: Springer-Verlag.

Home Office (1987) *The Use of Video Technology at Trials of Alleged Child Abusers.* London: Home Office.

Hedderman, C. (1987) Children's evidence: The need for corroboration. *Home Office Research and Planning Unit, Paper No. 41.* London: Home Office.

Jones, D.P.H. and Krugman, R. (1986) Can a three-year-old child bear witness to her sexual assault and attempted murder? *Child Abuse and Neglect, 10,* 253–258.

Jones, D.P.H. and McGraw, J. (1987) Reliable and fictitious accounts of sexual abuse to children. *The Journal of Interpersonal Violence, 2,* 27–45.

King, M.A. and Yuille, J.C. (1987) Suggestibility and the child witness. In S.J. Ceci, M.P. Toglia and D.F. Ross (eds) *Children's Eyewitness Memory.* New York: Springer-Verlag.

Loftus, E.F. (1979) *Eyewitness Testimony.* Cambridge, Mass.: Harvard University Press.

Marin, B.V., Holmes, D.L., Guth, M. and Kovac, P. (1979) The potential of children as eyewitnesses. *Law and Human Behavior, 3,* 295–305.

Peters, D.P. (1987) The impact of naturally occurring stress on children's memory. In S.J. Ceci, M.P. Toglia and D.F. Ross (eds) *Children's Eyewitness Memory.* New York: Springer-Verlag.

Scottish Law Commission (1988) The evidence of children and other potentially vulnerable witnesses. *Discussion Paper No. 75.* Edinburgh: Scottish Law Commission.

Seth, R. (1969) *Children Against Witches.* New York: Taplinger Publishing Co.

Spencer, J. (1987a) Child witnesses and the criminal justice bill. *New Law Journal*, November, 816–817.

Spencer, J. (1987b) Child witnesses, corroboration and expert evidence. *Criminal Law Review*, April, 267–269.

Spencer, J. (1988) How not to reform the law. *New Law Journal*, July 15, 497–499.

Sporer, S.L. (1982) A brief history of the psychology of testimony. *Current Psychological Reviews, 2*, 323–340.

Stellar, M., Raskin, D.C. and Yuille, J.C. (in press) *Sexually Abused Children: Interview and Assessment Techniques*. New York: Springer-Verlag.

Stern, W. (1939) The psychology of testimony. *Journal of Abnormal Psychology, 34*, 3–20.

Undeutsch, U. (1984) Courtroom evaluation of eyewitness testimony. *International Review of Applied Psychology, 33*, 51–67.

Varendonck, J. (1911) Les témoignages d'enfants dans un procès retentissant. *Archives de Psychologie, 11*, 129–171.

White, P.D., Strom, G.A., Santilli, G. and Haplin, B. (1986) Interviewing young sexual abuse victims with anatomically correct dolls. *Child Abuse and Neglect, 10*, 519–529.

THE STRANGE ACHIEVEMENTS OF IDIOTS SAVANTS

Michael J.A. Howe

'Idiot savant' is a descriptive term that has been applied to certain mentally handicapped individuals. These people, despite their disabilities, are capable of remarkable feats. From the viewpoint of scientific psychology, these accomplishments seem at first to be interesting mainly because of their apparently paradoxical nature. They challenge us to discover how it can be possible for certain people to gain abilities that seem to demand high levels of intelligence – which these individuals do not obviously possess.

But on closer examination we find that the scientific importance of idiots savants is greater than this. Their achievements are more than puzzling anomalies. The main significance for psychology of the extraordinary combinations of abilities and disabilities to be found in these people lies in the fact that they raise fundamental questions about the nature of human abilities, and about the causes of differences in abilities between people. Evidence from case studies of idiots savants, combined with findings from a variety of other sources, presents a challenge to the view that human intellectual abilities are in any real sense either unitary or centrally controlled by a global entity of general ability or intelligence.

THE FEATS THESE PEOPLE PERFORM

What do idiots savants actually do? What kind of people are they? They are in fact a varied group of individuals, who have little in common with one another apart from the unusual distinction of being at the same time mentally handicapped yet capable of highly impressive accomplishments. Many idiots savants are rather withdrawn, but by no means all of them. A substantial minority of the individuals who have been described as idiots savants are also autistic. That is to say, they lack social and communicative abilities, have restricted language development, and do not have the capacities that enable ordinary people to empathize with others and understand other people's points of view, but are likely to show less impairment of intellectual abilities that do not have a social component (Baron-Cohen *et al.*, 1985; Leslie, 1987).

Because these individuals differ so much, no one case is entirely typical, but a few brief descriptions of idiots savants will illustrate some of the characteristics they display.

Harriet was a mentally handicapped woman who, with much help from a very supportive younger sister, eventually managed to learn to cope with the demands of a job as an unskilled hospital kitchen assistant. (It took six months' careful training, through which Harriet acquired a fixed and unvarying routine which she was able to keep to on her own.) Her IQ was 73 on the Wechsler scale. She performed worse on verbal than non-verbal items, and did poorly on general knowledge questions. Her replies indicated that she thought that there were 10 feet in a yard and 48 weeks in a year. Her social deficiencies were equally striking. One Christmas day, when she was in her thirties, her father suddenly died, just before the family's Christmas dinner. To everyone's horror she sat down to eat as soon as the body had been carried out (Viscott, 1970).

Yet this same woman, despite her handicap, was a superb musician. Harriet was an excellent performer on the piano. She was able to transcribe from memory, and could make difficult key changes in the middle of playing a musical item. If she played a transcribed version of music written for a different instrument, she would carefully imitate the tone and phrasing of that instrument. When she was playing orchestral works, she would fill in parts from the full orchestral version that were not included in her piano score. Harriet could name each of the component notes of a four-note piano chord held for just half a second. She was able to name both of two randomly chosen notes struck at the same time, and could instantly tell the key and the mode of any chord.

Apart from her specific skills, Harriet the musician was in a number of respects a very different person from her non-musical self. Outside her musical life she was rigid, passive and unemotional. Her musical activities, in contrast, were expressive and creative. She often improvised when she played an instrument; and when she talked about music her language included words describing feelings, such as 'frightening', 'sweet', 'lovely' and 'sad', which she never uttered in non-musical contexts. Similarly, when she played or listened to music her face would light up with emotions and feelings that were never seen when she was doing other things. She liked most kinds of music, and had an encyclopaedic knowledge of it, contrasting with her ignorance of other aspects of life. For example, for virtually any classical piece she could supply the composer, key, opus number, and date of first performance. Her knowledge of opera was especially detailed. She had attended every Saturday concert given by the Boston Symphony Orchestra over a twenty-year period, and she could say what had been played at every single concert and who had conducted each performance. She knew about the musical experience and the qualifications of every single member of the orchestra. She also had a huge amount of biographical knowledge about the lives of composers and performers.

The combination seen in Harriet, of mental handicap and superb musicianship, is rare but not entirely unique. One man whose disability was more profound than Harriet's, and who was incapable of looking after himself without constant supervision, was nevertheless such an excellent musician that he was regularly asked by a leading chamber orchestra to play the piano at rehearsals (Anastasi and Levee, 1960; see also Charness et al., 1988; Lucci et al., 1988; Miller, 1987; Sloboda et al., 1985).

Very occasionally, there are reports of idiots savants who are extraordinarily accomplished in one of the visual arts. For instance, there is the widely reported case of a 13-year-old mentally handicapped boy who makes excellent drawings of large buildings. Another gifted artist was a profoundly retarded autistic man, with no speech, who made realistic and lifelike drawings of natural objects (Sacks, 1985). Like Harriet, whose imaginative and stylish performances on the piano contrasted with her rigid and unemotional demeanour when she was not involved with music, this man displayed qualities of humour and imagination in his art that were never glimpsed when he was not drawing.

Equally remarkable is the case of Nadia, a young autistic girl who lacked speech and was profoundly retarded (Selfe, 1977). Despite these handicaps, from the age of three years she produced drawings of animals that displayed an amazing degree of sophistication and technical expertise. Her drawings were not only vastly superior to anything else she could achieve, but were beyond the capabilities of even the brightest 'normal' children at twice her age.

Lorna Selfe, who carefully investigated Nadia's skills, subsequently made a careful search for other children with extraordinary skills in the visual arts. She eventually located eleven young people whose drawings demonstrated an exceptional ability to depict objects realistically (Selfe, 1983). Although she had not excluded ordinary children from her search, it turned out that all eleven were abnormal in some ways and most were mentally handicapped. Selfe was able to examine six of the children fairly closely. She discovered that all six, like Nadia, had some symptoms of autism. For instance, all had obsessions and unusual mannerisms; social development was impaired in all of them; and all showed restricted language development.

In about one-third of the published case histories of idiots savants, it is reported that the individual is capable of an unusual skill known as 'calendar calculating'. At its simplest, this involves the ability to state the day of the week on which a specified date falls. For instance, if a person who performs this skill is supplied with the date 16 August 1987, he or she will announce, usually within a few seconds, that this date fell on a Sunday. Some calendar calculators can solve problems of this kind for spans of dates extending several hundred years into the past and the future.

There has been one case in which both members of a pair of mentally handicapped twins were skilled calendar calculators (Horwitz *et al.*, 1965; Horwitz *et al.*, 1969; Sacks, 1985). The abler of the twins had a range of at least six thousand years. His skill extended into the future beyond the year 7000, but for dates before 1582 he gave the wrong answer, because he did not know about the calendar adjustment which was made at that time. (Ten days were eliminated. The alteration was necessitated by the inaccuracy of the Julian calendar system, which was then replaced by the more precise Gregorian one that is still in use.) Both twins could also answer calendar questions other than ones in the conventional form. For instance, if asked to state years in which 12 April fell on a Sunday, both of them would answer correctly. Both twins could state the correct date if appropriate specifications were provided. For example, to 'The fourth Monday in February, 1993?' they would correctly reply 'The 22nd'. One twin could also give the correct answer if asked to supply, say, the months in 2002 in which the 1st falls on a Friday (February, March and November).

However it is actually achieved, calendar calculating makes substantial demands on memory (Goldsmith and Feldman, 1988; Howe, 1988a; O'Connor and Hermelin, 1984; White, 1988). Quite a number of the accomplishments of idiots savants are essentially memory feats. As typical as any are those of a 7-year-old American boy whose mental age was 2 years and 6 months (Goodman, 1972).

He could recall numerous population statistics relating to American states and many other countries. He also recited lengthy lists of addresses, telephone numbers, and other sequences of detailed information. Other cases are described by Boygo and Ellis (1988) and Waterhouse (1988). One 6-year-old autistic girl who had no communicative use of language is said to have been able to repeat, word for word, lengthy conversations or dialogues from radio or television that had been heard more than a year earlier (Cain, 1969). The same girl was reported to read and reproduce (with correct spelling) any word that she had seen just once, even if it was years beyond her age level.

A. Lewis Hill (1978) has written a good general survey of the various skills demonstrated by idiots savants. Typically, the idiots savants described in case histories have had more than one special skill. For example, Harriet, whose musical accomplishments have already been mentioned, also performed some striking memory feats. As a child she could recall on request any of about three hundred telephone numbers which had been told her by members of her family or other people who visited her house. She also performed calendar calculating feats over a 35-year range.

HOW ARE THE SKILLS ACQUIRED? THE CASE OF CALENDAR CALCULATING

The many reports surveyed by Hill (1978) establish that the feats of idiots savants are genuine and that the individuals who perform them are indeed mentally handicapped. But in most cases the reports are largely descriptive. They make no serious attempt to explain how the individuals actually mastered their skills, and they do not come to grips with the challenge of understanding how it is possible for remarkable cognitive abilities and very severe intellectual limitations to exist simultaneously in the same person.

There are some exceptions, however. Here I shall summarize some of the attempts that have been made to explain how one particular skill, calendar calculating, has been mastered by mentally impaired individuals.

Being confronted by an uncommunicative person who has severe mental handicaps and yet nevertheless possesses a remarkable ability to give the correct answers to difficult questions about calendar dates is such an uncanny experience that it is difficult for an observer to imagine how one might even begin to explain the feats that have been observed (Howe, 1988a; Howe, in press; Howe and Smith, 1988; Smith and Howe, 1985). One possible starting-point is to ask whether or not an idiot savant calendar calculator might be following methods similar to ones that could be located by a person of ordinary intelligence. A number of such techniques can be found in printed form in certain encyclopaedias, handbooks and, occasionally, diaries. They differ in their details. Some require the user to consult a number of tables. Others dispense with this necessity but make heavy demands on memory, thereby enabling the user to produce, for each year, a twelve-digit sequence in which each digit corresponds to a fixed day (the first Sunday, say) in each month. An alternative method requires the user to consult or memorize a six-step algorithm which can be used to obtain the day of the week for any date. (Once memorized, the algorithm is not difficult to use, but solving calendar date problems in this way is a tedious activity. I found that even after considerable practice at this method, I was taking at least five times as long as the most skilled idiots savants to answer questions.)

It is quite likely that some stages of the available techniques for performing calendar date calculations are similar to elements of the methods that some idiots savants have arrived at. However, the evidence suggests that the majority of idiot savant calendar date calculators do not follow such techniques, at least not in their entirety. One reason for this is that many savant calculators, perhaps the majority, are illiterate. Even those with some reading ability seem unlikely to possess the information retrieval skills necessary for gaining access to the somewhat obscure sources in which the instructions are to be found. It is conceivable that an individual could have been taught one of the known methods by a literate adult, but in none of the reported cases does this appear to have happened.

A more powerful argument against the possibility that savant calculators generally make use of the published methods lies in the fact that many idiots savants are able to solve calendar date problems that such methods cannot deal with at all. For example, none of the known techniques would be entirely satisfactory for solving some of the problems that the twins studied by Horwitz and his colleagues were able to answer, such as the ones that asked for a list of years in which a particular date fell on a certain day of the week. The known methods would be similarly inappropriate for solving some of the problems which were successfully dealt with by a 14-year-old English boy (Smith and Howe, 1985; Howe and Smith, 1988). These included, for instance, one in which the boy was simply given a list of seven month–date combinations and asked to say which was the odd one out. This (essentially unspecified) problem could only be solved by a person who was able to notice that all but one of the months started on the same day of the week.

It is likely that most idiot savant calendar calculators have somehow or other been able to amass and remember a considerable amount of detailed information about particular calendar dates. Conceivably, an individual could simply memorize the day of the week for every single date over a period of years. It is possible that knowledge about particular dates is the main resource of some individuals whose calendar date skills extend over a range of several years. Such a range could be extended by remembering a large number of particular dates that would serve as anchor points or bench-marks, making it possible for someone to work forwards or backwards to a date for which the day of the week is requested.

But it seems very unlikely that the larger ranges of calendar-calculating skills, extending over hundreds of years (and in the case of one of the twins studied by Horwitz, thousands of years), could be achieved in this way. The most impressive calculators not only answer questions about the days of the week for particular dates, but can also deal with a variety of very different kinds of calendar date problems. For such feats to be possible, it seems that the individual must possess calendar information in some structured form. It is conceivable that some idiots savants know about some of the rules by which calendars are constructed. That would make it possible to generate information about specified dates.

How might a mentally handicapped person acquire a substantial body of stored information about calendar dates? At first sight, doing so might appear to demand exceptional memory skills, but in fact that is not necessarily the case (Howe, 1988d). Most people are good at remembering information about a topic that they find interesting, and to which they are happy to devote much of their time. As a result, many ordinary individuals can recall, for example, the words and tunes of numerous songs, or large quantities of information about football teams and match scores (Morris, 1988), or even the vast amount of linguistic information that is gained in the course of learning to speak a foreign language fluently. And the chances are that someone for whom calendars were a main interest in life, and who spent several hours every day thinking about them, would similarly end up retaining in memory a very considerable amount of calendar information. Something of this kind probably takes place with most idiot savant calendar calculators.

Of course, most people do not find calendar information interesting. They would find it hard to imagine someone spending hours every day on calendars. But this is one way in which idiots savants are not like ordinary people: for one reason or another, some mentally impaired individuals *are* interested in calendars, perhaps obsessively so. The point is that an important way in which these people are different from everyone else is in having an *interest* that is extraordinary, rather than in having a fundamental ability that other people lack.

A number of researchers investigating idiot savant calendar calculators have remarked upon their subjects' intense interest in calendar date information. The twins investigated by Horwitz *et al.* spent a great deal of time, as children, playing with a perpetual calendar device which they had been given. The boy studied by Smith and Howe (1985; Howe and Smith, 1988) spent much of his free time literally drawing calendar months. He would fill in the dates, in the appropriate positions, as they appear on the kind of calendar that displays one month at a time. Furthermore, some of his responses when he was solving problems indicated that he had particular calendar months in mind. For example, he answered one question by saying 'Thursday, that's black'. When asked what he meant by this, he said 'Thursdays are always in black', and, pressed to explain, he replied 'They're black on the kitchen calendar'. Moreover, Sacks (1985), who observed the twins previously investigated by Horwitz and his colleagues, noticed that when the twins were solving difficult calendar problems their eyes moved and fixed in peculiar ways, as though they were unrolling or scrutinizing some kind of inner landscape. When he asked the twins how they held a large number in their minds, they replied 'We see it'. Another man usually gazed at the ceiling before he answered calendar questions (Roberts, 1945). On one occasion when his answer was wrong, the experimenter advised him to 'look at it again', whereupon he did so, and answered that and the following questions correctly.

These indications that people draw upon a knowledge of the visual appearance of calendar data suggest that visual imagery has a place in the mental procedures that enable them to solve calendar problems. Is it possible that *all* idiot savant calendar calculators depend on visual imagery? The findings of other reports of calendar calculating make it seem unlikely that imagery played a role in the skills of at least some of the individuals concerned (see, for example, Hill, 1975). And there has been at least one case of calendar calculating in a congenitally blind person (Rubin and Monaghan, 1965).

One complication that adds to the difficulty of discovering exactly how an individual achieves calendar calculating feats is that it is often hard to discover exactly what skills a mentally handicapped person does possess. Such a person may have cognitive capacities which appear only in a particular context and are never applied to new or different situations. For example, in the investigation by Smith and Howe (1985; Howe and Smith, 1988) the investigators wanted to know whether or not the subject was capable of various subtraction tasks. He succeeded at simple problems such as 'What is 20 minus 8?', but failed at harder ones such as 'What is 1,981 minus 1,963?'. However, when difficult tasks were presented in the form of problems about calendar years, such as 'If I was born in 1908 how old would I be in 1973?', he found the questions easy, and answered correctly.

A more extreme instance of mentally handicapped individuals having unsuspected skills was discovered by Sacks (1985). He spent a considerable amount of time with the twins whose calendar abilities Horwitz and his colleagues had investigated more than a decade previously. It had been assumed that the twins' arithmetic skills were very limited, but Sacks discovered that they had a great interest in numbers. On one occasion, as Sacks watched and listened to the twins, he found that they were engaged in a kind of dialogue. One twin would say a six-digit number and the other would nod and smile, apparently enjoying the number, and then say another six-digit number, in his turn, to the delight of the first twin. It turned out that the twins were engaged in playing a sophisticated game involving the exchange of prime numbers. Eventually Sacks joined in, giving a number of his own, an eight-digit prime. At this the twins, after a long pause, suddenly and simultaneously broke into smiles, and proceeded to pursue the game with skill and enthusiasm. It is hard to know whether, or how, the twins made use of their impressive numerical abilities when they were solving calendar date problems, but this incident serves to alert us to the fact that our failure to detect particular abilities in idiots savants does not necessarily mean that such abilities are absent.

A related source of difficulty in investigating calendar date skills is that it is rarely possible to establish for certain whether or not an individual is able to draw upon knowledge about the rules by which calendars are constructed. Most idiots savants show no evidence of possessing such knowledge. (An interesting exception is a man examined by Kahr and Neisser (1982), but he differed considerably from the majority of savant calculators in being mentally impaired only to a mild extent.) When individuals are asked 'How do you do it?', replies are rarely at all illuminating: Howe and Smith's (1988) subject's response, 'I use me head!', was not untypical. However, an inability to articulate rules, or even to display awareness that rules exist, cannot be taken as evidence that rules are not followed. Most people, whenever they use language, are following a number of complex rules to which conscious access is extremely restricted.

It is clear that even when a number of people share an ability to do the same feat, the manner in which they actually perform the feat can differ very greatly from one person to another. The uniqueness of individuals' skills, as well as the incompleteness of our knowledge, makes it hard to draw generalizations about the abilities of idiots savants. Yet it is reasonably certain that in every case the individual has managed to acquire a great deal of knowledge relating to the area of expertise. Such knowledge, which is gained in the course of the lengthy periods of time for which the person engages his or her thoughts on the topic of interest, plays an important part in making difficult feats possible. Among people of normal intelligence, the kinds of skill that we label 'thinking' and 'reasoning' depend on, and are closely tied to, the particular domains of knowledge that an individual possesses, and on the way in which the individual has structured that knowledge (Carey, 1985; Chi and Ceci, 1987; Glaser, 1984). The same is true of mentally handicapped individuals.

We can think of an idiot savant calendar calculator as being in certain respects like an ordinary person who happens, for one reason or another, to become obsessively interested in calendar dates. Put in that light, the fact that calendar skills are gained may not seem altogether surprising. But the musical skills that were mentioned earlier, and the very rare artistic skills of individuals such as Nadia, seem to challenge our comprehension more severely. Perhaps, from early in life, certain mental computing systems become 'locked in' to a particular aspect of experience to an extreme degree. The person's cognitive facilities seem to become exclusively directed to processing experiences of one kind. The individual may be literally unable to engage his or her full attention, and accompanying mental processing systems, to events and experiences outside that particular area.

In some cases, savants' skills may only be possible when specific impairments exist. It is noteworthy that Nadia's best work was produced when she was without language (Selfe, 1977). Her ability to concentrate exclusively on the appearance of things, which would seem to have been essential for her to acquire her artistic skills, appears to have depended on an inability to process visual information as objects which have the kinds of meaning that language expresses. The artistic productions of ordinary children are influenced by their knowledge of the meaning and significance of the objects being depicted. They cannot choose to exclude meaning and concentrate exclusively on form. In all likelihood, the two are not distinct in the child's inner representation of an object. Moreover, the act of depicting an object cannot usually be divorced from the act of communicating conceptual knowledge about that object.

WHAT IDIOTS SAVANTS CAN TELL US ABOUT THE NATURE OF HUMAN ABILITIES

How is it possible for remarkable cognitive abilities and very severe intellectual limitations to coexist in the same person? Our attempts to discover how idiots savants perform particular feats have done little to help answer this broader question.

Try turning the question around. Instead of asking how the two states of affairs can exist together, ask why we find it so surprising that they can. Why do we presume that it should *not* be possible for a mentally handicapped person to have extraordinary skills? Why do we find that juxtaposition so puzzling?

The reason lies in our everyday assumptions about the nature of human abilities. Most people, including psychologists, assume that cognitive abilities are relatively cohesive and interdependent, and to some extent centrally controlled. Throughout this century there has been much debate about the roles of general and specific abilities in human intelligence, but it is still widely accepted that there exists some unitary global entity of general intellectual ability, or intelligence, and that this places limits on the degree of expertise that can be achieved at different intellectual skills. But within this conceptual framework, idiots savants are puzzling misfits: in appearing to contradict it, they are seen as a strange anomaly.

But there is another possibility. It is possible that the apparent unitariness and cohesiveness of human intelligence is, in fact, largely a figment of our imaginations. Perhaps each person's different intellectual skills are actually separate and autonomous to a considerably greater degree than has been realized. Conceivably, a person's different skills are neither closely dependent on one another nor governed by any limiting quality of general intelligence or mental capacity. If this alternative view of the structure of cognitive abilities is even partly correct, it can be seen that the contrasts observed in idiots savants between levels of ability at different skills are simply manifestations of something that is true of all people, namely that their different skills are to a large degree autonomous. The contrasts are certainly more striking in idiots savants that in other people, but that may be largely because savants' exceptional accomplishments are thrown into especially sharp relief against a backdrop of unimpressive levels of performance in other areas.

I am not suggesting that different abilities are totally independent; rather, that the degree of their interdependence may have been exaggerated. Even so, such a claim requires the backing of empirical evidence. Does such evidence exist?

Many accounts mirror the descriptions of idiots savants by recounting surprising limitations that have been encountered in people of genius, but the anecdotal nature of these stories restricts their scientific value. Investigations of the effects of brain damage provide one source of data that is more reliable. In hundreds of studies, it has been observed that the effects of such damage on skills can be remarkably specific (Ellis and Young, 1988). For example, damage that causes deficits in speech production may leave comprehension undamaged, and lesions at different locations may differentially affect retrieval of particular words, ability to utter grammatical sentences, and the capacity to speak in sentences that have a clear meaning. Brain damage may disrupt language but leave calculating skills intact, or vice versa. Sufferers from one kind of damage may be able to understand symbols and read numbers, but only if these are encountered in an arithmetical or numerical context. Other lesions may selectively impair the ability to transfer an activity from one hand to another, or the capacity to put one's clothes on, or the ability to carry out actions as requested even when the person can understand the request and is physically capable of undertaking the actions.

The fact that abilities may selectively be impaired or remain intact after brain damage does not necessarily justify the inference that they function in isolation in the intact brain (Mehler, Morton and Juscyk, 1984). Yet the neuropsychological evidence does establish that there exists a considerable degree of specificity in the mechanisms underlying different intellectual functions, even ones that have similar outputs. Further evidence consistent with the view that intellectual skills function separately, rather than being centrally controlled by broader or more general abilities, has been provided by studies in which people's performance at certain tasks is correlated with the same individuals' performance at other tasks. It is found, for instance, that when people are assessed on a number of different and unrelated learning tasks, performance correlations are close to zero

(Estes, 1971, 1982; Howe, 1976, 1988b) and that within-individual correlations in performance at different memory tasks are also very small (Martin, 1978; Wilding and Valentine, 1988). Moreover, when people are given tasks involving forms of learning that do not depend on knowledge or experience, young children and mentally handicapped individuals tend to do just as well as intelligent adults (Estes, 1971). Additional evidence that individuals' different abilities are relatively independent of one another has been provided by studies that have examined the relationships between general measures of ability or intelligence and measures of effectiveness at skills required in daily living. Important indexes of success in the real world are found to be uncorrelated with measured intelligence, contrary to what would be expected if it were true that different mental abilities are either closely connected to each other or under some kind of central control (Klemp and McClelland, 1986; McClelland, 1973; Zigler and Seitz, 1982).

On the other hand, however, levels of performance at different tests of intellectual abilities often *are* positively correlated, and the existence of such correlations makes it possible to derive a substantial *g* factor. Also, correlations of up to 0.4 or so are observed between performance on intelligence tests and performance on tests assessing the speed at which certain very simple (and apparently 'basic') cognitive tasks are accomplished (Barrett and Eysenck, 1988; Nettelbeck, 1987). This evidence is sometimes interpreted by psychologists as indicating that a common parameter, such as speed of cognitive processing (Eysenck, 1988), functions as the fundamental variable underlying differences in intellectual ability.

But the existence of correlations and general factors does not, in fact, provide firm ground for arguing that there exists any one intellectual process or variable that is common to all, or even most, of the tasks at which measures of performance are correlated (Horn, 1986; Howe, 1988b, 1988c; Rabbitt, 1988). There are many other possible reasons for correlations in a person's performance at different intellectual tasks, even when the cognitive mechanisms underlying such tasks are clearly distinct. Correlations are likely to occur whenever two or more tasks are similarly influenced by any of a variety of personal traits, states and attributes such as mood, temperament, competitiveness, attention, perseverance, self-confidence, desire to succeed, optimism, self-directedness, persistence in the face of failure, interest in the task, desire to impress, need to achieve, and so on. We ought perhaps to be more surprised by the finding that individuals' performances at certain tests of ability are *not* correlated than by the finding that many are.

So the strange feats of idiots savants are more than a puzzling anomaly. They draw our attention to the fact that it is quite possible for complex intellectual skills to exist in relative isolation. They also alert us to the possibility that different abilities in people of all ability levels are largely autonomous. When examined in conjunction with evidence from additional sources, idiots savants' achievements contradict the assumption (which the fact that the *g* factor can be extracted has been taken to indicate) that a person's intellectual abilities are limited by a cognitive process or quality that is common to all intellectual tasks.

It is beginning to seem more likely that each person possesses a conglomeration of cognitive skills (or 'intelligences', as Gardner (1984) would say) that operate as relatively autonomous modules (Fodor, 1983). Only to a limited extent do they function in coordination with each other. They may bear the imprint of having evolved from mental computing systems that were designed for specialized purposes. These can be inaccessible to other systems and not readily exploited for cognitive needs other than the ones for which they were originally intended (Rozin, 1976). So far as people's abilities are concerned, the operation of the human brain appears to be neither unitary nor centrally controlled. It is a 'loose federation' (Geschwind, 1983) of separate parts that work together but are not perfectly connected.

REFERENCES

Anastasia, A. and Levee, R.F. (1960) Intellectual defect and musical talent: A case report. *American Journal of Mental Deficiency, 64*, 695–703.

Baron-Cohen, S., Leslie, A.M. and Frith, U. (1985) Does the autistic child have a 'theory of mind'? *Cognition, 21*, 27–46.

Barrett, P.T. and Eysenck, H.J. (1988) Brain electrical potentials and intelligence. In A. Gale and M. Eysenck (eds) *Handbook of Psychophysiology, Volume 3*. Chichester: Wiley.

Boygo, L. and Ellis, R. (1988) Elly: A study in contrasts. In L.K. Obler and D. Fein (eds) *The Exceptional Brain: Neuropsychology of Talent and Special Abilities*. New York: Guilford Press.

Cain, A.C. (1969) Special 'isolated' abilities in severely psychotic young children. *Psychiatry, 32*, 137–147.

Carey, S. (1985) Are children fundamentally different kinds of thinkers and learners than adults? In S.F. Chipman, J.W. Segal and R. Glaser (eds) *Thinking and Learning Skills, Volume 2: Research and Open Questions.* Hillsdale, NJ: Erlbaum.

Charness, N., Clifton, J. and Macdonald, L. (1988) Case study of a musical 'mono-savant': A cognitive-psychological focus. In L.K. Obler and D. Fein (eds) *The Exceptional Brain: Neuropsychology of Talent and Special Abilities.* New York: Guilford Press.

Chi, M.T.H. and Ceci, S.J. (1987) Content knowledge: Its role, representation, and restructuring in memory development. *Advances in Child Development,* 20, 91–142.

Ellis, A.W. and Young, A.W. (1988) *Human Cognitive Neuropsychology.* Hove, Sussex: Erlbaum.

Estes, W.K. (1971) *Learning Theory and Mental Development.* New York: Academic Press.

Estes, W.K. (1982) Learning, memory, and intelligence. In R.J. Sternberg (ed.) *Handbook of Human Intelligence.* New York: Cambridge University Press.

Eysenck, H.J. (1988) The concept of 'intelligence': useful or useless? *Intelligence,* 12, 1–16.

Fodor, J.A. (1983) *The Modularity of Mind.* Cambridge, Ma: MIT Press.

Gardner, H. (1984) *Frames of Mind.* London: Heinemann.

Geschwind, N. (1983) The organization of the living brain. In J. Miller (ed.) *States of Mind: Conversations with Psychological Investigators.* London: BBC.

Glaser, R. (1984) Education and thinking: The role of knowledge. *American Psychologist,* 39, 93–104.

Goldsmith, L.T. and Feldman, D.H. (1988) Idiots savants – thinking about remembering: A response to White. *New Ideas in Psychology,* 6, 15–23.

Goodman, J. (1972) A case study of an 'autistic-savant': Mental function in the psychotic child with markedly discrepant abilities. *Journal of Child Psychology and Psychiatry,* 13, 267–278.

Hill, A.L. (1975) An investigation of calendar calculating in an idiot savant. *American Journal of Psychiatry,* 132, 557–560.

Hill, A.L. (1978) Savants: Mentally retarded individuals with special skills. In N.R. Ellis (ed.) *International Review of Research in Mental Retardation, Volume 9.* New York: Academic Press.

Horn, J. (1986) Intellectual ability concepts. In R.J. Sternberg (ed.) *Advances in the Psychology of Human Intelligence, Volume 3.* Hillsdale, NJ: Erlbaum.

Horwitz, W.A., Deming, W.E. and Winter, R.F. (1969) A further account of the idiots savants, experts with the calendar. *American Journal of Psychiatry,* 126, 160–163.

Horwitz, W.A., Kestenbaum, C., Person, E. and Jarvik, L. (1965) Identical twin – 'idiot savants' – calendar calculators. *American Journal of Psychiatry,* 121, 1075–1079.

Howe, M.J.A. (1976) Good learners and poor learners. *Bulletin of the British Psychological Society,* 29, 16–19.

Howe, M.J.A. (1988a) Context, memory and education. In G.M. Davies and D.M. Thomson (eds) *Memory in Context: Context in Memory.* Chichester: Wiley.

Howe, M.J.A. (1988b) Intelligence as an explanation. *British Journal of Psychology,* 79, 349–360.

Howe, M.J.A. (1988c) The hazards of using correlational evidence as a means of identifying the causes of individual ability differences: A rejoinder to Sternberg and a reply to Miles. *British Journal of Psychology, 79,* 539–546.

Howe, M.J.A. (1988d) Memory in mentally retarded 'idiots savants'. In M.M. Gruneberg, P.E. Morris and R.N. Sykes (eds) *Practical Aspects of Memory, Volume 2.* Chichester: Wiley.

Howe, M.J.A. (in press) *Fragments of Genius: Investigations of the Strange Feats of Mentally Retarded Idiots Savants.* London: Routledge.

Howe, M.J.A. and Smith, J. (1988) Calendar calculating in 'idiots savants': How do they do it? *British Journal of Psychology, 79,* 371–386.

Kahr, B.E. and Neisser, U. (1982) The cognitive strategies of a calendar calculator. Unpublished manuscript, Cornell University.

Klemp, G.O. and McClelland, D.C. (1986) What characterizes intelligent functioning among senior managers? In R.J. Sternberg and R.K. Wagner (eds) *Practical Intelligence: Nature and Origins of Competence in the Everyday World.* Cambridge: Cambridge University Press.

Leslie, A.M. (1987) Pretense and representation: The origins of 'theory of mind'. *Psychological Review, 94,* 412–426.

Lucci, D., Fein, D., Holevas, A. and Kaplan, E. (1988) Paul: A musically gifted autistic boy. In L.K. Obler and D. Fein (eds) *The Exceptional Brain: Neuropsychology of Talent and Special Abilities.* New York: Guilford Press.

McClelland, D.C. (1973) Testing for competence rather than for 'intelligence'. *American Psychologist, 28,* 1–14.

Martin, M. (1978) Assessment of individual variation in memory ability. In M.M. Gruneberg, P.E. Morris and R.N. Skyes (eds) *Practical Aspects of Memory.* London: Academic Press.

Mehler, J., Morton, J. and Juscyk, P.W. (1984) On reducing language to biology. *Cognitive Neuropsychology, 1,* 83–116.

Miller, L.K. (1987) Determinants of melody span in a developmentally disabled musical savant. *Psychology of Music, 15,* 76–89.

Morris, P.E. (1988) Expertise and everyday memory. In M.M. Gruneberg, P.E. Morris and R.N. Sykes (eds) *Practical Aspects of Memory: Current Research and Issues, Volume 1: Memory in Everyday Life.* Chichester: Wiley.

Nettelbeck, T. (1987) Inspection time and intelligence. In P.A. Vernon (ed.) *Speed of Information Processing and Intelligence.* Norwood, NJ: Ablex.

O'Connor, N. and Hermelin, B. (1984) Idiot savant calendrical calculators: Maths or memory? *Psychological Medicine, 14,* 801-806.

Rabbitt, P.M.A. (1988) Critical notice of R.J. Sternberg (ed.) *Handbook of Human Intelligence: Advances in the Psychology of Human Intelligence,* vol. 1: *Human Abilities;* vol. 2: *Beyond IQ: A Triarchic Theory of Human Intelligence. Quarterly Journal of Experimental Psychology, 40A,* 167–185.

Roberts, A.D. (1945) Case history of a so-called idiot savant. *Journal of Genetic Psychology, 66,* 259–265.

Rozin, P. (1976) The evolution of intelligence and access to the cognitive unconscious. *Progress in Psychobiology, Physiology and Psychology, 6,* 245–280.

Rubin, E.J. and Monaghan, S. (1965) Calendar calculating in a multiple-handicapped blind person. *Journal of Mental Deficiency, 70,* 478–485.

Sacks, O. (1985) *The Man who Mistook his Wife for a Hat.* London: Duckworth.

Selfe, L. (1977) *Nadia: A Case of Extraordinary Drawing Ability in an Autistic Child.* London: Academic Press.

Selfe, L. (1983) *Normal and Anomalous Representational Drawing Ability in Children*. London: Academic Press.

Sloboda, J.A., Hermelin, B. and O'Connor, N. (1985) An exceptional musical memory. *Music Perception, 3,* 155–170.

Smith, J. and Howe, M.J.A. (1985) An investigation of calendar-calculating skills in an 'idiot savant'. *International Journal of Rehabilitation Research, 8,* 77–79.

Viscott, D.S. (1970) A musical idiot savant. *Psychiatry, 33,* 494–515.

Waterhouse, L. (1988) Extraordinary visual memory and pattern perception in an autistic boy. In L.K. Obler and D. Fein (eds) *The Exceptional Brain: Neuropsychology of Talent and Special Abilities*. New York: Guilford Press.

White, P.A. (1988) The structured representation of information in long-term memory: A possible explanation for the accomplishments of 'idiots savants'. *New Ideas in Psychology, 6,* 3–14.

Wilding, J. and Valentine, E. (1988) Searching for superior memories. In M.M. Gruneberg, P.E. Morris and R.N. Sykes (eds) *Practical Aspects of Memory: Current Research and Issues, Volume 1: Memory in Everyday Life*. Chichester: Wiley.

Zigler, E. and Seitz, V. (1982) Social policy and intelligence. In R.J. Sternberg (ed.) *Handbook of Human Intelligence*. New York: Cambridge University Press.

SPORT PSYCHOLOGY
Lew Hardy

Not surprisingly, sport psychology is usually regarded as the application of psychology to sport. However, in reality, it is considerably broader than this and includes the application of psychology to many forms of physical activity that are not (strictly speaking) sports, as well as the use of physical activities as a medium to answer fundamental psychological questions. Examples of these extensions include the study of non-competitive activities such as solo long-distance running and rock-climbing, and the rapidly developing area of exercise psychology.

Sport psychology is generally deemed to have started in 1897, when Triplett studied the effects of audiences upon competitive cycling performance. However, sport psychology first became recognized as an academic discipline in Britain around the late 1960s. Indeed, although many Eastern European countries had been very active in applied sport psychology (working with élite performers) since the end of the Second World War, the first International Congress of Sport Psychology was not held until 1965 in Rome. During these early years, sport psychology was dominated first by the Eastern bloc countries, and then later by the North Americans. However, since the early 1980s sport psychology has gone from strength to strength in Britain, with the psychology content of undergraduate sports science degrees gradually increasing (and improving), and a steady stream of good-quality doctoral theses being produced. Consequently, Britain now has an international reputation for producing small quantities of good-quality research. (This is in marked contrast to some other countries which have a reputation for producing large quantities of poor-quality research.)

The growth and expansion of sport psychology was welcomed by sports coaches and performers, but led to inevitable territorial disputes over who was qualified to do what. As is often the case with academic disciplines which span two fields, specialists from each field claimed that specialists from the other field did not have sufficient knowledge of the area. This situation, together with the need to safeguard naive consumers, has recently led to the British Association of Sports Sciences setting up a Register of Sport Psychologists. To become registered, sport psychologists are normally expected to have a first degree in sports science and a higher degree in psychology, or vice versa.

Current issues in British sport psychology reflect world-wide trends, and include:

1 developing ecologically valid methodologies to answer applied questions in the field in a rigorous way;
2 identifying the factors which determine peak performance (including stress, motivation, and mental preparation);
3 the development of skill (including children in sport, and performers with special needs);
4 exercise and sport for health.

THE DEVELOPMENT OF SKILL

British psychology has a strong tradition in the area of motor skill development. It is therefore not surprising that early sport psychology courses (taught as a component of physical education degrees) included a fairly substantial quantity of motor control and learning in their syllabuses. Today, motor skill remains an important aspect of sport psychology, but its domination of the area has ceased. Nevertheless, from an historical point of view, it is a logical place for this review to start.

Interest in motor skill expanded when behavioural psychology 'went cognitive', and information-processing models of performance became fashionable (see, for example, Whiting, 1969). Much of this early work focused upon questions about the conditions of practice which were required to produce optimal learning. These included the distribution of practice, the role of feedback and augmented feedback in the learning process, and the use of mental rehearsal for the enhancement of learning (see Schmidt, 1982, for a review, and the chapter on *Skills* by John Annett in this volume).

At about this time, Henry and Rogers (1960) refined the notion of motor programmes as a natural extension of the analogy between human beings and computers as processors of information. Fleishman

(1964) took his analogy a stage further by making a distinction between what he called abilities and skill. According to this distinction, abilities were regarded as the fundamental subroutines from which a motor programme (or skill) could be constructed. Over the next 20 years, Fleishman derived a large number of these perceptual-motor abilities by factor analytic techniques. They included such abilities as manual dexterity, arm/hand steadiness, control precision, multi-limb coordination, movement prediction, perceptual speed and reaction time. More recently, it has been suggested that the identification of abilities which are not properly developed may be a key to solving the motor dysfunction problems of 'clumsy' children (Henderson and Hall, 1982).

Interest in motor programmes reached its zenith in the late 1970s, as researchers investigated Schmidt's (1975) 'schema theory'. In crude terms, schema theory proposed that simple movements are controlled by generalizable motor programmes which govern a small class of 'similar' movements. One of the basic predictions of schema theory was that practice which is variable in nature would develop stronger schema than practice which is very specific in nature (essentially, because varied practice should develop the whole schema class). Furthermore, most of the early experiments which tested this variability of practice hypothesis found support for it (Schmidt, 1982). Consequently, for several years, this theory was regarded by many as the answer to the question of how movements were recalled and executed. However, the discovery by Western psychologists of Bernstein's (1967) coordinative structures led to considerable controversy regarding the involvement of cognition in motor control.

This controversy has been inflamed by a small but influential group of (so-styled) ecological psychologists, who have argued that movement is controlled by direct links between the perceptual and action systems (Reed, 1982; Turvey and Kugler, 1984). Although there is considerable evidence to suggest that certain movements may be controlled in this way by skilled performers, it requires a substantial logical leap to deduce that cognition is unnecessary for any action! (See Harvey (in press), for an excellent review of this controversy.)

Recent research by Fazey (1985) is also interesting in the light of the direct perception controversy. This suggests that augmented feedback of a verbal nature – the type most typically used by coaches – might actually be detrimental to performance in skilled or semi-skilled performers. On the basis of these and other findings, Fazey argues that error corrections, which are made at a high level in the nervous system, are very crude and lack the precision of lower level (subconscious) corrections.

Another area which developed out of schema theory is contextual interference. This literature (Shea and Morgan, 1979) addresses the question of whether it is variability of practice *per se* which enhances schema development, or if any sort of interference will produce the same effect. Shea and Morgan argued that contextual interference effects occur because deeper levels of processing are necessary under interference conditions.

Finally, the use of imagery and mental rehearsal strategies in motor learning and performance continues to attract its share of research interest. It is now reasonably well established that mental rehearsal can enhance both motor learning (see Feltz and Landers, 1983, for a review) and motor performance (Ainscoe and Hardy, 1987). Consequently, current research is more concerned with *how*, rather than *whether*, mental rehearsal works. [Note that several of these issues are also addressed in the chapter on *Skills* by John Annett in this volume.]

PERSONALITY

In the late 1960s and early 1970s, personality research was quite popular amongst sport psychologists. Generally, this research focused upon the problems of identifying the personality profiles which were hypothesized to underlie élite performance and involvement in different sports. Although some weak trends were observed (see Morgan, 1980, for a review), this line of research was stunningly unsuccessful and heavily criticized from within the field. The rest of this section focuses upon these criticisms and the influence which they have had on subsequent research.

Early criticisms

Perhaps the most damning criticism of research in this area was its atheoretical nature, the most popular design being the shotgun approach. Researchers grabbed the nearest group of élite performers they could find, blasted them with a personality inventory, and then looked at what was left standing. In fact, in an early review of the sport personality literature, Martens (1975) reported that less than 10 per cent of the empirical studies reviewed involved any experimental manipulation. The rest were correlational in nature, with all the attendant problems regarding inferences of causality. What was needed were longitudinal studies in which samples were randomly selected and personality development monitored across time.

Another methodological criticism related to the use of only one assessment device (often by untrained personnel). In the clinical setting, personality is usually assessed by several different techniques, so that the clinician can cross-validate the results before arriving at a final decision. Furthermore, this criticism was compounded by the fact that the measurement devices which were employed were essentially designed to identify people with clinical disorders, rather than people with supranormal abilities.

Finally, most of this early research considered personality in terms of *traits*, which were presumed to be very stable across both time and situations. However, more recent formulations of personality have considered it to reflect a person-by-situation interaction, rather than a person main effect. Two consequences of this interactionist approach are that a distinction is usually made between 'state' and 'trait' measures (Spielberger, 1966; Bandura, 1977), and that personality is often evaluated in sports settings using situationally-specific measurement devices (Martens, 1977; Thill, 1983; MacAuley and Gill, 1983).

States versus traits. The state/trait distinction has been most strongly formulated in the study of anxiety and self-confidence. For example, trait anxiety is generally described in terms of a predisposition to regard relatively neutral stimuli as threatening, whilst state anxiety is regarded as a transitory emotional state in which the individual perceives him- or herself to be threatened (Spielberger, 1966). It should be clear from this relationship that individuals who have high trait anxiety are more likely to demonstrate symptoms of high state anxiety in any given situation than individuals who have low trait anxiety (Shedlestsky and Endler, 1974).

The importance of distinguishing between state and trait self-confidence has been most forcefully expounded by Bandura (1977) in his theory of 'self-efficacy'. This proposes that the most important determinants of self-confidence in a stressful situation are previous performance accomplishments in similar situations, vicarious experience (for example, seeing others succeed), verbal persuasion, and the individual's interpretation of his or her physiological state. This theory has now received considerable experimental support in sports settings (Feltz, 1984) although it has also had its critics (Borkovec, 1978). The influence of self-confidence and anxiety upon performance will be considered in more detail later.

Situational specificity. The desire to examine personality in different situations led in two directions. Early work by Ogilvie and Tutko (1966) and others attempted to develop trait-like sports personality measures which could then be used for selection and training purposes. This work was criticized on several grounds, not the least of which was the lack of empirical support. It was eventually laid to rest by Martens (1975) in a ferocious attack which concluded that:

> if [Ogilvie and Tutko's] unavailable research can substantiate their sale of personality assessment and diagnoses, their discovery will doubtless be considered the most remarkable advance in all of the social sciences in the twentieth century. (Martens, 1975, p. 125)

The second wave of research in this area was more successful. It led to the development of trait and state competitive sports anxiety inventories by Martens (1977), and a sports self-confidence inventory by MacAuley and Gill (1983), both of which have proved to be very useful.

Current situation

Personality research in sport got off to a bad start, and was subsequently rejected by many British sport psychologists. This is a shame, because several lines of research by sport psychologists from other countries, and British psychologists from different branches, appear to offer considerable promise for the development of interactionist personality theories. For example, Eysenck (1988) has used an interactionist approach to predict vulnerability to several stress-related diseases with considerable success. Whilst, at the Institut National du Sport et de l'Education Physique in France, Thill's (1983) *Questionnaire de Personalité pour Sportifs* is used, together with a Sports Thematic Apperception Test and a standardized clinical interview, to pair newly selected members of the Institut with appropriate coaches (Thill, 1983).

STRESS AND PERFORMANCE

The stress–performance literature grew out of an early interest in social facilitation. As mentioned at the beginning of this chapter, some of the earliest studies in sport psychology investigated the phenomenon of audience effects upon performance (for example, Triplett, 1897). By the 1970s, three different aspects of social facilitation had been identified and studied using different paradigms (see Landers and McCullagh, 1976, for a review). These were audience effects, coaction effects (performing with others), and competition effects (performing against others). Although the results of these studies were fairly mixed, interpretations were usually attempted in terms of increases in drive, or general arousal (Landers and McCullagh, 1976).

Eventually, social facilitation studies became unfashionable, probably because of the considerable difficulty experienced in trying to achieve experimental control. Quite apart from the methodological difficulties identified by Jones (1984), there were just too many variables – personality, perception of the threat or challenge of the situation, ability, the nature and difficulty of the task, and so on. In the face of these difficulties, researchers appeared to decide that a better strategy would be to examine some of the specific variables which were thought to underlie social facilitation.

Anxiety and performance

Many introductory (and advanced) texts try to explain the anxiety–performance relationship in terms of the inverted-U hypothesis (Yerkes and Dodson, 1908). The general line of reasoning goes like this: increases in anxiety lead to increases in arousal which cause performance to first of all increase and then later decrease when arousal becomes very high. Various reasons for this inverted-U shaped curve have been suggested, ranging from Easterbrook's (1959) theory of attentional narrowing to Revelle and Michaels' (1976) motivational theory which, put crudely, states that the 'tough get going when the going gets tough', but, 'wise men do not beat their heads against brick walls'!

Despite its intuitive appeal, the inverted-U hypothesis has been criticized at many levels. It makes little or no distinction between the basic concepts of stress, arousal, and anxiety; it assumes the existence of a unidimensional arousal construct which mediates performance; it ignores the role of higher level cognition; and it ignores the possibly multidimensional nature of performance and anxiety (see Jones and Hardy (in press) for a review). Rather than spend time discussing these various criticisms in detail, it seems more appropriate to discuss some of the alternative approaches which have been proposed for the study of the anxiety–performance relationship.

Recent conceptualizations of anxiety from North America view it as a multidimensional phenomenon having at least two components:

cognitive and somatic anxiety (Davidson and Schwartz, 1976; Martens *et al.*, 1984). These two components are characterized by negative expectations about performance or coping, and awareness of the current physiological state (butterflies, racing pulse, sweaty hands, etc.). Because expectations regarding performance can change at any time throughout the competition, it has been proposed that cognitive anxiety should be a more powerful predictor of performance than somatic anxiety which (it is argued) should disperse once the competition has started (Martens *et al.*, 1984). However, it has also been argued that somatic anxiety should be an important influence upon performance in motor settings (Parfitt and Hardy, 1987; Burton, 1988).

The European approach to anxiety research has been characterized by the examination of the influence of anxiety upon different aspects of performance (Idzikowski and Baddeley, 1983; Baddeley and Idzikowski, 1985). Despite early promise (Idzikowski and Baddeley, 1983), this approach has been generally disappointing, in that patterned effects for anxiety upon different aspects of performance (for example: perception, working memory, long-term recall) have not been found. However, recent studies examining the separate influences of cognitive and somatic anxiety upon different aspects of motor performance have been much more productive (Parfitt and Hardy, 1987; Parfitt, 1988).

The self-confidence–performance relationship

Self-confidence has been thought to be an important performance variable for some time (Bandura, 1977; Mahoney, 1979), and recent research by Burton (1988) has demonstrated a significant linear trend between self-confidence and performance. This relationship is thought to occur because confident performers choose harder goals (Locke *et al.*, 1984) and persist longer at those goals (see Feltz, 1984) than non-confident performers.

Despite substantial evidence supporting it, Bandura's theory has not been without its critics. For example, Borkovec (1978) has described self-confidence (or, more precisely, self-efficacy) as simply an epiphenomenon resulting from a lack of anxiety. Conversely, Bandura (1977) has implied that anxiety is simply an epiphenomenon resulting from a lack of self-efficacy. Which, if either, of these two positions is the more accurate remains unclear at the moment (Feltz, 1984), although there is an increasing quantity of evidence to suggest that cognitive anxiety and self-confidence should be regarded as independent factors, rather than opposite ends of the same continuum (Thayer, 1978; Martens *et al.*, 1984; Hardy and Whitehead, 1984).

Current situation. Current issues in the area include the identification of conditions which lead to stressful situations being perceived as challenging or threatening; investigation of the processes by which anxiety and self-confidence affect performance; and the role of self-control and other skills in these processes. Two recent developments which appear to offer some promise are the use of biochemical measures to assess effort expenditure and distress (Sothman *et al.*, 1988) and the use of catastrophe theory to model the stress–performance relationship (Hardy and Fazey, 1987).

MOTIVATION

Participation and attrition

Early work on reasons for participation in sport by Alderman and Wood (1976) proposed seven major incentive systems:

success (seeking prestige, status, etc.)

independence (doing things without help)

power (controlling others)

affiliation (making friends)

stress (seeking excitement)

aggression (intimidating others)

excellence (becoming skilful).

Subsequent research by Alderman and others indicated that the majority of young (North American) performers had multiple reasons for participating in sport (Carron, 1984, pp. 74–83). The most common reasons given were:

affiliation

skill development

excitement

success and status

fitness

energy release

whilst a need for independence, power and aggression were very rarely given. Social pressure (from parents, for example) was also very rarely given.

More recently, factor analytical studies have reduced the number of motives for participation to four: the need to

demonstrate competence

master the task

gain social approval

experience adventure and excitement.

Furthermore, Roberts (1986) proposes a developmental trend whereby young children are motivated more by task mastery and social approval than are older children, who are more motivated by the need to demonstrate competence. This research also suggests that children whose prime motive for participating in sport is to demonstrate their competence by beating others are more likely to drop out than children with other motives. The implications of these findings may be far-reaching, particularly in the areas of health promotion and mental training.

Rewards. Just as people's reasons for participating in sport may by instrinsic or extrinsic to the task in hand, so the rewards which they receive as a result of participating may also be instrinsic or extrinsic. For example, praise, prizes, and publicity are usually thought of as extrinsic rewards, whilst satisfaction, enjoyment, and a sense of achievement are usually thought of as intrinsic rewards (Carron, 1984, pp. 96–105). Recent research in this area has focused upon identifying those conditions under which extrinsic rewards enhance intrinsic motivation, and those conditions under which extrinsic rewards reduce intrinsic motivation. This paradox has been superbly illustrated by Casady (1974).

> [An] old man lived alone on a street where boys played noisily every afternoon. One day the din became too much, and he called the boys into his house. He told them he liked to listen to them play, but his hearing was failing and he could no longer hear their games. He asked them to come around each day and play noisily in front of his house. If they did he would give them each a quarter. The youngsters raced back the next day and made a tremendous racket in front of the house. The old man paid them,

and asked them to return the next day. Again they made noise, and again the old man paid them for it. But this time he gave each boy only 20 cents, explaining that he was running out of money. On the following day, they got only 15 cents each. Furthermore, the old man told them, he would reduce the fee to five cents on the 4th day. The boys became angry, and told the old man they would not be back. It was not worth the effort, they said, to make noise for only five cents a day. (Casady, 1974, p. 52)

Deci's (1975) theory of 'self-determination' attempted to explain this phenomenon by arguing that extrinsic rewards will enhance intrinsic motivation whenever the information which they convey infers an increase in competence. Conversely, extrinsic rewards which convey information inferring a decrease in competence, or a reduction in the degree of control which the performer has over the situation, lead to a reduction in intrinsic motivation. These predictions have been confirmed in several empirical studies (for a review, see Deci and Ryan, 1985).

In many ways, self-determination can be thought of as a model of mental health which is complementary to Abramson *et al.*'s (1978) reformulated 'learned helplessness' model of ill-health. Furthermore, like the learned helplessness model, Deci's theory relates motivation to both rewards and attributions. Attributions are also thought to be an important motivational variable for emotional reactions, the acceptance of unsuccessful outcomes, and the study of coach–performer conflict (see Carron, 1984, pp. 84–96).

Group dynamics

Developing team cohesion and synergies are clearly important considerations for sport psychologists. One line of research has been to try and identify the components of cohesion; for example, Carron (1980) suggested that communication, 'fairness', active involvement in team planning, and homogeneity of skill level were all important factors. Other variables which are thought to influence team cohesion include the team's success, external threats, interpersonal tension, and the coach's leadership style (Browne and Mahoney, 1984).

Current situation. Current interests in exercise and health have provided a new impetus for motivation research, particularly in terms of participation and adherence. Furthermore, the social psychology of teams is still very poorly understood, so that these areas of research are ready for much-needed development (Browne and Mahoney, 1984).

SPORT AND HEALTH

Psychological effects of participation

Active involvement in sport at any level provides several opportunities to enhance mental, as well as physical, health. These opportunities include the enhancement of: self-concept *via* body image (Sonstroem, 1978); locus of control and self-confidence *via* goal planning and achievement (Bandura, 1977; Biddle, 1987); social integration (Mehrabian and Bekken, 1986); relaxation *via* regular exercise or 'time outs' (Morgan, 1980); and self-regulation skills, as a result of learning to cope with stressful environments (Mahoney and Avener, 1977; Mahoney *et al.*, 1987).

Although the experimental literature which has examined the efficacy of exercise in terms of the above variables is fraught with methodological problems, it does seem fairly consistently to find positive effects in favour of sport and exercise. More (rigorous) studies are clearly needed to confirm these tentative findings.

Health promotion

The recent upsurge of interest in exercise as a means of promoting health and, in particular, reducing the incidence of coronary heart disease (CHD) has focused largely upon aerobic activities. This is understandable because these activities have the potential to produce both physiological training effects and post-exercise relaxation. Whether or not these therapeutic effects are psychologically or biochemically mediated is not yet clear (Dishman, 1985).

Current research by Eysenck and associates (Eysenck, 1988) offers several other exciting opportunities for sport and exercise psychologists. In a series of ten-year longitudinal studies, Eysenck *et al.* found that personality variables predicted death by both cancer and coronary heart disease much better than did smoking. In these studies, personality type was defined in terms of different coping strategies for dealing with interpersonal stress; it was also found that stress was a potent cause of death. However, a close examination of Eysenck's typologies suggests the distinct possibility that they might be modifiable by the use of interventions which alter self-esteem, locus of control, and self-confidence. These are, of course, the very variables which, it is hypothesized, participation in sport and exercise enhances.

Exercise as therapy

Despite serious research design problems (Browne and Mahoney, 1984), the available literature suggests that exercise may be at least as effective in the treatment of depression as more conventional drug treatment or cognitive therapies (Dishman, 1985). Furthermore, it may be longer lasting in its effect, has positive rather than negative side effects, and may also prove useful in the treatment of other psychological disorders (Biddle, 1987).

Exercise adherence. Adherence to exercise programmes is a major problem for exercise and sport psychologists. Despite the considerable volume of literature which now exists on exercise adherence, the drop-out rate for supervised exercise programmes remains at about 50 per cent after 6–9 months (Biddle, 1987). Dishman (1985) and others have reported that exercise adoption is relatively easily influenced by perceptions of health benefits. However, exercise adherence appears to be more affected by instrinsic motivation as a result of enjoyment and well-being (Biddle, 1987). Consequently, those who might benefit most from an exercise programme, such as the obese or very unfit, tend to be the very people who drop out.

Current situation. This is an area of massive growth in sport and exercise psychology, with many important questions as yet unanswered. For example, (how) can sport be used to aid psychological development and social integration? What can be done to help participants adhere to health exercise programmes? What are the psychological or biochemical mechanisms by which sport and exercise exert their influence? Do long-term exercise programmes reduce vulnerability to stress-related disorders?

PEAK PERFORMANCE

Some of the characteristics which have been found to contribute to ideal performance states and peak performance include: intentionality, clear focus, total absorption in the task, effortless concentration, feelings of the body performing on its own without fatigue, loss of fear, and certainty of success (Ravizza, 1977; Unestahl, 1983, pp. 15–18). Similarly, researchers investigating the characteristics of élite performance have identified that élite performers have greater motivation for their sport, better attention control strategies, more

224 / *Lew Hardy*

confidence and less anxiety than their non-élite counterparts (Mahoney and Avener, 1977; Mahoney *et al.*, 1987).

There is also a growing body of evidence which indicates that the meta-cognitive skills underlying such self-regulation can be taught using mental training programmes (MTPs), rather than just one-to-one clinical tuition (see Hardy and Nelson, 1989). This development is important, because the clinical approach is usually reserved for élite or professional performers. The MTP approach represents an opportunity for ordinary performers to develop self-regulation skills which may enhance both their sports performance and the quality of their everday lives.

At least four meta-cognitive skills can be identified which the experimental literature suggests are important determinants of peak performance. These are: goal-setting, imagery, anxiety and activation control, and attention control skills.

Goal-setting

Goal-setting is thought to exert its influence upon performance by enhancing motivation and the allocation of attention to priority sources (Locke and Latham, 1985). However, it is clear from Bandura's (1977) work that goal-setting should also enhance self-confidence, particularly if long-term goals are broken down into short-term goals which can be readily achieved. Furthermore, Locke *et al.* (1984) have shown that this process is cyclical. Greater self-confidence leads to harder goals being set, the achievement of which leads to even greater self-confidence. Conversely, it should be noted that this effect is mediated by goal acceptance and commitment, which may change under conditions of high anxiety (Hardy *et al.*, 1986).

Imagery

Imagery is well established as an important skill for the enhancement of both learning (Feltz and Landers, 1983) and performance (Ainscoe and Hardy, 1987). However, it is an enormously powerful skill, which can also be used in a number of other ways. For example, it can be used to increase self-confidence (Bandura, 1977), to reduce anxiety (Davidson and Schwartz, 1976) and restructure negative experiences (Meichenbaum, 1977).

Imagery may be defined as symbolic sensory experience which can occur in any sensory mode, although the most important are generally considered to be visual, kinaesthetic, and auditory. Furthermore, visual imagery may be used from either a first-person or a third-person perspective. It has been suggested (Feltz and Landers, 1983; Mahoney *et al.*, 1987) that internal visual imagery is more powerful than external visual imagery. However, this conclusion seems to have been drawn from data which confounds internal visual images with kinaesthetic images (Mahoney and Avener, 1977), and seems unlikely to be true in all situations. One of the major problems here is that although there is a considerable body of evidence showing that imagery does work, there is still considerable disagreement on exactly how it works.

Activation and anxiety control

The ability to control anxiety is clearly a fundamental one for sports performers to possess (Mahoney and Avener, 1977). Research from both clinical and sport psychology has identified that it is important to distinguish between cognitive and somatic relaxation strategies (Davidson and Schwartz, 1976; Jones and Hardy (in press); Burton, 1988). Furthermore, recent research (Parfitt, 1988; Burton, 1988) confirms the potential benefits which might be had from employing appropriate activation, or 'psyching up', strategies in tasks which have a low cognitive, but a high effort, demand. The ideal content of such activation strategies is not yet well understood.

Attention control skills

Given that information-processing capacity is generally regarded as limited, and that effective processing capacity may also be reduced under conditions of high stress (Eysenck, 1982; Parfitt, 1988), the need for attention control skills in sports performance is clear. Unfortunately, the number of controlled experimental studies which have directly measured attention control in a sports setting is very small.

Early work by Wachtel (1967), identified two dimensions to perceptual attention: focus and scanning. Wachtel explained these dimensions by means of an analogy. He linked focus to the breadth of a beam of light, and scanning to the movement of the beam about the field of vision. Thus, perceptual attention can be broad and slow-moving, or narrow and quick-moving, for example. Wachtel also proposed a dimension called selectivity, which represented the notion of attending to a particular class (or classes) of information, for example, only that information relevant to performance.

An alternative typology was proposed by Nideffer (1976). He classified attentional focus into four types: broad external, broad internal, narrow external, and narrow internal. Despite its popularity, the experimental evidence has not always supported Nideffer's typology (Van Schoyck and Grasha, 1981). Indeed, in view of the fact that Nideffer's typology makes no distinction between relevant and irrelevant sources of information, this is perhaps not surprising.

Another interesting approach has been to try and identify where attention should lie in different activities, with a view to then teaching performers appropriate strategies to control their attention (Morgan *et al.*, 1983; Schomer, 1987). A variation on this approach has been to identify those aspects of performance which are most likely to suffer under stress, so that performers can be taught strategies to reduce these negative effects (Baddeley and Idzikowski, 1985; Parfitt and Hardy, 1987). Finally, Klinger *et al.* (1981) examined the thought content of basketball players during effective and poor play. They found that process-oriented thoughts were typically associated with periods of effective play, whilst evaluative thoughts were typically associated with periods of poor play.

Attentional research in sport is still at a very early stage of development. Interesting questions include: the identification of attentional processes required for different sports (for example, perceptual attention, working memory, long-term recall); the identification of process availability and disruption under high performance anxiety (see, for example, Baddeley and Idzikowski, 1985; Parfitt and Hardy, 1987); the development of pedagogical techniques to enhance attention control (Parfitt, 1988); and the measurement of 'on the job' attention control.

Current situation in peak performance. It has been suggested that one of the principal functions of sport psychology is to develop mental training programmes for the enhancement of sports performance. However, more recently, sport psychologists have recognized that the self-regulation skills which can be acquired through mental training are important skills in their own right that can enhance the lifelong development of the individual (Unestahl, 1983; Hardy and Nelson, 1989). It is perhaps ironic that most 'normal' people would not attempt to acquire these skills were it not for their involvement in sport.

Although there are clearly limitations to the mental training programme approach when it is compared to the specialist individual attention which a clinical psychologist can give in a one-to-one situation, it is thought that mental training programmes have much to offer when they are carefully constructed and properly supervised. A major issue in this area is the assessment of mental training programmes in terms of the skills which they purport to develop.

CONCLUDING REMARKS

Despite its poor start, these are exciting times for sport psychology. Much new and interesting ground remains to be explored, particularly in the areas of mental training and sport, health and exercise. Indeed, some areas have not yet been touched, for example the application of sport psychology to sport officials.

Perhaps inevitably, the areas of sport psychology which have been reviewed in this chapter reflect to some extent the author's own interests and knowledge, as much as the obvious space restriction. For example, the psychological development of children in sport could have been included as a separate section, as could lifelong development through sport, the female athlete, aggression and sport, and many other issues of considerable interest and importance.

There is now a steadily increasing number of British sport psychologists who also have fairly eclectic interests in general psychology. This has led to the establishment of links between sport psychology and various other branches of psychology, including health psychology, occupational psychology, industrial psychology, educational psychology and the psychology of people with special needs. These links will undoubtedly be strengthened as more psychologists from other fields recognize the potential which sport possesses as a medium for the study of theoretically significant, but ethically difficult, areas of psychology. At the risk of being contentious, it is therefore suggested that sport psychology is not some sort of fringe offshoot of 'mainstream' psychology. Rather, it is a microcosm of the whole of psychology. This point is perhaps best illustrated by two quotations which constitute a fitting end to this review. The first is from a psychologist whose contribution to cognitive behaviourism represents a milestone in the development of psychology.

Competitive athletics . . . may represent an invaluable microcosm within which we may test and refine our understanding of human adaptation. The athlete must learn to cope with a wide range of stressors – performance standards, the experience of failure, ageing, and so on. In evaluating our theories and developing new treatment techniques, the athlete may, therefore, be an able and willing ally. My own recent attempts to bridge the gap between clinical and sports psychology have convinced me that we can learn much about the former from the latter. It may be the case, then, that the athlete is not only a willing ally, but also a welcome one. (Mahoney, 1979, p. 441)

At the opposite end of the fame continuum, the second quotation is from a research student of mine:

Take virtually any disorder which is studied in mainstream psychology, and somebody in sport does it for enjoyment! (Nelson and Hardy, 1988)

REFERENCES

Abramson, L.Y., Seligman, M.E.P. and Teasdale, J.D. (1978) Learned helplessness in humans: Critique and reformulation. *Journal of Abnormal Psychology, 87,* 49–74.

Ainscoe, M. and Hardy, L. (1987) Cognitive warm up in a cyclical gymnastic skill. *International Journal of Sport Psychology, 18,* 269–275.

Alderman, R.B. and Wood, N.L. (1976) An analysis of incentive motivation in young Canadian athletes. *Canadian Journal of Applied Sport Sciences, 1,* 169–176.

Baddeley, A. and Idzikowski, C. (1985) Anxiety, manual dexterity and diver performance. *Ergonomics, 28,* 1475–1482.

Bandura, A. (1977) Self-efficacy theory: Towards a unifying theory of behavioural change. *Psychological Review, 84,* 191–215.

Bernstein, N. (1967) *The Coordination and Regulation of Movements.* Oxford: Pergamon Press.

Biddle, S. (1987) Exercise physiology: A new direction for British sports science. Unpublished paper presented to the Annual Conference of the British Association of Sports Sciences. West London Institute of Higher Education.

Borkovec, T.D. (1978) Self-efficacy: Cause or reflection of behavioural change. In S. Rachman (ed.) *Advances in Behaviour Research and Therapy (Vol. 1.).* Oxford: Pergamon.

Browne, M.A. and Mahoney, M.J. (1984) Sport psychology. *Annual Reviews in Psychology, 35,* 605–625.

Burton, D. (1988) Do anxious swimmers swim slower? Re-examining the elusive anxiety–performance relationship. *Journal of Sport Psychology, 10,* 45–61.

Carron, A.V. (1980) *Social Psychology of Sport.* Ontario: University of Ontario Press.

Carron, A.V. (1984) *Motivation: Implications for Coaching and Teaching.* London: Sports Dynamics.

Casady, M. (1974) The tricky business of giving rewards. *Psychology Today, 8,* 52.

Davidson, R.J. and Schwartz, G.E. (1976) The psychobiology of relaxation and related states: A multiprocess theory. In D.I. Mostofsky, *Behaviour Control and Modification of Physiological Activity*. Englewood Cliffs, NJ: Prentice-Hall.

Deci, E.L. (1975) *Intrinsic Motivation*. New York: Plenum Press.

Deci, E.L. and Ryan, R.M. (1985) *Intrinsic Motivation and Self-Determination in Human Behaviour*. New York: Plenum Press.

Dishman, R.K. (1985) *Exercise Adherence: Its Impact on Public Health*. Champaign, Illinois: Human Kinetics.

Easterbrook, J.A. (1959) The effect of emotion on cue utilization and the organization of behaviour. *Psychological Review*, 66, 183–201.

Eysenck, H.J. (1988) Personality, stress and cancer: Prediction and prophylaxis. *British Journal of Medical Psychology*, 61, 57–75.

Eysenck, M.W. (1982) *Attention and Arousal: Cognition and Performance*. Berlin: Springer-Verlag.

Fazey, J.A. (1985) Schema theory: The development of a model for the control and learning of motor skills. Unpublished doctoral thesis, University of Wales.

Feltz, D.L. (1984) Self-efficacy as a cognitive mediator of athletic performance. In W.F. Straub and J.M. Williams (eds) *Cognitive Sport Psychology*. Lansing, New York: Sport Science Associates.

Feltz, D.L. and Landers, D.M. (1983) The effects of mental practice on motor skill learning and performance. *Journal of Sport Psychology*, 5, 25–57.

Fleishman, E.A. (1964) *The Structure and Measurement of Physical Fitness*. Englewood Cliffs, NJ: Prentice-Hall.

Hardy, L. and Fazey, J.A. (1987) The inverted-U hypothesis: A catastrophe for sport psychology. *Technical Reports in Physical Education No. 1*. Bangor: University College of North Wales.

Hardy, L., Maiden, D.S. and Sherry, K. (1986) Goal-setting and performance: The effects of performance anxiety. *Journal of Sports Science*, 4, 233–234.

Hardy, L. and Nelson, D. (1989) Self-regulation training in sport and work. *Ergonomics*, 31, 1573–1585.

Hardy, L. and Whitehead, R. (1984) Specific modes of anxiety and arousal. *Current Psychological Research and Reviews*, 3, 14–24.

Harvey, N. (in press) The psychology of action: Current controversies. In G. Claxton (ed.) *New Horizons in Cognition*. London: Routledge & Kegan Paul.

Henderson, S.E. and Hall, D. (1982) Concomitants of clumsiness in young school children. *Developmental Medicine and Child Neurology*, 24, 448–460.

Henry, F.M. and Rogers, D.E. (1960) Increased response latency for complicated movements and a 'memory drum' theory of neuromotor reaction. *Research Quarterly*, 31, 448–458.

Idzikowski, C. and Baddeley, A. (1983) Waiting in the wings: Apprehension, public speaking and performance. *Ergonomics*, 26, 575–583.

Jones, J.G. (1984) Problems in social facilitation: An examination of post-1965 studies which have examined audience effects on performance. *Physical Education Review*, 7, 41–46.

Klinger, E., Barta, S.J. and Glas, R.A. (1981) Thought content and gap time in basketball. *Cognitive Therapy and Research*, 5, 109–114.

Landers, D.M. and McCullagh, P.D. (1976) Social facilitation and motor performance. *Exercise and Sport Science Reviews*, 4, 125–162.

Locke, E.A., Frederick, E., Lee, C. and Bobko, P. (1984) Effect of self-efficacy, goals and task strategies on task performance. *Journal of Applied Psychology, 69*, 241–251.

Locke, E.A. and Latham, G.P. (1985) The application of goal-setting to sports. *Journal of Sport Psychology, 7*, 205–222.

MacAuley, E. and Gill, D. (1983) Reliability and validity of the Physical Self-Efficacy Scale in a competitive sport setting. *Journal of Sport Psychology, 5*, 410–418.

Mahoney, M.J. (1979) Cognitive skills and cognitive performance. In P.C. Kendall and S.D. Hollon (eds) *Cognitive-Behavioural Intervention: Theory, Research and Practice.* New York: Academic Press.

Mahoney, M.J. and Avener, M. (1977) Psychology of the élite athlete: An exploratory study. *Cognitive Research and Therapy, 1*, 135–141.

Mahoney, M.J., Gabriel, T.J. and Perkins, T.S. (1987) Psychological skills and exceptional athletic performance. *The Sport Psychologist, 1*, 181–199.

Martens, R. (1975) *Social Psychology and Physical Activity.* New York: Harper and Row.

Martens, R. (1977) *Sport Competition Anxiety Test.* Champaign, Illinois: Human Kinetics.

Martens, R., Burton, D., Vealey, R.S., Bump, L.A. and Smith, D.E. (1984) Competitive state anxiety inventory-2. (Unpublished.)

Mehrabian, A. and Bekken, M.L. (1986) Temperament characteristics of individuals who participate in strenuous sports. *Research Quarterly for Exercise and Sport, 57*, 160–166.

Meichenbaum, D. (1977) *Cognitive Behaviour Modification.* New York: Plenum Press.

Morgan, W.P. (1980) The trait psychology controversy. *Research Quarterly for Exercise and Sport, 51*, 50–76.

Morgan, W.P., Horstman, D.H., Cymerman, A. and Stokes, J. (1983) Facilitation of physical performance by means of a cognitive strategy. *Cognitive Therapy and Research, 7*, 251–264.

Nelson, D. and Hardy, L. (1988) The behaviour approach in the context of sport and exercise. Unpublished paper presented to the Behavioural Therapy World Congress. Edinburgh, 1987.

Nideffer, R.M. (1976) The test of attentional and inter-personal style. *Journal of Personality and Social Psychology, 34*, 394–404.

Ogilvie, B.C. and Tutko, T.A. (1966) *Problem Athletes and How to Handle Them.* London: Pelham.

Parfitt, C.G. (1988) Interactions of models of stress and models of motor control. Unpublished doctoral thesis, University College of North Wales.

Parfitt, C.G. and Hardy, L. (1987) Further evidence for the differential effects of competitive anxiety upon a number of cognitive and motor sub-components. *Journal of Sports Science, 5*, 62–63.

Ravizza, K. (1977) Peak experience in sport. *Journal of Humanistic Psychology, 17*, 35–40.

Reed, E.S. (1982) An outline of a theory of action systems. *Journal of Motor Behaviour, 14*, 98–134.

Revelle, W. and Michaels, E.J. (1976) The theory of achievement motivation revisited: The implications of inertial tendencies. *Psychological Review, 83*, 394–404.

Roberts, G. (1986) The growing child and the perception of competitive stress in sport. In G. Gleeson (ed.) *The Growing Child in Competitive Sport*. London: Hodder and Stoughton.

Shea, J.B. and Morgan, R.L. (1979) Contextual interference effects on the acquisition, retention and transfer of a motor skill. *Journal of Experimental Psychology: Human Learning and Memory*, 5, 179–187.

Schmidt, R.A. (1975) A schema theory of discrete motor skill learning. *Psychological Review*, 82, 225–260.

Schmidt, R.A. (1982) *Motor Control and Learning: A Behavioural Emphasis*. Champaign, Illinois: Human Kinetics.

Schomer, H.H. (1987) Mental strategy training programme for marathon runners. *International Journal of Sport Psychology*, 18, 133–151.

Shedlestsky, R. and Endler, N.S. (1974) Anxiety: The state-trait model and the interaction model. *Journal of Personality*, 42, 511–527.

Sonstroem, R.J. (1978) Physical estimation and attraction scales: Rationale and Research. *Medicine and Science in Sports*, 10, 97–102.

Sothmann, M.S., Hart, B.A., Horn, T.S. and Gustafson, A.B. (1988) Plasma catecholamine and performance association during psychological stress: Evidence for peripheral noradrenergic involvement with an attention-demanding task. *Human Performance*, 1, 31–43.

Spielberger, C.D. (1966) Anxiety as an emotional state. In C.D. Spielberger (ed.) *Anxiety: Current Trends in Theory and Research*. New York: Academic Press.

Thayer, R.E. (1978) Toward a psychological theory of multidimensional activation (arousal). *Motivation and Emotion*, 2, 1–34.

Thill, E. (1983) *Questionnaire de Personalité pour Sportifs (Q.P.S.)*. Paris: Les Editions du Centre de Psychologie Appliquée.

Triplett, N. (1897) Dynamogenic factors in pacemaking and competition. *American Journal of Psychology*, 9, 507–533.

Turvey, M.T. and Kugler, P.N. (1984) An ecological approach to perception and action. In H.T.A. Whiting (ed.) *Human Motor Actions: Bernstein Reassessed*. Amsterdam: North-Holland.

Unestahl, L.E. (ed.) (1983) *The Mental Aspects of Gymnastics*. Orebro: Veje.

Van Schoyck, S.R. and Grasha, A.F. (1981) Attentional style variations and athletic ability: The advantages of a sports specific test. *Journal of Sports Psychology*, 3, 149–165.

Wachtel, P.L. (1967) Conceptions of broad and narrow attention. *Psychological Bulletin*, 68, 417–429.

Whiting, H.T.A. (1969) *Acquiring Ball Skill*. London: Bell & Sons.

Yerkes, R.M. and Dodson, J.D. (1908) The relation of strength of stimulus to rapidity of habit formation. *Journal of Comparative and Neurological Psychology*, 18, 459–482.

PARAPSYCHOLOGY
Robert L. Morris

Parapsychology can be defined as 'the study of apparent new means of communication between organism and environment'. It thus falls within anomalistic psychology, the study of anomalous or unusual experiences and behaviour (see Zusne and Jones, 1982, for a fuller description of the domain of anomalistic psychology).

Traditionally, parapsychology has studied two classes of experience and behaviour: those suggesting extrasensory perception or ESP abilities, and those suggestive of psychokinesis or PK abilities. ESP refers to the apparent ability to acquire information about external events without access to presently understood means, such as the known senses or rational inference. Within ESP, three subcategories have come to be used in the literature. Telepathy refers to circumstances in which one individual appears to have knowledge of, or be influenced by, the thoughts and experiences of another. Clairvoyance refers to the apparent ability to gain knowledge about remote or concealed physical events, not necessarily known to anyone else at the time. Precognition is the apparent ability to access information about future events before they happen. In all cases, some individual appears to have knowledge about, or be influenced by, some aspect of the environment that is sufficiently physically removed that we cannot see how any presently understood mechanism could have been responsible. In PK, the direction of influence seems to be reversed, going from organism to environment. An individual appears to be able to influence physical events simply by a direct volitional act of some sort, by wanting the event to happen in a certain way. These hypothetical abilities are often lumped together and referred to as psychic ability, or psi. The individual is often referred to as a psychic, and the relevant aspect of the environment is called the target.

The range of experiences encompassed by the above definitions is considerable, and the boundaries between psychic and non-psychic experiences are very fuzzy. I have argued elsewhere (for example, Morris, 1980) that it is heuristically useful to regard psychic ability in simple communication terms. For ESP, it looks as though the organism is serving as a receiver in a communication system. Some aspect of the environment is acting as a source, or sender, so that a message (or influence) appears to be conveyed from source to receiver. The only difference is that, for psychic communication, we cannot yet specify a channel, or means of conducting the information from sender to receiver. For PK, the direction of transfer of information or influence is reversed. Now the organism appears to be the source, and some aspect of the environment appears to be receiving the influence. Once again, no channel or physical means of conveying the influence can yet be specified.

Such an approach is relatively free of assumptions about the nature of the channels involved. We are not committed, for instance, to an interpretation of psychic phenomena as evidence of a non-physical 'mind' which somehow interacts directly with the environment, bypassing the known biophysical mediators of exchange.

What evidence really exists to be evaluated? Some of it is anecdotal, represented in extensive compilations of case collections, ranging from early Society for Psychical Research surveys such as Gurney *et al.* (1886) and Sidgwick *et al.* (1894) to more recent collections such as those of Rhine (1951, 1969) and Sannwald (1963). Most of the evidence, however, comes from an experimental literature sum-marized effectively in the *Handbook of Parapsychology* (Wolman, 1977); *Advances in Parapsychological Research* (Krippner, 1977–1987, 5 vols); and *Foundations of Parapsychology* (Edge *et al.*, 1986). The findings of parapsychology have been challenged both conceptually and methodologically, especially in recent years (for example, Alcock, 1981; Hansel, 1966, 1980; Kurtz, 1985; Marks and Kammann, 1980; and Zusne and Jones, 1982).

A COMMUNICATION MODEL OF PSI

As defined above, the term psi has come to be used to describe apparent communication or transfer of influence between organism and environment through some additional, not presently understood means. Someone observes that there has been a coincidence between events in an organism and events in the environment, and attributes special meaning to that coincidence.

The observer is saying, 'I observed two events that resembled each other and I cannot understand why this should be, unless somebody involved was being psychic.' Expressed in more detail, the observer is saying the following:

1 I observed two sets of events and observed them well.
   a My direct observations were made accurately.
   b My indirect observations relied upon descriptions (measurements and recordings) produced by others with accuracy.
2 The two sets resembled each other quite a bit.
3 The resemblance was unlikely to be mere coincidence.
4 Neither set of events influenced the other through presently understood means.
5 The two sets of events did not share common antecedent influences.
6 I am aware of the concept of psi, and infer that it was responsible.

If we are to assess the evidence for psi, we must understand this six-step process, and what psychology can tell us about how things may go wrong at each stage. Bearing these problems in mind, we can then consider the logic behind the basic experimental strategies of parapsychology.

THE PSYCHOLOGY OF OBSERVATION

Observing external events

Psychology knows a great deal about how we go about observing the external world, and factors that can lead to errors in that process. There are several stages in the course of observation of complex systems where problems can arise, as I have described in detail elsewhere (Morris, 1986, 1987).

The observer may be denied access to important information. Observers may not fully understand what information is relevant, and may thus fail to look for it or ignore such information when it is available. The information may simply not be available at all, for physical reasons. Information may also have been withheld or concealed by a deliberate deceiver (a pseudopsychic). Pseudopsychics may present a 'cover story' to bias the observer's understanding of what is relevant and what is not. A confederate offers a broken watch to be fixed by a psychic. As observers we accept that the watch is ordinary and do not think to inspect it in advance. However, it could have been altered earlier so that sharp movement or heat from the psychic's hand might free the mechanism and start the watch.

The observer may be given inaccurate information. Sometimes information is available, but is inaccurate or misleading. We see an image in a mirror, unaware that it is a mirror. Sound travels along a wall, sounding louder and therefore closer in source. An effective pseudopsychic may arrange for deceptive physical signals to be sent to the observer, signals which will produce a false impression when processed. In a darkened seance room, a pinhole camera can be used to project a transparency onto a cloud of steam, thus making a shimmery image which will get brighter or dimmer as the steam density changes.

The observer may misperceive the information. Unfortunately, our mechanisms for processing information can deceive us. In camouflage, we are unable to separate an object or event (including a 'negative object' such as a hole or opening) from its background. There is too little information available to enable us to detect meaningful differences. Camouflage can also involve concealing any boundary where one object stops and another begins. Similarly, an important object or event, like a thin thread or rapid movement, may simply emit too little information, regardless of the background. Environmental factors can reduce perceptual aspects of observation if, for instance, there is too little light, or poor atmospheric conditions, or a partial barrier (a 'dirty window'), or some source of environmental noise.

As human beings develop, they build up an organized picture of the way the world works. This involves learning to make various assumptions about causal relationships, the laws of motion, what characteristics familiar objects will have, how our bodies work, and so on. This may lead to over-learned, quite unconscious strategies of perception which can mislead us. For a thorough description of various kinds of visual illusion, see Coren and Girgus (1978); for auditory illusions, Warren and Warren (1970) provide an effective summary. Many such illusions occur very naturally, for instance those that involve systematic patterns of eye movements, and may be difficult to overcome even when we are aware of them. Others may be more under our conscious control, driven by assumptions that can be more readily set aside once we are aware of them. Many of these involve principles articulated first by the Gestalt psychologists (for example, Koffka, 1935). We tend to group things perceptually according to similar characteristics; we assume that what happened before will happen again under similar circumstances, that things occur in organized wholes, and that objects with similar patterns of motion belong together. We tend to experience what we expect to experience, so that if portions of an organized whole are missing, we may fill them in without even being aware of having done so. Our reliance on such principles serves us well for the most part, but can mislead us innocently and is easily exploited by pseudopsychics. A sword is pushed into one side of a box and the blade appears to come out through the other side. But in fact the blade may have collapsed inside the sword handle and someone in the box, supposedly being skewered, is in fact pushing another blade out. If the two movements are coordinated, we assume they belong to the same object.

Fisher (1979) provides a good overview of techniques used to exploit our assumptions about how the body works in order to simulate special powers such as superstrength and the ability to change one's own body weight. Some of our assumptions may be based on information acquired about specific aspects of our own individual experiences, and are thus more idiosyncratic. Familiar objects such as top-hats, canes, silk scarves and so on are frequently used as props because we regard them as natural and readily accept that they are not special gimmicks. A performer introducing an unfamiliar item cannot rely on observer expectation because the observer does not know enough to have specific expectations. Most strategies for deceiving exploit the knowledge and sophistication as much as the ignorance of the observer.

The observer's attention may be diverted. Sometimes, important information is readily available to us and is not observed because we are attending elsewhere. Zusne and Jones (1982) summarize the extensive role that expectancies and beliefs can play in determining how we deploy our attention when observing anomalous phenomena, and explain how attention focused on one locus decreases attention given to others.

The extent of the problem may be made clearer by considering some of the writings of professional magicians on the manipulation of attention. A pseudopsychic or magician attempting to deceive an observer may need to shift the observer's attention away from certain important, accurate information, and towards other information, designed to mislead, to guarantee that the observer is building up the desired misunderstanding of what is going on. Nelms (1969) focuses on techniques for capturing and holding attention. He states that to keep an observer's attention fixed on something, one must make it interesting. This can be done by employing something that is inherently interesting, such as a sensuous assistant or a jewelled box. Alternatively, one can attract attention to something in various ways: (a) by pointing, with angular body parts such as hand, foot or bent elbow, direction of gaze, and so on; (b) by using objects containing sharp contrasts or which themselves contrast sharply with their backgrounds; (c) by the use of movement; (d) by producing frequent change of any sort, and keeping the background relatively constant; (e) by treating the object as though it were important, but without overdoing it; (f) by producing something of interest that is apparently outside the main routine and seems unexpected; and (g) by stating or implying verbally that the object or event deserves attention.

Fitzkee (1975) deals more with strategies for directing an observer's attention away from an undesired location. *Anticipation* involves leading the observer to anticipate that the crucial action will take place at a later time, then performing the action in advance, before the observer is paying attention properly. Pseudopsychics welcome being 'watched like a hawk' five minutes after the real action is over. *Monotony* concerns circumstances in which attention must be directed away from a particular event, such as an odd gesture, that would ordinarily stand out and attract attention. The problem is solved by presenting the novel event repeatedly in the earlier parts of the demonstration, under harmless circumstances, so that its presence no longer attracts attention later on, when it truly is important. *Confusion* is the strategy of having many things going on all at once while the crucial event is taking place, so that the observer has too much to monitor and nothing gets adequate attention. Famous performers travelling with retinues can often use this procedure, as such groups can be quite chaotic naturally. *Diversion* and *distraction* are very similar, and both involve dramatic, attention-grabbing external events. In diversion, the external event is natural, part of the ordinary flow of things, likely to go unrecalled later on. The pseudopsychic asks if there is any metal around, claiming that it can interfere. While everyone looks at the big metal filing cabinet, the spoon-bending takes place quickly by physical force. Later on, everyone claims they were watching the spoon all the time. Distraction is similar, but involves a more obvious event such as a sudden noise or the arrival of an assistant. *Premature consummation* is the reverse of anticipation.

The observer is persuaded that the important events have all taken place, and that vigilance can now be relaxed. Then the real trick takes place. Pseudopsychics can use this method when asked to perform while being too closely observed. They 'try' hard, announce that they have failed and that the test is over, and request a break before the next test. Once the observers relax sufficiently, the metal is bent surreptitiously and left to be discovered by someone, thereafter to be regarded as a 'delayed effort' effect.

The writings of Nelms and Fitzkee can be regarded as 'folk psychology', as descriptions of real-world practitioners of what they have learned, and of how they have come to structure knowledge about their craft. Their models are the products of observation rather than experimental research, but what they say can have important heuristic value.

Observers may misinterpret information perceived correctly. Sometimes what is perceived is not well understood. Observers interpret their perceptions most accurately when they have an appropriate understanding of the true context of those perceptions. Observers, according to Nelms (1969), are more likely to misinterpret their perceptions either when they have been given a false context or when they have been prevented from building up an adequate picture of the true context. False context may be the product of the observer's own misconstruction. Or it may be deliberately induced by a pseudopsychic, who is essentially an actor playing the part of a psychic and thus attempts to have the observer regard him as such. Nelms suggests that by providing erroneous explanations and motivations for the actions he is taking, he breaks up the observer's logic and leads him to misunderstand the sequence of events being observed. A muscle-reader may need to hold your arm in order to be guided by your muscular movements. If he persuades you that he needs to touch you in order to pick up 'psychic vibes', then you will perceive his hand on your arm but misinterpret its purpose.

The observer may misremember the information perceived. Distortions of memory are common, and pseudopsychics can enhance the process of distortion in a variety of ways. Some involve disruption of memory consolidation, such as the use of backward masking. A strong stimulus is inserted into a demonstration just after something has happened that the pseudopsychic does not want the observer to remember. This serves as a distraction and interferes with the process of consolidation. Another strategy is to provide later information which conflicts with the observer's earlier impressions. This may involve the subtle presentation of contrary physical evidence, or personal assertions about what in fact happened. A related strategy is to suggest a different context for the event after the fact, to lead the observer to reinterpret his memories. Social influences in the remembrance of past events can be very powerful.

Secondary observations can be distorted as well. All the factors considered so far relate to primary, direct observations. But many observations can be regarded as secondary, based on someone else's descriptions of primary observations. Any primary distortion is thus likely to be passed on and augmented in the course of preparing a description, and perhaps enhanced even further by the expectations and motivations of the secondary observers. Elsewhere (Morris, 1978a) I have described various stages in the organization of descriptive material in which the biases of primary observers, interviewers, investigators and journalists describing the research of others can all contribute to misinformation.

Biases in the description stage can be exploited by pseudopsychics. Measurement and recording of the ostensibly psychic individual's experience can be influenced by those with knowledge of the nature of the target, when such knowledge is available. The very act of recording an event can itself produce additional information (impressions left behind on the pad, characteristic movements of the visible tip of the pen, etc.). Once there is a record of a target event, that record itself, if not safeguarded, can serve as an additional source of information. The process of measuring and recording a target event can also be biased if someone involved is aware of the description of the experience with which it will be compared. Knowledge of either description can bias preparation of the other.

Autobiographical memory

Much of this reasoning applies also to the process of observing one's own experiences, especially when one is attempting to remember those experiences after the fact. In recalling dreams, for instance, factors such as vividness and cohesion may aid in recall. Time between awakening and recall attempt may be a factor as well. Once we start the recall process, we may further process the information as it comes to mind, filtering, selecting, paying attention to features more readily expressed and understood. In conveying the contents to others, and even in rehearsing them to oneself, further distortion and elaboration can take place. Rubin (1986) provides a good overview of the problems involved in autobiographical memory retrieval in general. Johnson (1988) notes that we may often have difficulty in discriminating between actions we have taken and actions we vividly imagined taking but never actually did. Her research also indicates that people can be trained to improve their ability to do so.

Assessing similarity of pattern

The second step generally taken in the overall process of inferring that something psychic has taken place involves deciding how much the two sets of events resemble each other. One of the long-standing problems in parapsychology is that observers attempting to assess the degree of similarity between two complex sets of events can be influenced heavily by their own expectations and biases. This is especially true if the two sets of descriptions are ambiguously or flexibly expressed, or where there are many potential descriptions to choose from and no fixed rules for determining what is to be compared with what. A pseudopsychic can easily guide the observer to focus only on favourable sets of comparisons, ignoring all others; or the observer can be encouraged to interpret ambiguous descriptions in a favourable light.

A major part of the problem lies in the ambiguous nature of the process of estimating similarity between two sets of somewhat complex patterns. We are good at noticing patterns and pattern similarities, but not always able to tell whether we have detected a real or an imposed similarity. Alcock (1981) and Zusne and Jones (1982) present good discussions of the effects of bias, expectation and need upon the ways we organize our perceptions of the world and notice similarities. Marks and Kammann (1980) note that one way we impose pattern is by selectively noticing similar pairs and ignoring dissimilar ones. They describe the 'clustering illusion', whereby objects and events which are similar seem to cluster together in space and time; and the 'gremlin illusion', whereby negative events seem to happen all at once ('when it rains, it pours'). Once we notice such an overall pattern developing, we then scan for further examples and ignore all exceptions.

THE PSYCHOLOGY OF EVALUATING EVIDENCE FOR PSI

Once we are impressed with the resemblance between two sets of events, we have the problem of assessing the likelihood that such a resemblance can be readily explained and does not in fact constitute support for some new means of influence transfer in operation.

Assessing the role of chance

Coincidences do arise by chance, without meaningful causal linkages of any sort. In a series of ingenious experiments, Tversky and Kahneman (1973, 1986) have shown that people in general have a very poor intuitive grasp of probability theory, of the likelihood of classes of similar events occurring 'just by chance'. In one of their studies, deficits in understanding were even shown by professional mathematical psychologists.

Kammann (in Marks and Kammann, 1980) offers five biases in human perception and judgement that contribute to our tendency to regard any given coincidence, noticed after the fact, as more unlikely than it really is. First, people do tend to notice coincidences when they occur. We have learned to be good at it, and it is a useful skill. Second, we do not notice failed opportunities for coincidences to occur. If we spent much time doing this, we would be quite overloaded with relatively useless information. Third, by not noticing failed opportunities, we fall prey to the 'short-run illusion'; that is, the coincidences we do observe in a short period of time stand out against the background of unrelated preceding or following events, which makes them look more impressive and rare. Fourth, we are poor at estimating the probabilities of combinations of events, because we tend to be biased by how easily we can recall simple events as opposed to complex combinations, which do not spring to mind so readily and thus are likely to be regarded as rarer. Fifth, we ignore the 'principle of equivalent oddmatches', the idea that one coincidence is as good as another. When we notice a particular coincidence, we single it out and regard it as especially meaningful, whereas in fact there are many other coincidences which did not happen, but which we would also regard as meaningful should they suddenly do so.

For additional general treatment of problems of human judgement and assessing the role of chance, see Nisbett and Ross (1980), Alcock (1981) and Arkes and Hammond (1986). Lopes (1986) treats the specific situation of judgements based on random orders of events. Dow (1988) describes how failure in human judgement can produce both false positive and false negative decisions about evidence for anomalous events.

Assessing the role of real-time influences

Sometimes when there appears to be an adequate barrier between organism and target, such as to preclude known means of communication, the barrier is actually ineffective or even non-existent. There are several principles involved, as I have detailed elsewhere (Morris, 1986).

Organisms can detect and process a wide variety of information. We have a wide variety of senses, including several in our skin, in our muscles and around our joints, and chemical sensors throughout our bodies, all providing us with a constant and diverse stream of information. We tend to be unaware of them until things go wrong or until our attention is called to them, as in exercises where we are directed to 'turn our attention inward, to feel our psychic energies building'. We may also be able to detect, or be influenced by, a variety of additional sources of information without needing specialized sensors. NcNulty et al. (1975), for example, found that when charged particles such as pions and muons pass through the retina, they produce visual sensations of the kind reported as mysterious flashes of light by astronauts beyond the Van Allen radiation belt, where such particles are common. Adey (1981) and Becker and Marino (1982) summarize evidence that we can respond behaviourally to changes in the strength of magnetic fields, electrostatic fields and electromagnetic radiation.

In each of our known sensory modalities, acuity can vary in accordance with a variety of factors including those that affect our distribution of attention. Dixon (1981) and others have described evidence that information presented to us below our threshold of awareness may nevertheless influence our mental processes and behaviour. Once information has been perceived, we may subsequently forget it, only to have it surface in our awareness later on as ostensibly fresh information. Examples of this phenomenon, known as cryptomnesia or buried memories, have been cited by Reed (1988) and Kline (1956), and can sometimes be mistaken as evidence for psi. Special skills in memory and mathematics can be learned and displayed as evidence for unusual mental powers (Higbee, 1977; Corinda, 1968). Some individuals do have exceptional information-processing abilities, and we are only slowly beginning to understand their neuropsychological bases (Obler and Fein, 1988).

Objects and events in the environment also emit considerable information, not always noticeable, and therefore potentially exploitable by a pseudopsychic. Some of this is information available naturally from the target. Many psychic claims involve being especially sensitive to other people and their problems, and people display a great deal of information about themselves through their behaviour and appearance, including clothing, mannerisms, gesture, speech patterns, and even body physiology (sweating, blushing and so on). Professional muscle-readers rely upon small muscle movements to reveal aspects of people's thoughts, such as the location of objects, whether something is liked or disliked, or whether a statement is correct or incorrect. Cumberland (1975, originally published 1888) gives a practitioner's description of muscle-reading (often called Cumberlandism or Hellstromism), and Christopher (1970) provides a good general survey. Some domestic animals seem able to use similar cues, and may perform as 'talking' animals, mental marvels or psychics (for example, Pfungst, 1965). Pseudopsychics may train themselves to have heightened sensory skills of various sorts in order to circumvent existing barriers. They may also arrange for the target or target environment to emit useful information, as with marked cards or the coding systems used by confederates in mind-reading acts. Sophisticated electronic systems can be used as well.

Sometimes there can be problems with the apparent barriers themselves. Often, a barrier to information transfer can be rendered ineffective for just a short time, thereby allowing a brief glimpse of the target. This can involve skilled manipulation of a device used to conceal a target (for example, the clasp on a folder or container) while the observer is distracted. Strategically placed small convex mirrors, including hand-held ones, can be manipulated to provide a brief but effective wide-angle view. In backlighting, a target concealed in something partly translucent like a manilla envelope is illuminated briefly from behind, so that the shadow of whatever is inside (such as a simple line drawing) is temporarily visible. Some volatile substances such as alcohol can render coverings of certain materials like paper temporarily transparent, until they evaporate. Glimpses can be obtained by applying analogous substances to devices such as blindfolds designed to conceal the pseudopsychic rather than the target.

Occasionally, an observer is persuaded that a barrier is present when in fact it is not. This can easily be the case where precognition is concerned. It looks as though time itself serves as a barrier. But precognition can be simulated in several ways. A prophecy once made may stimulate people in all innocence to take steps to ensure that it comes true (self-fulfilling prophecy). Or a pseudopsychic may deliberately influence events, clandestinely, to make a prediction come true. Some predictions may be made in such abundance that some of them are bound to come true, and the observer's attention will later be focused only on the good ones.

Assessing shared antecedent influences

If the two sets of events being compared share antecedent influences, then they are likely to resemble each other. There are three general ways this is likely to happen, either naturally or through the deliberate efforts of a pseudopsychic. First, factors affecting the nature of the target events may become known to the ostensible psychic. We all build up considerable lore, formal and informal, about the way the world works, such that we can generate inferences about what will probably happen next. Thus what appear to be psychic hunches may be the product of considerable conscious or unconscious synthesizing of past lore and present circumstances. Psychics who make public predictions about sociopolitical events or the private lives of famous people may maintain extensive information-gathering networks, including cultivated resources and expertise in many areas of specialization. Background information gathering on specific clients and on audience members is also common practice (for example, Keene, 1976; Wilson, 1987).

Second, factors determining the target may be influenced so as to conform to the psychic's likely response. This can be accomplished by a pseudopsychic or by those who know what the response of someone being tested is likely to be. If someone wishes to persuade us that we are psychic, they may make use of knowledge of response biases we all have, and select our target accordingly. If we are asked to think of a European city, Paris is a common response; Minsk is not. When asked to select 'randomly', most of us tend to choose alternatives that seem very random and ignore those that are not. From a line of five options, we choose the second or fourth, rather than the middle or either end. Asked to choose a number from one to a hundred, we will lean towards numbers that 'look random', like 19, 37 or 71, rather than 1, 25, 50, or 99. This tendency can be exploited in large audience demonstrations especially. Marks and Kammann

(1980) provide a good discussion of how such general behaviour patterns can be exploited (or merely misunderstood) so as to create the impression that we are psychic. Even idiosyncratic behaviour patterns can be exploited once someone learns them.

Finally, common factors may influence both sets of events, leading them to resemble each other. Similarities in the actions and experiences of acquaintances may reflect shared recent events such as the weather, media events, situations at work and so on. As I have said above, someone might persuade us we are psychic through knowing our naturally-occurring behavioural or choice biases; they might also decide to 'force' us to make a specific choice, then ensure that the target matches that choice. Some 'forces' rely on linguistic ambiguities, and not letting the observers know in advance just what the rules of the game are. Suppose I have two face-down cards side by side in front of me, and you are standing opposite. I can force you to choose the card on my left by asking you which card you pick, the one on the left or the one on the right. If you say 'left', I announce I am picking up the card on *my left,* and do so. If you say 'right', I state that I am taking the card on *your right,* and do so. Other forces may rely on what Triplett (1900) calls 'The Law of Economy of Effort', which states that in general we tend to do whatever is easiest for us. To force a particular action or decision, just make sure that the desired decision is the easiest one to make.

Assessing the likelihood that psychic functioning has occurred

In evaluating the likelihood of non-obvious but real alternatives to psi, one must be aware of the factors summarized above and use knowledge of them with considerable cleverness. My summaries have only skimmed the surface, and it is difficult to win a mental battle with a skilled pseudopsychic unless you really know what you are doing, can insist upon fixed experimental procedures designed to rule out the above strategies, and can also guarantee that those procedures have been adhered to faithfully.

Before moving on, we should note that sometimes evidence for psychic functioning may be claimed when there is a very powerful, anomalous set of events in either the psychic or the environment without there being a comparable validating set of events in the other. For ESP, this may take the form of vivid perception-like experiences, such as hallucinations and visions. In each case, the anomaly in and of itself suggests to some observers that there must have been an external source, to account for it. Our knowledge of the cognitive and physiological bases for the occurrence of hallucinations is growing (for example, Reed, 1988; Julien, 1981); our understanding of the bases of their content is still meagre (for example, Hufford, 1982). Maher (1988), in commenting on the aetiology of delusional beliefs, hypothesizes that, for apparently neurological reasons, we may very occasionally have the experience that whatever we are attending to at the time is extremely meaningful, and that such experiences can have a great impact upon how we interpret later experiences.

In PK, the anomalous set of events occurs in the environment, as in poltergeist cases or physical oddities taking place around a psychic claimant, and may include seemingly miraculous improvements in health as well. Our knowledge of how the physical world works is extensive but far from perfect. Fitzkee (1944) provides an excellent organization of the basic strategies conjurors can use to produce physical anomalies such as appearances, vanishes, transformations, destruction and restoration, or levitation and adhesion. Rothman (1988) provides a recent summary of physical principles and observed anomaly, although more oriented toward general theory than toward explaining specific kinds of observations. With regard to health, the growing discipline of psychoneuroimmunology (PNI) has given new impetus to psychosomatic medicine in general and is suggesting that some alternative healing practices may produce favourable results, but for physiologically-mediated reasons not necessarily calling for a psi component (see Locke et al., 1985; Braud, 1986).

THE METHODS OF PARAPSYCHOLOGY

Spontaneous cases and field investigations

Much of the evidence that has impressed people throughout the ages has come from isolated, unintended, but meaningful and often intense experiences validated by external events, at least in the eyes of an observer. Stevenson (1970) has argued that individual cases can be impressive enough and sufficiently documented to be considered a firm demonstration of psi in and of themselves. Others such as Rhine (1969) and Schouten (1982) have argued that, for reasons such as those developed above in detail, individual cases are inevitably imperfect and should be valued primarily as providing research hypotheses and complementing the findings of more controlled laboratory studies. Unfortunately, it is only in recent years that psychology has started to put together a sufficiently detailed view of human information processing to allow the development of models complete enough to guide the systematic collection of descriptive data from such cases. The early case studies vary considerably in quality, with respect to the effectiveness with which each of the important aspects presented earlier was assessed, either by the experiencer or by secondary observers acting as investigators after the fact. More recent efforts have tended to involve general surveys of the rates of incidence of various kinds of experience (for example, Palmer, 1979).

Similar problems exist with field investigations, which generally centre on the study of repeated anomalous events in a particular location or with a particular person. In the field, it is difficult to know the full range of factors contributing to the effect observed. Experimentation in the field is possible, assuming the full cooperation of parties concerned. Given the sophistication of the pseudopsychic, however, and the lack of it in most investigators, it is difficult for the reader of field reports to know how much confidence to put in their findings. True experiments have been done upon occasion, generally involving at least some studies under controlled conditions, both for poltergeist cases (for example, Roll and Pratt, 1971) and for psychic claimants (for example, Roll *et al.*, 1973; Schmeidler, 1973). Surveys of methodological issues in non-laboratory studies can be found in Rhine (1977), Morris (1982) and Rush (1986). Methodology in these areas leaves much to be desired, although we have now learned a considerable amount about how we can be misled in our interpretation of such evidence.

Experimental methodology

Experimental attempts to investigate psi under controlled conditions tend to follow the communication model outlined earlier.

For ESP tests, there are three rough groupings of procedures. All involve selecting and setting out a target in the environment that is construed as a potential source of information, such as a concealed card or picture. Once chosen, the subject serves as a hypothetical receiver of that information. Barriers such as shielding and distance are placed between the two. The characteristics of the source are varied in some way, so as to constitute a message. The message has a randomized component, to ensure that it has no pattern that may inadvertently match a bias in the pattern of the receiver's response. That randomized component ideally occurs shortly before the monitored communication attempt (except for precognition), so as to minimize the likelihood that the receiver could gain knowledge of it in advance or otherwise be influenced by knowledge of target determinants. During the experimental session itself, the receiver is monitored and asked to respond to the message being sent. Usually this is done in real time, unless precognition is under investigation, in which case the receiver is asked to respond to a message to be determined at a later time. For precognition, especially careful monitoring of the target determinants is necessary, to ensure that someone with knowledge of the receiver's responses cannot bias the selection of the target.

In restricted choice ESP tests, the target material is a series of finite and known options, such as the suits in a deck of cards, or the binary decisions of a random event generator. The receiver's task is thus analogous to a guessing game. The rate of hitting, of making a correct choice, comes to be the performance measure. In free response ESP tests, the target is more variable, such as an art print, a physical location, the characteristics of a person, and so on. The receiver may know the general target category but not the identity of any particular target, and thus is free to respond with whatever imagery or impressions come to mind. The target for a given trial is selected randomly from a small pool of possible targets. Later the receiver's response is compared with each of the possible targets, either by blind judges, or through use of a fixed coding system for responses and for target characteristics. The performance measure can vary, but in each case reflects the extent to which the receiver's responses resembled the actual target as opposed to the non-target controls. In somatic ESP tests, the source is a physiologically activating event occurring at random intervals to a sender. The receiver is physiologically monitored and may also be asked to indicate changes in arousal, by a simple action such as a button press. The performance measure is receiver arousal during the time of sender activation, as compared with arousal during control periods within the same session.

For PK tests, the direction of influence is reversed. Now the subject becomes the source, and the target in the environment is designated as receiver. The subject is asked to engage in volitional activity of some sort, to attempt to influence the behaviour of the receiver system in some specified way. Or, more rarely, the subject may be unaware of the existence of the target, but the target nevertheless can change in ways that are potentially salient for the subject. In each case, the subject is motivated to want the target to change, barriers are erected which should eliminate known means of influence, and the receiver/target system is monitored to see if it changes in accordance with the assigned wants of the subject.

There are three general strategies. In discrete outcome procedures, the target is a dynamic system which periodically comes to rest, producing a discrete outcome, such as the fall of dice or the binary output of a random number generator. The instructions to the subject generally incorporate random or counterbalanced instructions about which outcome to produce at what time. For example, each die face would be assigned as target an equal number of times, but in random or counterbalanced order. The target system is tested in advance for randomness, and is monitored during the experiment to see if it deviates in accordance with the intended influences. Controls may be run between sessions or within sessions, in the form of comparisons between effort and non-effort periods, or effort in direction *A* versus effort in direction *B*. Performance measure is either the rate of successful outcomes as opposed to that expected by chance, if the system has been shown to perform at chance consistently in the absence of influence; or, preferably, rate during effort versus rate during control periods within the session.

In stable system PK tests, the target is a measurable system having some degree of lability, but nevertheless relatively stable. Examples would be temperature recordings in a sealed container or monitored physiological activity. The subject is asked to alter the target system activity level in accordance with prior instructions, and the system is monitored to see if it changes in accordance with the instructions. Controls occur within the session, in terms of randomly selected periods of effort versus no effort, high versus low effort, or effort in direction *A* versus effort in direction *B*. Performance measures involve a comparison of system activity level and assigned instructions to the subject.

A third set of procedures involves attempts to influence the properties of a static object, either by inducing movement in it when it is at rest, or deforming it or altering it in some way as in metal bending. The procedures employed can vary considerably, depending on the nature of the claim being tested and the properties of the target system used. All involve efforts to seal off the target system from relevant sources of influence, plus monitoring both the target system and the intending subject. Performance measures involve prespecified effects on the target system, but may also include additional anomalous effects. Researchers must be careful of the tendency to include unspecified anomalies, bearing in mind the diversity of strategies to which a skilled pseudopsychic may have access.

For each of these sets of methods for evaluating psi, it should be borne in mind that the logic can be easier to describe than to apply, especially in making sure the target is determined in an unbiased way. Many of the studies found in the parapsychological literature appear upon closer examination to be flawed, some more seriously than others. In general, methodology has gradually improved, profiting from the often vigorous interaction between critic and researcher. Researchers are increasingly aware of the need to describe conditions much more fully than they might do when conducting research in less controversial areas. Any experiment evaluating psi is by its nature very complex, often quite hard to isolate from external influences. In most other areas, researchers have not needed to take seriously the issue of deliberate, organized fraud on the part of subjects. Unfortunately, fraud does occur in parapsychology (see Kurtz, 1985, for several examples). An outstanding example of productive interaction between critic and researcher over points of methodology is the debate between Hyman and Honorton over the Ganzfeld technique, a sensory deprivation procedure for stimulating imagery and thus, hypothetically, improving free response performance (Honorton, 1985; Hyman, 1985; Hyman and Honorton, 1986; Rosenthal, 1986). For overviews in more detail of ESP and PK experimental methods, see Morris (1978b), plus relevant chapters by Palmer, and Palmer and Rush, in Edge *et al.* (1986).

EXPERIMENTAL FINDINGS IN PARAPSYCHOLOGY

Several hundred research reports have been published, without producing either a strong confirmation or a refutation of the concept of psi. Some information does appear to be emerging, however.

Results bearing on the existence of psi

Results vary considerably, as do methods. Effect sizes can range widely, but are generally small. There have been a few recent attempts at meta-analysis of large groups of data. Rosenthal (1986) and others have argued that such analyses, based on effect size as well as significance level, may provide a truer assessment of replication rate in parapsychology than a simple tally of the proportion of significant studies. Honorton (1985) and Hyman (1985) both analysed studies employing the Ganzfeld technique to facilitate free response performance. Both agree (Hyman and Honorton, 1986) that there is a real effect that cannot be reasonably explained away, and that there is ample justification for further research, better conducted and more adequately described, to assess whether Ganzfeld procedures truly do facilitate a psi factor that has assessable properties. Hyman remains sceptical. Honorton found no significant correlation between indices of study quality and study outcome. Hyman, using a slightly larger data base, found no significant correlation between study outcome and procedural flaws involving multiple analysis, sensory leakage, statistics and security, but did find positive correlation with inadequate randomization, use of feedback, and inadequate documentation. Saunders (in Honorton, 1985), however, has challenged the applicability of Hyman's statistical procedure and also notes that he makes no attempt to correct for multiple analysis himself. Nelson and Radin (1988) assessed the outcomes of 597 random number generator PK experimental series and found that the mean effect size was over six standard deviations from that expected by chance, in the direction of participants' intentions, whereas the mean effect size in 235 control series was well within chance expectation. They, like Honorton, found no significant correlation between effect size and methodological quality of study. Honorton (1988), reviewing all restricted choice experiments using precognition procedures published in English (over 300 in all), found overall results more than twelve standard deviations from chance expectation. He also found no significant relationship between any of eight different indices of study quality and study outcome. Each of these surveys, although drawing from three separate data bases, concluded that the so-called file drawer problem, of unreported non-significant studies, would be quite unlikely to account for the results, in terms of the sheer volume of such studies needed.

These surveys need to be replicated, and more such meta-analyses done, to help us develop an effective overall picture of the degree of consistency in previous research. Taken as a whole, the results seem to suggest a weak and noisy but real effect; they deserve much closer collective scrutiny, and follow-up studies using the testing procedures that have appeared best to combine methodological safeguards and positive results. Certainly, the results indicate as well that if there are any new means of communication, they are not ones that are readily and naturally available to us with little special effort. If such were the case, they would have shown up more strongly in the studies done and would surely be more evident in our daily lives.

Results relating to psi-favourable conditions

There are clusters of thematically related findings, suggesting that, for ESP at least, we may have access to some means of communication that is ordinarily very weak and sporadic. It is unreliable, especially in controlled laboratory research where for ethical reasons we have been compelled to employ rather low-intensity messages. Irwin (1979) has attempted to develop a testable information-processing model of how such information may be received and distorted so as to fail ordinarily to have sufficient impact upon our experience and behaviour. Braud (1978, 1981) has developed a model of eight interfering noise sources capable of masking weak signals, and summarizes experimental evidence that techniques to reduce each source of noise appear to enhance overall results. Such models are vital in organizing existing findings and predicting research procedures which should improve results. Compatible with Braud's model is the general finding that people less likely to feel uncomfortable in a strange laboratory setting, such as those high on extraversion, low on neuroticism, and more open to the possibility of psi, tend to be the most successful in controlled laboratory ESP studies. For summaries of the state and trait variables most correlated with psi success, see Palmer (in Edge *et al.*, 1986); for a recent assessment of the internal state research and its interpretations, see Stanford (1987).

Although there are other clusters of findings, they have tended to involve fewer studies and their relevance awaits further research and conceptual integration.

SUMMARY

Parapsychology is a complex endeavour, but is amenable to systematic investigation. Much of what we have learned deals with how we may misinterpret evidence. A sizeable number of studies of varying quality have been done, and are starting to be analysed collectively in the search for overall trends in what are at best noisy data. The strongest evidence seems to come from studies showing functional relationships between state and trait variables and psi performance. Future research will be focusing on apparent psi optimization procedures, and more emotionally salient target conditions. Models are being developed, primarily to deal with the potential information-processing characteristics of ESP, with some apparent success, but are badly in need of further evaluation and systematic research. Theoretical systems are also being developed to grapple with the more challenging question of the actual means by which such information transfer could be achieved (see Stokes, 1987, for an overview) but they are still in the process of being refined so as to be testable. As can be seen from the meta-analyses cited earlier, there appears to be considerable empirical support both for precognition and for PK effects upon random processes, both of which seem especially counter-intuitive or characteristic of 'magical thinking'. Even within parapsychological theory, however, each can be interpreted in a variety of other ways, as described by Stokes. The evidence for at least some form of real-time ESP is regarded by this writer as strongly suggestive but not compelling, such that much further systematic research is needed if we are to understand fully the processes that go on in ostensibly psychic events.

REFERENCES

Adey, W.R. (1981) Tissue interactions with non-ionizing electromagnetic fields. *Physiological Review, 61*, 435–514.
Alcock, J.E. (1981) *Parapsychology: Science or Magic?* Oxford: Pergamon Press.
Arkes, H. and Hammond, K. (eds) (1986) *Judgment and Decision Making.* Cambridge: Cambridge University Press.
Becker, R.O. and Marino, A.A. (1982) *Electromagnetism and Life.* Albany, NY: SUNY Press.
Braud, W. (1978) Psi conducive conditions: Explorations and interpretations. In B. Shapin and L. Coly (eds) *Psi and States of Awareness.* New York: Parapsychology Foundation.
Braud, W. (1981) Lability and inertia in psychic functioning. In B. Shapin and L. Coly (eds) *Concepts and Theories of Parapsychology.* New York: Parapsychology Foundation.
Braud, W. (1986) Psi and PNI: Exploring the interface between parapsychology and psychoneurology. *Parapsychology Review, 17*, No. 4, 1–5.
Christopher, M. (1970) *ESP, Seers and Psychics.* New York: Crowell Press.
Coren, S. and Girgus, J.S. (1978) *Seeing is Deceiving: The Psychology of Visual Illusions.* Hillsdale, NJ: Lawrence Erlbaum.
Corinda, T. (1968) *Thirteen Steps to Mental Magic.* New York: Tannen Magic.
Cumberland, S. (1975) *A Thought-Reader's Thoughts.* New York: Arno Press (original work published in 1888).
Dixon, N. (1981) *Preconscious Processing.* Chichester: Wiley.
Dow, C. (1988) Factors affecting judgments about the occurrence of psi in spontaneous settings. *Research in Parapsychology 1987*, 105–109.
Edge, H., Morris, R.L., Palmer, J. and Rush, J. (1986) *Foundations of Parapsychology.* London: Routledge & Kegan Paul.

Fisher, J. (1979) *Body Magic*. London: Hodder & Stoughton.

Fitzkee, D. (1944) *The Trick Brain*, 2nd ed. Oakland, Ca: Magic Limited.

Fitzkee, D. (1975) *Misdirection*. Oakland, Ca: Magic Limited.

Gurney, E., Myers, F.W.H. and Podmore, F. (1886) *Phantasms of the Living*. London: Trubners.

Hansel, C.E.M. (1966) *ESP: A Scientific Evaluation*. New York: Scribners.

Hansel, C.E.M. (1980) *ESP and Parapsychology: A Critical Reevaluation*. Buffalo, NY: Prometheus.

Higbee, K.L. (1977) *Your Memory: How It Works and How To Improve It*. Englewood Cliffs, NJ: Prentice-Hall.

Honorton, C. (1985) Meta-analysis of psi Ganzfeld research: A response to Hyman. *Journal of Parapsychology, 49*, 51–91.

Honorton, C. (1988) Summarizing research findings: Meta-analytic methods and their use in parapsychology. Paper presented at *Psi Research Methodology: A Reexamination. Thirty-seventh Annual International Conference of the Parapsychology Foundation*. Held at Chapel Hill, NC.

Hufford, D. (1982) *The Terror That Comes in the Night*. Philadelphia: University of Pennsylvania Press.

Hyman, R. (1985) The Ganzfeld psi experiment: A critical appraisal. *Journal of Parapsychology, 49*, 3–49.

Hyman, R. and Honorton, C. (1986) A joint communique: The psi Ganzfeld controversy. *Journal of Parapsychology, 50*, 351–364.

Irwin, H. (1979) *Psi and the Mind: An Information Processing Approach*. London: Scarecrow Press.

Johnson, M. (1988) Discriminating the origin of information. In T. Oltmanns and B. Maher (eds) *Delusional Beliefs*. Chichester: Wiley.

Julien, R.M. (1981) *A Primer of Drug Action*, 3rd ed. San Francisco: W.H. Freeman.

Keene, M.L. (1976) *The Psychic Mafia*. New York: Dell.

Kline, M. (ed.) (1956) *A Scientific Report on 'The Search for Bridey Murphy'*. New York: Julien Press.

Koffka, K. (1935) *The Principles of Gestalt Psychology*. New York: Harcourt & Brace.

Krippner, S. (ed.) (1977) *Advances in Parapsychological Research, Vol. 1: Psychokinesis*. New York: Plenum Press.

Krippner, S. (ed.) (1978) *Advances in Parapsychological Research, Vol. 2: Extrasensory Perception*. New York: Plenum Press.

Krippner, S. (ed.) (1982) *Advances in Parapsychological Research, Vol. 3*. New York: Plenum Press.

Krippner, S. (ed.) (1984) *Advances in Parapsychological Research, Vol. 4*. London: McFarland.

Krippner, S. (ed.) (1987) *Advances in Parapsychological Research, Vol. 5*. London: McFarland.

Kurtz, P. (ed.) (1985) *A Skeptic's Handbook of Parapsychology*. Buffalo, NY: Prometheus.

Locke, S., Ader, R., Besedovsky, H., Hall, N., Solomon, G. and Strom, T. (eds) (1985) *Foundations of Psychoneuroimmunology*. New York: Aldine.

Lopes, L. (1986) Doing the impossible: A note on induction and the experience of randomness. In H. Arkes and K. Hammond (eds) *Judgment and Decision Making*. Cambridge: Cambridge University Press.

Maher, B. (1988) Anomalous experience and delusional thinking: The logic of explanations. In T. Oltmanns and B.A. Maher (eds) *Delusional Beliefs*. Chichester: Wiley.

Marks, D. and Kammann, R. (1980) *The Psychology of the Psychic*. Buffalo, NY: Prometheus.

McNulty, P.J., Pease, V.P. and Bond, V.P. (1975) Visual sensations induced by cerenkov radiation. *Science, 189*, 453–454.

Morris, R.L. (1978a) Review of Anson, J., *The Amityville Horror*. *Skeptical Inquirer, 2*, No. 2, 95–101.

Morris, R.L. (1978b) A survey of methods and issues in ESP research. In S. Krippner (ed.) *Advances in Parapsychological Research, Vol. 2: Extrasensory Perception*. New York: Plenum Press.

Morris, R.L. (1980) Psi within a simple communication model. In B. Shapin and L. Coly (eds) *Communication and Parapsychology*. New York: Parapsychology Foundation.

Morris, R.L. (1982) An updated survey of methods and issues in ESP research. In S. Krippner (ed.) *Advances in Parapsychology, Vol. 3*. New York: Plenum Press.

Morris, R.L. (1986) What psi is not: The necessity for experiments. In H. Edge, R.L. Morris, J. Palmer and J. Rush, *Foundations of Parapsychology*. London: Routledge & Kegan Paul.

Morris, R.L. (1987) Parapsychology, paradox and exploration of the impossible. *Speculations in Science and Technology, 10*, 303–309.

Nelms, H. (1969) *Magic and Showmanship*. New York: Dover.

Nelson, R. and Radin, D. (1988) Statistically robust anomalous effects: Replication in random event generator experiments. *Parapsychological Association 31st Annual Convention: Proceedings of Presented Papers*, 74–86.

Nisbett, R. and Ross, L. (1980) *Human Inference: Strategies and Shortcomings of Social Judgment*. Englewood Cliffs, NJ: Prentice-Hall.

Obler, L. and Fein, D. (1988) *The Exceptional Brain: Neuropsychology of Talent and Special Abilities*. London: Guilford Press.

Palmer, J. (1979) A community mail survey of psychic experiences. *Journal of the American Society for Psychical Research, 73*, 221–251.

Pfungst, O. (1965) *Clever Hans* (ed. R. Rosenthal). New York: Holt, Rinehart & Winston.

Reed, G. (1988) *The Psychology of Anomalous Experience* (revised edition). Buffalo, NY: Prometheus.

Rhine, L.E. (1951) Conviction and associated conditions in spontaneous cases. *Journal of Parapsychology, 15*, 164–191.

Rhine, L.E. (1969) Case study review. *Journal of Parapsychology, 33*, 228–266.

Rhine, L.E. (1977) Research methods with spontaneous cases. In B. Wolman (ed.) *Handbook of Parapsychology*. London: Van Nostrand Reinhold.

Roll, W. and Pratt, J. (1971) The Miami disturbances. *Journal of the American Society for Psychical Research, 65*, 409–454.

Roll, W., Morris, R., Damgaard, J., Klein, J. and Roll, M.R. (1973) Free verbal response experiments with Lalsingh Harribance. *Journal of the American Society for Psychical Research, 67*, 197–207.

Rosenthal, R. (1986) Meta-analytic procedures and the nature of replication: The Ganzfeld debate. *Journal of Parapsychology, 50*, 315–336.

Rothman, M. (1988) *A Physicist's Guide to Skepticism*. Buffalo, NY: Prometheus.

256 / *Robert L. Morris*

Rubin, D.C. (ed.) (1986) *Autobiographical Memory*. Cambridge: Cambridge University Press.
Rush, J. (1986) Spontaneous psi phenomena: Case studies and field investigations. In H. Edge, R.L. Morris, J. Palmer and J. Rush, *Foundations of Parapsychology*. London: Routledge & Kegan Paul.
Sannwald, G. (1963) On the psychology of spontaneous paranormal phenomena. *International Journal of Parapsychology, 5*, 274–292.
Schmeidler, G. (1973) PK effects upon continuously recorded temperature. *Journal of the American Society for Psychical Research, 67*, 325–340.
Schouten, S. (1982) Analyzing spontaneous cases: A replication based on the Rhine collection. *European Journal of Parapsychology, 4*, 113–158.
Sidgwick, H., Johnson, A., Myers, F.W.H., Podmore, F. and Sidgwick, E.M. (1894) Report of the Census of Hallucinations. *Proceedings of the Society for Psychical Research, 10*, 25–422.
Stanford, R.G. (1987) Ganzfeld and hypnotic-induction procedures in ESP research: Toward understanding their success. In S. Krippner (ed.) *Advances in Parapsychology, Vol. 5*. London: McFarland.
Stevenson, I. (1970) *Telepathic Impressions*. Charlottesville: University of Virginia Press.
Stokes, D. (1987) Theoretical parapsychology. In S. Krippner (ed.) *Advances in Parapsychology, Vol. 5*. London: McFarland.
Triplett, N. (1900) The psychology of conjuring deceptions. *American Journal of Psychology, 11*, 439–510.
Tversky, A. and Kahneman, D. (1973) Availability: A heuristic for judging frequency and probability. *Cognitive Psychology, 5*, 207–232.
Tversky, A. and Kahneman, D. (1986) Judgment under uncertainty: Heuristics and biases. In H. Arkes and K. Hammond (eds) *Judgment and Decision Making*. Cambridge: Cambridge University Press.
Warren, R.M. and Warren, R.P. (1970) Auditory illusions and confusions. *Scientific American*, December, *223*, 30–36.
Wilson, I. (1987) *The After Death Experience*. London: Sidgwick & Jackson.
Wolman, B.B. (ed.) (1977) *Handbook of Parapsychology*. New York: Van Nostrand Reinhold.
Zusne, L. and Jones, W. (1982) *Anomalistic Psychology*. Hillsdale, NJ: Lawrence Erlbaum.

THE PSYCHOLOGY OF AIDS

Keith Phillips

Acquired Immune Deficiency Syndrome (AIDS) was unheard of before 1981, when a few cases were reported in the USA (CDC, 1981). The emergence of AIDS as a novel and life-threatening illness has had an enormous impact upon our psychological construction of the world. Since 1981 we have become all too familiar with the tragic consequences. AIDS has been described as the public health issue of the decade and it has had a dramatic impact upon social institutions, with major implications for health economics and the organization of health care, and for individual rights and public health. Psychology has several roles to play in combating AIDS and the social injustices that have arisen as a reaction to it.

This review will focus upon the role for psychology in preventing the spread of AIDS and will draw upon evidence available from studies conducted in North America and Western Europe. It is important to recognize, however, that the incidence and spread of AIDS differs in other parts of the world. To date, few international collaborative studies have been carried out, though these are clearly needed to examine cultural similarities and differences and to compare the effectiveness of different approaches to health promotion. Research into prevention, however, is not the only contribution that psychologists are making. They are also significantly involved in meeting the psychological needs of those infected with the virus that allows AIDS to develop, of those with AIDS, and of their friends and relatives. Important contributions are being made in this area, and a separate review would be necessary to do justice to these.

AIDS: WHY BEHAVIOURAL CONTROL IS NECESSARY

The sudden emergence of AIDS presented dramatic challenges to medical sciences: epidemiology, immunology, virology. They have responded with alacrity. The virus responsible for AIDS has been identified, and the mechanisms by which it causes immunodeficiency are largely understood (Hersh and Petersen, 1988).

AIDS is an illness diagnosed after a person has been infected by a virus, the human immunodeficiency virus, on the evidence of disease symptoms that do not occur in people whose immune system is working normally. The human immunodeficiency virus attacks one variety of the body's white blood cells, the T-helper lymphocytes. The consequent reduced effectiveness of the immune system renders the body vulnerable to opportunistic attack by malignancies and infections. Most AIDS fatalities are caused by a particular form of pneumonia (*Pneumocystis carinii*), by an otherwise rare cancer of the skin called Kaposi's sarcoma, or by other tumours of the lymphatic system (lymphomas).

It cannot be emphasized too strongly that infection with human immunodeficiency virus (HIV) is not the same as AIDS. HIV infection may be entirely asymptomatic, or it may be accompanied by a range of symptoms including swollen glands, weight loss, diarrhoea, fever, and fatigue. The presence of these symptoms is referred to as AIDS-related complex (ARC). The diagnosis of full-blown AIDS involves, in addition to the ARC symptoms, the identification of an opportunistic infection or malignancies that do not otherwise normally occur in humans.

It should also be appreciated that mere exposure to HIV does not automatically result in infection. The virus is poorly transmitted. Moreover, the progression from HIV infection to AIDS is influenced by additional factors. Different populations of people with AIDS show different mortality rates, and the progression rate from HIV infection to full-blown AIDS is not equal. Significant co-factors may include malnutrition and other causes of chronic suppression of the immune system such as alcohol and drug abuse. The contribution of these and other co-factors may in part explain the epidemiological variations between different countries. For example, the high rate of AIDS in some African countries may reflect the impact of widespread malnutrition. Finally, AIDS is not inevitably fatal. There is a place for recovery treatment programmes for patients with AIDS involving drugs that treat the symptoms or the opportunistic infections associated with it, and for psychological therapies involving stress

The Psychology of AIDS / 259

reduction, since stressors acts as co-factors aiding progression from infection with HIV to full-blown AIDS (Siegel, 1988).

AIDS is caused by the effect of HIV upon the body's immune system, and the ultimate weapon against AIDS will be a vaccine against HIV. So far, however, the development of vaccines against HIV has proved more difficult than early optimistic reports suggested. It is now recognized that because the HIV has a lengthy incubation period of 5–8 years, it is unlikely that a vaccine will be developed for at least a further five years (Zuckerman, 1989). In the absence of an effective medical treatment for prevention of AIDS, behavioural strategies directed towards reducing the risks of transmission of HIV are the only viable means of limiting the AIDS epidemic (Phillips, 1988). Psychologists can assist campaigns to prevent AIDS by promoting effective behavioural interventions for limiting the spread of HIV infection. To be effective, those interventions must also eliminate the myth that AIDS is spread by particular groups such as gay men, rather than by behaviours that cause the transfer of body fluids from any infected person to someone non-infected.

HIV TRANSMISSION AND AIDS WORLD-WIDE

The spread of AIDS has been rapid. In the USA, the first four cases were reported in 1981, and it is estimated by the Centers for Disease Control that there are currently between 1 and 1.5 million American people infected with HIV. In the UK, the number of confirmed cases of AIDS in December 1988 was reported to be 1,982, of which 1,509 had resulted in death; and 9,603 individuals were estimated to be infected by HIV. The World Health Organisation (1987) has predicted that between 50 and 100 million people world-wide will become infected with HIV within the next decade.

AIDS first spread within epicentres of infection such as San Francisco, New York and Los Angeles, and was associated with individuals who had histories of homosexual or bisexual lifestyles. Though the statistics show that HIV infection has been and remains associated with homosexual or bisexual males and with intravenous drug users, it is not confined to these groups. Heterosexual transmission is increasing in the USA and the UK, as too is perinatal transmission. In Central Africa, AIDS is a heterosexual disease (Sher, 1987). It is important to recognize that there are no risk groups, but only behaviours that present risks for individuals.

Transmission of HIV occurs by several routes, but primarily by the transfer from an infected to a non-infected individual of sexual fluids (male to male, male to female, female to male) or the transfer of blood that has not been screened for HIV (haemophiliacs, blood trans-fusions, injection with non-sterile needles, perinatal transfer from mother to child).

Particular behaviours that have been identified as potential risks are: unprotected vaginal or anal intercourse (without the use of condom) with a partner who is HIV-infected; and exchanging blood with an infected person via non-sterile needles and syringes, as may occur by the sharing of 'works' between intravenous drug abusers. Engaging in high-risk behaviours with many partners further increases an individual's personal risk of encountering HIV. These risk behaviours account for the vast majority of cases of AIDS in the USA and the UK. Though HIV has been detected in blood, semen, saliva and tears, no transmission has been reported from either saliva or tears (CDC, 1985); and there is no evidence that the virus is transmitted through casual or social contacts such as kissing, touching, or sharing cutlery (Fischl et al., 1987).

It has been established from the world-wide statistics that three distinct patterns of transmission can be recognized (Piot et al., 1988). Pattern 1 has been seen in North America and Western Europe, and is characterized initially by sexual transmission among homosexual and bisexual men, followed by a slower rate of heterosexual transmission. Blood-borne transmission occurs primarily via intravenous drug abuse. Pattern 2 shows sexual transmission to be predominantly heterosexual. Further transmission occurs through blood trans-fusions, and perinatally. This pattern is seen in Central Africa and Latin America. Pattern 3 has emerged more recently in Eastern Europe, the Middle East and Asia; there is little endemic infection with HIV, and instances of AIDS appear to have resulted from transmission via individuals from areas of patterns 1 and 2. Campaigns against AIDS must take into account these differences in transmission patterns, and interventions must be judged accordingly.

SOCIAL PERCEPTIONS OF AIDS

AIDS is not simply a medical condition. The concept of AIDS has a significant social dimension (Aggleton and Homans, 1988). It exists as a social representation that is constructed upon knowledge in association with 'values, images, social stigma, beliefs and myths' (Markova and Wilkie, 1987). Psychologists can make an important contribution to the destruction of the myth that AIDS is confined to deviant or marginal groups. This myth leads not only to social injustice and the victimization of individuals with HIV or AIDS, but also acts as an obstacle to the adoption of appropriate behavioural responses against the spread of HIV by encouraging notions of invulnerability in persons who do not see themselves as belonging to 'risk groups'. AIDS should be seen as an issue of behavioural health, not one of public morality. Unfortunately, the evidence suggests that perceptions of AIDS are governed by ideological and moral values rather than accurate information about the disease.

A national survey of the French general public (Moatti *et al.*, 1988) found that 21.9 per cent agreed that AIDS patients should be isolated from society and 73.1 per cent that there should be mandatory screening for HIV. Beliefs supporting these coercive measures were associated with false beliefs about the possibility of HIV transmission through casual or environmental contacts such as donating blood or the bite of a mosquito. Thus false beliefs relate to a willingness to adopt coercive measures leading to the stigmatization and victimization of individuals (by compulsory isolation, for example).

Metaphors used by the media reinforce the myths about AIDS (Wellings, 1988) and the language used even by well-informed individuals suggests that they have internalized these, since language that refers to 'innocent victims' confirms the suspicion that perceptions exist of innocence for some and therefore, by implication, guilt for others (Boyle *et al.*, 1989). The moral judgements implied may have significant implications for intentions to modify one's own behaviour as well as the judgements that are made of others (Clift and Stears, 1988; Markova and Wilkie, 1987; Semin, 1989).

Fears and concerns about AIDS are expressed by individuals and by the actions of governments. Moatti *et al.* (1988) found that almost a quarter of the French public declared that AIDS is the disease they fear the most, and for the 18- to 24-year-olds the figure was 40.9 per cent, despite the fact that at the time of the survey in 1987 there were only 2,523 reported cases of AIDS in France. Similarly, the Swedish public regard AIDS as the most significant social problem, and this perception is held regardless of the respondents' age or sex (Brorsson and Herlitz, 1988a).

National reactions have varied from the introduction of health education campaigns, as in the UK, to the adoption of authoritarian and coercive measures including compulsory notifying of HIV, as has been reported in Japan. Even in the UK there has been considerable uncertainty and debate about the desirability of anonymous screening for HIV. AIDS has raised important ethical issues concerning the rights of individuals, confidentiality, and the preservation of public health (Gostin and Curran, 1987). The phenomenon of AIDS has thrown into sharp relief issues of enduring interest for psychology, including stereotyping, stigmatization and scapegoating. The original public perception of AIDS as a disease of young male homosexuals and intravenous drug abusers has persisted. Coercive measures directed against target groups confirm the myths and hinder effective health education. A first step in the campaign against AIDS must be the dissemination of accurate information to individuals. This by itself, however, will not be sufficient to alter social representations of AIDS, which reflect the relationship between the individual and society. To change these representations it will be necessary to modify perceived social norms and values.

KNOWLEDGE, ATTITUDES AND BELIEFS ABOUT AIDS

Recognizing that the spread of HIV infection can be limited only by persuading individuals to modify risk behaviours has prompted several countries, including the UK, to introduce public health education campaigns. Their objectives were to raise awareness about the existence of AIDS, to inform about the medical facts concerning HIV and AIDS, and to produce changes in behaviour that will contain the spread of HIV. It has been assumed that knowledge, attitudes and beliefs will determine behaviour, and there has been considerable interest in the relationship between these measures. One aspect that has been well examined is the extent to which knowledge about HIV and AIDS has been accurately taken up by the general population and by particular groups.

In the UK, several surveys have been conducted since the Department of Health and Social Security introduced its public education campaigns about AIDS in February 1986. Those campaigns involved the print and broadcasting media as well as the distribution of leaflets to individual homes. An early postal survey of Southampton residents by Mills et al. (1986) reported that a newspaper advertisement campaign run in the spring of 1986 had little effect upon the knowledge of AIDS. A later evaluation of the impact of the newspaper coverage (Sher, 1987) compared a high-risk with a lower-risk group before and after the campaign. Though knowledge increased slightly in both groups, it was found that there remained alarming gaps, especially concerning the risks of transmission through casual contacts. Anxiety about AIDS was not reduced by the campaign, and there was no evidence of intentions to modify behaviour as a result of the campaign. The DHSS campaign was monitored by means of a series of surveys conducted by the British Market Research Bureau (DHSS, 1987). It was found that the campaign was effective in increasing awareness of AIDS, and between February 1986 and February 1987 the number of people reporting having 'heard' anything about the disease increased from 44 per cent to 94 per cent. Respondents claimed to know more and to have talked with others more about AIDS. This survey, and others too (Campbell and Waters, 1987), indicated that knowledge about AIDS had increased. Attitudes showed favourable shifts for some individuals, though not all, and there remained widespread intolerance of homosexuals. There was no evidence of changes in behaviour for the general population, though a sample of homosexual males reported adopting changes towards safer sex, including greater use of condoms and reducing their numbers of sexual partners. It is likely, however, that changes had begun before the campaigns were introduced.

In Sweden, too, it has been found that a national AIDS information campaign was effective in raising awareness but had little influence on people's own behaviours (Brorsson and Herlitz, 1988b).

Several surveys of public opinion have been carried out in the USA since 1981 (Singer *et al.*, 1987), and there are clear trends indicating increased awareness of AIDS. In particular, these surveys have revealed that worry is linked negatively with knowledge about AIDS but positively with estimates of personal risk for AIDS. Knowledge about transmission has increased in general, though uncertainty remains concerning transmission by casual contacts. Attitudes have changed far less, and the number of people reporting that they have changed their own behaviours has increased only slightly. The media, and especially television, are widely reported as being the public's principal source of information about AIDS, and they clearly have a major responsibility for supplying the public with accurate information as scientific knowledge about the disease improves.

Surveys indicate that similar perceptions of AIDS exist in other countries. For example, Webb (1988) reports a survey of 33 nations which indicates that there is widespread awareness of AIDS as a life-threatening epidemic and generally good knowledge of the ways in which HIV may be transmitted from one individual to another, though there are also areas of ignorance (about casual transmission, for example). Obviously, the importance attached to various routes of transmission varies from country to country, since, as the statistics indicate, transmission patterns vary world-wide. It is important that health education messages about effective preventive measures do reflect the particular transmission risks for different countries.

A spin-off from the public education campaigns is that AIDS has become newsworthy, and there has been widespread media coverage – some accurate and informative, some false, misleading, and fear-provoking (Wellings, 1988). Nevertheless, despite the uneven coverage, knowledge about AIDS ought to be increasing. Though useful for tracking the trends in knowledge and attitudes, surveys of the general public are too blunt an instrument for dissecting the reasons why knowledge, attitudes and behaviours change, or fail to change, in groups or individuals.

Several studies have used questionnaires to measure the knowledge base of specific groups of individuals selected on the basis of demographic variables such as age or occupation. Two groups picked out for particular attention have been students, who are assumed to be at risk in that they represent a young, sexually active group, and adolescents. If education is to be the major weapon against AIDS, then adolescents are an important group requiring special consideration (Melton, 1988). Trends that can be discerned from these studies suggest that knowledge has increased over the years. Early studies (Simkins and Eberhage, 1984; Price *et al.*, 1985) reported only moderate levels of knowledge about AIDS compared to the high levels reported by more recent studies (DiClemente *et al.*, 1986, 1988; White *et al.*, 1989). Despite these gains in knowledge, there is little evidence of intentions to alter behaviour. Strunin and Hingson (1987) found that although 70 per cent of teenagers reported themselves as sexually active, only 15 per cent had changed their behaviour as a result of AIDS. Even well-informed adolescents are reporting a desire for more information, and the source of their information will be important. The majority report that television is their principal source of information. Unfortunately, though television is an effective medium for raising awareness of an issue, it is not the best medium for conveying complex messages. There is an important role for schools in this respect. Adolescents need more than simply the facts about AIDS; they require knowledge and understanding of relationships, intimacy, and social pressures if they are to apply their knowledge about AIDS and the transmission of HIV effectively within their own lives (White *et al.*, 1988; 1989).

Clift and Stears (1988) conducted a questionnaire survey of students' AIDS-related knowledge, worry and moral perceptions between November 1986 and May 1987. During the interim, the national AIDS campaign received wide coverage in the media. They found over this period that although there was a significant reduction in worry about AIDS, there was no change in moral attitudes; and though the students were more knowledgeable about AIDS, there was little evidence that they believed that behaviours to reduce the risk of HIV infection (for example, the use of condoms) would be adopted. Similar conclusions can be drawn from other studies with undergraduates (Boyle *et al.*, 1989; Turner *et al.*, 1988).

A different approach has used discussion, interviews and open-ended questions to assess lay beliefs about HIV and AIDS, since these underlie individuals' perceptions of their own vulnerability and their assessments of risks for themselves and others. In turn, these will influence their social responses to individuals with AIDS or groups they perceive to be at risk. Using an exploratory approach, with open-ended questions delivered to groups of homosexual and heterosexual youths, Warwick *et al.* (1988) found that in the main their knowledge of the medical facts was comparable to that of older people but that there was a disquieting failure to differentiate between HIV infection and AIDS and a consequent misperception of both as contagious or infectious. Using a similar exploratory technique with single-sex discussion groups of undergraduates, we (Boyle *et al.*, 1989) have found it to be useful both as a method of inquiry and as an educational intervention. It exposes concerns and gaps in knowledge that may not be evident from replies to closed-item questionnaires, and allows members of the groups to share their knowledge and concerns and to compare their perceptions with those of others. The technique is one that our research team is continuing to employ in exploring the structuring of knowledge about AIDS in young people aged between 13 and 18 years in schools (Clifford and Murphy, 1989).

It is quite clear from the studies reported above that knowledge-ability by itself does not lead to the changes in behaviour which are necessary to minimize the risk of HIV infection. The participants in those studies, of course, are for the most part at rather low risk. Other research has concentrated upon the sexual and drug-using behaviours associated with greater risk.

SEXUAL BEHAVIOURS AND AIDS

People who abstain from sex, or share a monogamous relationship with a partner who does not have HIV, do not risk sexual transmission of HIV. Other sexually active individuals face some risk depending upon their particular sexual behaviours. Promoting safer sex has been and remains a primary strategy for reducing HIV infection within the general population. Some activities are considered to involve little risk, including non-penetrative sex such as masturbation or oral-genital contact protected by a condom. The risks associated with penetrative sex are reduced by the use of condoms with a water-based lubricant in combination with the spermicide nonoxynol-9. Protection is not absolute as condoms may fail. Other preventive measures include reducing the number of sexual partners and avoiding partners that are likely to have been exposed to HIV, such as intravenous drug users or prostitutes.

Health education messages delivered through media campaigns or community-based programmes can offer information about safer sex practices. But the information by itself does not automatically result in their adoption now or intentions to adopt them in the future. This problem is not unique to AIDS; it is a persistent finding in studies of preventive health, and other areas requiring changes in behaviour, that the translation of knowledge into action is difficult to achieve (Costanzo et al., 1986). Even with the knowledge about transmission of HIV and AIDS, there are several obstacles to the adoption of safer sex (Ingham, 1988).

An important cognitive factor that acts against the adoption of safer sex practices is that individuals may not see themselves as being at risk and may regard their personal vulnerability to HIV infection as low. Several studies of risk have found that individuals are unrealistically optimistic about their own health and that they see themselves as being less at risk than others (Weinstein, 1987). This 'illusion of invulnerability' (Perloff and Fetzer, 1986) is a systematic distortion that acts as a powerful bias against the avoidance of behaviours known to be associated with risk for HIV or the adoption of appropriate precautions against HIV infection such as the use of a condom for penetrative sex.

Evidence from a survey of sexual behaviours and contraceptive practice among students at Oxford University (Turner et al., 1988) indicates that they estimated their own personal risk of contracting AIDS as lower than average for people of their age and sex. This was true even for the majority of those who were engaged in sexual intercourse with bisexual partners, intravenous drug users, multiple and casual partners, and prostitutes. Of those students who were sexually active, 49 per cent of women and 30 per cent of men reported that they had reduced or would reduce their number of sexual partners. Also, 35 per cent of women and 44 per cent of men reported that they were more likely to use a condom because of fear of AIDS. However, only 50 per cent of those engaging in the higher-risk sexual activities reported being more likely to use a condom in the light of AIDS; the remainder were presumably denying the risks to themselves.

Estimates of personal vulnerability are based upon social comparisons. If there are to be effective changes in behaviour, there must first be shifts in perceived social norms. These probably operate at the level of local social networks, and so would best be approached by educational programmes developed and implemented at the local community level.

Other factors will also influence decisions about behaviour, including the costs–benefits pay-off associated with behaviours and precautions, the perceived efficacy of precautions, and expectations that advocated precautions might reasonably be employed. Our studies with young people (undergraduates and schoolchildren) indicate that they favour preventive measures that are likely to be ineffective against HIV infection. For example, the idea of mandatory screening for HIV is popular; and another precaution often mentioned was personal vetting of partners' previous sexual histories. The obvious unreliability of this measure seems to be ignored by these young people (Boyle *et al.*, 1989; White *et al.*, 1988, 1989).

Much of the research into changes in sexual behaviour because of AIDS has looked at groups of homosexual men in the USA (Becker and Joseph, 1988). It has been found that behaviours are changing in favour of risk reduction, though the changes are relative and there is no absolute elimination of high-risk activities such as receptive anal intercourse. Several factors influence the adoption of safer sex, including the local prevalence of HIV, age (young people are more resistant to change than old), and HIV status (gay men who know they are HIV-infected show greater reductions in risk behaviours).

There is much less evidence that equivalent reductions of risk are occurring in the young heterosexual population. Strunin and Hingson (1987) found from a telephone survey of adolescents that though their level of knowledge about AIDS was high, only 15 per cent reported taking any precautions against AIDS, and even then 80 per cent of the measures taken would be ineffective. There is little evidence that young heterosexuals have significantly changed their intentions to adopt the simple precaution of using condoms during intercourse (Kegeles *et al.*, 1988). A postal survey of Californian undergraduates (Baldwin and Baldwin, 1988) found that few sexually active students were adopting the preventive measures of condom use, restricting the number of sexual partners, and avoiding casual sex. Accurate knowledge about AIDS was not associated with the adoption of safer sex; and individuals who judged themselves to be at higher risk than others were more likely to be engaging in higher-risk sexual activities, without apparent intentions to change.

Studies of risk reduction by individuals may miss one important aspect of sexual behaviours, namely that they are social acts involving interaction and negotiation between partners (Peplau *et al.*, 1977). The process of negotiation may not be equitable and may involve disagreements about the preferred degree or nature of sexual intimacy. In turn, disagreements may give rise to compliance or coercion (Byers and Lewis, 1988) that cause an individual to engage in behaviours that contravene their prior intentions for safer sex. Such contraventions increase the risks of HIV infection, and there is an urgent need for research into individuals' adherence to behavioural intentions for risk reduction within the context of intimate relationships.

The current indications are that sexually active heterosexuals are not adopting behaviours for safer sex to any significant degree; but this may not be entirely surprising, since adoption would involve prior acceptance that the changes advocated are necessary and attainable. When changes of behaviour do occur in individuals, then a model derived from communication studies predicts that the new behaviour or 'innovation' may diffuse throughout a community over a period of time by sharing of information and objectives. The adoption of an innovation – safer sex, for example – is influenced by perceptions of the innovation itself (is it reasonable or attainable?); by the channels available for its communication (interpersonal and media channels are both appropriate); by the time available for transition from awareness of the innovation to its implementation and to confirmation of its effectiveness; and by the characteristics of the social system and its particular social norms. It should be expected that the objectives of preventive health programmes of the type being used to combat AIDS can only be met by allowing time for their innovative messages to diffuse throughout communities, but also that different communities will have different social systems that will have different effects upon the diffusion process (Rogers, 1987).

It is clear that behaviour has changed to an extent in some groups.

For example, there is widespread evidence that certain high-risk activities, such as receptive anal intercourse, have significantly declined among male homosexuals in a number of American cities (Winkelstein *et al.*, 1987). These changes appear to have been largely independent of media messages and national campaigns, arising rather within the community by sharing of knowledge and concern – that is, through social diffusion.

INTRAVENOUS DRUG ABUSE AND AIDS

The risks of HIV infection for injecting drug users are substantial. First, the criminal status of drug abuse means that users may be dependent upon syringes and needles that are shared with others, some of whom may be HIV-infected. Second, we know that the progression from HIV infection to AIDS depends upon the presence of co-factors which are often associated with intravenous drug use: for example, poor general health, homelessness, and the absence of 'good nutrition', which may debilitate the immune system. Third, the drugs injected, especially opiates, can have a direct effect on the immune system, reducing its effectiveness. Fourth, drug abuse may be associated with episodes of financial emergency that are relieved by prostitution. Sexual clients may themselves be engaging in practices that present risks. Finally, the intoxicant effects of the drugs injected may produce non-compliance with risk-reducing behaviours that might otherwise be adopted, such as the use of a condom during intercourse (Stall *et al.*, 1986).

As if this were not serious enough, there is further cause for alarm in the fact that intravenous drug users represent what is known as a 'bridging group' for the spread of HIV into the general population (Newmeyer, 1988). HIV-infected drug users may have sexual intercourse with regular or occasional non-drug-using partners. Both they and their partners may be unaware of their HIV status. Perinatal transmission of HIV is often from an intravenous drug-using mother to her child. It is clear from the statistics that a substantial proportion of the instances of heterosexual transmission of HIV are associated with transmission via injecting drug users (Mulleady, 1987).

Preventing or reducing risk behaviours for intravenous drug users presents a tremendous challenge; they are a heterogeneous group, and research is confounded by the unreliability of their self-report data, and often by their limited literacy and education. Despite the difficulties, however, there are strategies for reducing the spread of

HIV infection among intravenous drug users. These depend upon a shift from treating drug users simply for chemical dependency to stabilizing their drug use and eliminating the risk practices attached to it. Such a shift, which implies a decriminalization of drug abuse in favour of health education, is essential if the epidemic of HIV infection among injecting drug users is to be contained.

One strategy for reducing high-risk practices involves utilizing a hierarchy of messages for harm minimization (Landrey and Smith, 1988; Mulleady, 1987). The reduction that would be most effective is to stop using drugs entirely, but this is unlikely to be adopted by the majority of users. A more realistic approach is to stabilize the drug user's intake of heroin (the most popular drug for intravenous injection) by replacement with oral doses of methadone. The advantage of this approach is that injecting is reduced, though it may not be eliminated as users may continue to have occasional 'fixes' by injecting heroin. In addition, it brings the drug user into contact with drug service agencies where further advice about healthy practices and risk avoidance can be given. It may result in the user deciding to take a test for HIV antibodies. If positive, this can produce significant reductions in risky practices (Westley-Clark and Washburn, 1988). This does not mean, however, that there should be mandatory testing, since this would serve only to deter potential clients from attending the drug services and adopting the advice being offered.

Methadone maintenance will not be popular with all users. Many will wish to continue injecting, and in this case they must be persuaded that they should not share needles, syringes and associated equipment. Syringe sharing is a common practice among injecting drug users, and it allows for the very efficient transmission of HIV by the transfer of infected blood from one individual to another. The reasons for sharing are complex: drug abuse is a social activity involving deals, conspiracies and shared experiences; often, sharing occurs between partners in long-term relationships or between dealer and client; convenience or necessity are more obvious reasons. In some cities, such as Edinburgh, groups of users make use of shared equipment at so-called 'shooting galleries' (locations where users meet to share otherwise scarce equipment for injecting drugs), with dramatic and alarming consequences. In Edinburgh and New York, where shooting galleries are popular, HIV is endemic among injecting drug users (Des Jarlais et al., 1985; Robertson et al., 1986). One preventive measure that can discourage shooting galleries and reduce sharing involves allowing users legally to exchange used needles and syringes for new ones. Needle exchange schemes were pioneered in Amsterdam and are now being evaluated in the UK (Stimson *et al.*, 1988). Though some may feel that this approach condones or even encourages drug abuse, there is no evidence that this is so (Mulleady, 1987). The lowest-level approach in the harm minimization hierarchy is to persuade injecting users that if they do share, any needles or equipment must be sterilized by boiling or by using bleach between each injection. Unfortunately, adherence to even this simple message requires a degree of planning or organization that may not be possible in a user's chaotic life.

Major resources are necessary if these messages are to be promoted effectively. A diversity of drug services are required, including drug dependency units, therapeutic and residential communities, and needle exchange schemes (Association of Metropolitan Authorities, 1988). Many drug users will only be contacted in their local communities by outreach workers. Evidence from the USA indicates that these community-based approaches can be effective in encouraging risk-reducing practices among injecting drug users (Watters, 1988).

In addition to the drug messages, users also require advice about safer-sex practices to reduce the spread of HIV through sexual and perinatal transmission. The clinical psychologists and counsellors presenting these messages need adequate resource support through national schemes. It has been found in the USA, for example, that directors and counsellors in substance abuse clinics were not equipped with the knowledge and experience they themselves thought necessary to deal with HIV or AIDS clients (Mejta *et al.*, 1988). The provision of appropriate training for service personnel must be made if the challenges posed by HIV infection are to be met. The most effective measure of all, of course, is primary prevention of drug abuse by educating young people not to take drugs. Governments and health educators have a major responsibility to implement national and community-based programmes for primary prevention.

PSYCHOLOGY AND THE PRIMARY PREVENTION OF AIDS

Much of the AIDS research has involved data gathering and has not been directed by theoretical models. There is a need for systematic examinations of psychological models that identify the determinants of behavioural change for preventive health. Only then will it be possible to devise and implement effective interventions for combating

AIDS. It is known that cognitive processes including heuristics and judgements of risk influence decision making. However, studies of preventive health have largely rejected models of rational decision making in favour of models that emphasize the combined effects of cognitive and social factors. Two models that have been particularly influential are the health belief model (Becker, 1974; Rosenstock, 1974) and the theory of reasoned action (Ajzen and Fishbein, 1980).

The health belief model attempts to explain health behaviours by identifying the factors that influence individuals' decisions about the perceived utility of their actions. It must be remembered that preventive measures are directed to individuals who are currently well and who may not perceive much risk to themselves. According to this model, the significant variables that determine behaviour in relation to a health threat are perceived vulnerability to the particular threat, its perceived severity, and the cost–benefit pay-off associated with adopting preventive behaviours. The model has been applied to several health issues, and the evidence is that the variables are important predictors of health behaviours (Janz and Becker, 1984). Another factor that may be added to this model is cues to action – that is, prompts that provoke decisions about health behaviours – and health education campaigns may play a valuable role in this regard by reminding individuals of the need for risk reduction.

The theory of reasoned action also includes cognitive variables as determinants of behaviour. In this case they are identified as attitudes and beliefs which are held to exert a shared influence upon intentions to behave in a particular way, together with an individual's perceptions of the subjective norms for the health issue in question. The model identifies behavioural intentions as the immediate determinants of behaviour. Recently the model has been extended, as the theory of planned behaviour, to include the influence of the individual's perceived control over the behaviours to be performed (Ajzen and Madden, 1986).

The literature upon AIDS indicates that the variables identified by these two models are likely to be important in determining the adoption of preventive measures (Cleary, 1987). However, direct evidence is lacking, since there have been few attempts to make comparisons of these and similar models (Rutter, 1988). Moreover, the indirect evidence – from studies of attitudes and intentions, for example – has seldom measured the behaviours themselves. There is an urgent need for studies that do measure relevant sexual and drug-using behaviours in relation to HIV infection, and which test the psychological models for preventive health. Ideally, such tests would use prospective studies to assess the impact of variables, singly and in combination, assumed to be predictors of changes in behaviour.

However, as Cleary points out (1987), health behaviour is determined by combinations of cultural, social and psychological factors, and the impact of situational variables should not be ignored. Health behaviours are not easily separated from the complexity of other behaviours that make up an individual's life. It may be that structural models are inappropriate and that the adoption of preventive health measures involves dynamic processes that have many determinants (Weinstein, 1988). In order to fully dissect the effects of situational variables upon adherence to intended precautionary measures, it is likely that longitudinal studies of intentions and diary reports of actual behaviours are necessary. Such studies would provide powerful tests of the robustness of the models of preventive health; and, though methodologically difficult, they have been used (Coxon, 1987). They require considerable commitment on the part of researchers and their volunteer respondents, but provide the data within their natural contexts that are needed to understand the determinants of health behaviour within someone's life. We are currently conducting studies of this type with a group of volunteers in order to compare the predictive powers of the health belief and reasoned action models.

While developments of theory are proceeding, AIDS remains with us; and until our psychological models are further refined, psychologists and health educators will continue to offer pragmatic solutions. In the immediate short term, it may be that the best approach is to utilize social marketing of health, where specific messages are sold as commodities to particular groups. Health promotion campaigns, in common with other areas of health behaviour research, face the problem that services and messages about health may not appeal to large proportions of the population at whom they are aimed. A study of predictors of health practices (Rakowski, 1988) found that they were not consistent across different age bands, nor between men and women in those age bands chosen. If the predictors are different, then different messages about health care would need to be devised and targeted to reflect those differences. The social marketing approach (Fredrickson *et al.*, 1984) segments the population into separate audiences to whom the specific and appropriate messages can be delivered. Of course, health issues are multi-determined; and the evidence suggests that segmentation of the population, based upon all of the significant segmenting variables, would lead to such small target groups that mass campaigns for health promotion would be inappropriate. Community-based programmes that are sensitive to the differences between individuals rather than their similarities are more likely to be effective.

Psychologists are currently involved in the design of educational interventions to limit the spread of HIV infection, particularly for young people. They must become further involved in determining the policies by which such interventions are implemented. They may then facilitate social changes which will alter the social representation of AIDS, thus fostering the recognition that AIDS concerns each of us and that its future spread will be determined by our own behaviours.

REFERENCES

Aggleton, P. and Homans, H. (eds) (1988) *Social Aspects of AIDS.* London: Falmer Press.

Ajzen, I. and Fishbein, M. (1980) *Understanding Attitudes and Predicting Social Behavior.* Englewood Cliffs, NJ: Prentice-Hall.

Ajzen, I. and Madden, T.J. (1986) Prediction of goal-directed behavior: Attitudes, intentions and perceived behavioral control. *Journal of Experimental and Social Psychology, 22,* 453–474.

Association of Metropolitan Authorities (1988) *The Challenge to Local Authorities: HIV Infection and Drug Use.* London.

Baldwin, J.D. and Baldwin, J.I. (1988) Factors affecting AIDS-related sexual risk-taking behavior among college students. *Journal of Sex Research, 25,* 181–196.

Becker, M.H. (ed.) (1974) *The Health Belief Model and Personal Health Behavior.* Thorofare, NJ: Slack.

Becker, M.H. and Joseph, J.G. (1988) AIDS and behavior change to reduce risk: A review. *American Journal of Public Health, 78,* 462–467.

Boyle, M.E., Pitts, M.K., Phillips, K.C., White, D.G., Clifford, B. and Woollett, E.A. (1989) Exploring young people's attitudes to and knowledge of AIDS: The value of focussed group discussions. *Health Education Journal* (in press).

Brorsson, B. and Herlitz, C. (1988a) AIDS epidemic ranked as 'Public Enemy Number One'. *Scandinavian Journal of Social Medicine, 16,* 73–74.

Brorsson, B. and Herlitz, C. (1988b) The AIDS epidemic in Sweden: Changes in awareness, attitudes and behavior. *Scandinavian Journal of Social Medicine, 16,* 67–71.

Byers, E.S. and Lewis, K. (1988) Dating couples' disagreements over the desired level of sexual intimacy. *Journal of Sex Research, 24,* 15–29.

Campbell, M.J. and Waters, W.E. (1987) Public knowledge about AIDS increasing. *British Medical Journal, 294,* 892–893.

CDC (Centers for Disease Control) (1981) Kaposi's sarcoma and pneumocystis pneumonia among homosexual men – New York City and California. *Morbidity and Mortality Weekly Reports 1981, 30,* 305–308.

CDC (Centers for Disease Control) (1985) Education and foster care of children infected with Human T-lymphotropic virus type 3/lymphadeno-pathy associated virus. Atlanta, Georgia.

Cleary, P.D. (1987) Why people take precautions against health risks. In N.D. Weinstein (ed.) *Taking Care: Understanding and Encouraging Self-Protective Behavior*. Cambridge: Cambridge University Press.

Clifford, B.R. and Murphy, S. (1989) Knowledge structuring of AIDS information in school children. Unpublished paper presented to The Annual Conference of the British Psychological Society, St Andrews, April 1989.

Clift, S.M. and Stears, D.F. (1988) Beliefs and attitudes regarding AIDS among British college students: A preliminary study of change between November 1986 and May 1987. *Health Education Research, 3*, 75–88.

Costanzo, M., Archer, D., Aronson, E. and Pettigrew, T. (1986) Energy conservation behavior: The difficult path from information to action. *American Psychologist, 41*, 521–528.

Coxon, T. (1987) 'Something sensational': The sexual diary as a tool for mapping detailed sexual behaviour. *Sociological Review, 63*, 353–367.

Des Jarlais, D., Friedman, S. and Hopkins, W. (1985) Risk reduction for the Acquired Immune Deficiency Syndrome among intravenous drug users. *Annals of Internal Medicine, 103*, 755–759.

DHSS and Welsh Office (1987) *AIDS: Monitoring Response to the Public Education Campaign February 1986–February 1987*. London: HMSO.

DiClemente, R.J., Boyer, C.B. and Morales, E.S. (1988) Minorities and AIDS: Knowledge, attitudes and misconceptions among black and Latino adolescents. *American Journal of Public Health, 78*, 55-57.

DiClemente, R.J., Zorn, J. and Temoshok, L. (1986) Adolescents and AIDS: A survey of knowledge, attitudes and beliefs about AIDS in San Francisco. *American Journal of Public Health, 76*, 1443–1445.

Fischl, M.A., Dickinson, G.M., Scott, G.B., Klimas, N., Fletcher, M.A. and Parks, W. (1987) Evaluation of heterosexual partners, children and household contacts of adults with AIDS. *Journal of the American Medical Association, 257*, 640–644.

Fredrickson, L., Solomon, L.J. and Brehony, K.A. (eds) (1984) *Marketing Health Behavior*. New York: Plenum.

Gostin, L. and Curran, W.J. (1987) AIDS screening, confidentiality and the duty to warn. *American Journal of Public Health, 77*, 361–365.

Hersh, E.M. and Petersen, E.A. (1988) Editorial. The AIDS epidemic: AIDS research in the life sciences. *Life Sciences, 42*, i–iv.

Ingham, R. (1988) Behaviour change and safe sex: A social psychology approach. *Proceedings of the First Conference of the Health Psychology Section*. Leicester: The British Psychological Society.

Janz, N.K. and Becker, M.H. (1984) The health belief model: A decade later. *Health Education Quarterly, 11*, 1–47.

Kegeles, S.M., Allen, N.E. and Irwin, C.E. (1988) Sexually active adolescents and condoms: Changes over one year in knowledge, attitudes and use. *American Journal of Public Health, 78*, 460–461.

Landrey, M.J. and Smith, D.E. (1988) AIDS and chemical dependency: An overview. *Journal of Psychoactive Drugs, 20*, 141–147.

Markova, I. and Wilkie, P. (1987) Representations, concepts and social change: The phenomenon of AIDS. *Journal for the Theory of Social Behaviour*, 17, 389–409.

Mejta, C.L., Denton, E., Krems, M. and Hiatt, R.A. (1988) Acquired Immunodeficiency Syndrome (AIDS): A survey of substance abuse clinic directors' and counselors' perceived knowledge, attitudes and reactions. *Journal of Drug Issues*, 18, 403–419.

Melton, G. (1988) Adolescents and prevention of AIDS. *Professional Psychology: Research and Practice*, 19, 403–408.

Mills, S., Campbell, M.J. and Waters, W.E. (1986) Public knowledge of AIDS and the DHSS advertisement campaign. *British Medical Journal*, 293, 1089–1090.

Moatti, J.P., Manesse, L., Le Gales, C., Pages, J.P. and Fagnani, F. (1988) Social perception of AIDS in the general public: A French study. *Health Policy*, 9, 1–8.

Mulleady, G. (1987) A review of drug abuse and HIV infection. *Psychology and Health*, 1, 149–163.

Newmeyer, J.A. (1988) The intravenous drug user and secondary spread of AIDS. *Journal of Psychoactive Drugs*, 20, 169–172.

Peplau, L.A., Rubin, Z. and Hill, C. (1977) Sexual intimacy in dating relationships. *Journal of Social Issues*, 33, 86–109.

Perloff, L.S. and Fetzer, B.K. (1986) Self–other judgements and perceived vulnerability to victimisation. *Journal of Personality and Social Personality*, 50, 502–510.

Phillips, K.C. (1988) Strategies against AIDS. *The Psychologist* (incorporating The Bulletin of The British Psychological Society), 1, 46–47.

Piot, P., Plummer, F., Mhalu, F., Lamboray, J-L., Chin, J. and Mann, J.M. (1988) AIDS: An international perspective. *Science*, 239, 573–579.

Price, J.H., Desmond, S. and Kukulka, G. (1985) High school students' perceptions and misperceptions of AIDS. *Journal of School Health*, 76, 494–495.

Rakowski, W. (1988) Predictors of health practices within age–sex groups: National survey of personal health practices and consequences, 1979. *Public Health Reports*, 103, 376–383.

Robertson, J. R., Bucknall, A., Welsby, P., Inglis, J., Peutherer, J. and Brettle, R. (1986) Epidemic of AIDS-related virus (HTLV III/LAV) infection among intravenous drug users. *British Medical Journal*, 292, 527–529.

Rogers, E.M. (1987) The diffusions of innovation perspective. In N.D. Weinstein (ed.) *Taking Care: Understanding and Encouraging Self-Protective Behavior*. Cambridge: Cambridge University Press.

Rosenstock, I.M. (1974) Historical origins of the health belief model. *Health Education Monographs*, 2, 409–419.

Rutter, D. (1988) Personal influences. Unpublished paper presented to The Joint Meeting of the Health Psychology Section of The British Psychological Society and The Health Education Authority. Royal Free Hospital, London, October 1988.

Semin, G. (1989) Adolescents' AIDS-related knowledge, attitudes, sexual morality and sexual intentions. Unpublished paper presented to The Annual Conference of The British Psychological Society, St Andrews, April 1989.

Sher, L. (1987) An evaluation of the UK Government health education campaign on AIDS. *Psychology and Health, 1,* 61–72.

Siegel, L. (1988) AIDS: Perceptions versus realities. *Journal of Psychoactive Drugs, 20,* 149–152.

Simkins, L. and Eberhage, M.G. (1984) Attitudes towards AIDS, herpes II and toxic shock syndrome. *Psychological Reports, 55,* 779–786.

Singer, E., Rogers, T.F. and Corcoran, M. (1987) The Polls. A report – AIDS. *Public Opinion Quarterly, 51,* 580–595.

Stall, R., McKusick, L., Wiley, J., Coates, T.J. and Ostrow, D.G. (1986) Alcohol and drug abuse during sexual activity and compliance with safe sex guidelines for AIDS: The AIDS Behavioral Research Project. *Health Education Quarterly, 13,* 359–371.

Stimson, G., Alldritt, L., Dolan, K. and Donoghoe, M. (1988) *Injecting Equipment Exchange Schemes: A Preliminary Report on Research.* London: University of London, Monitoring Research Group.

Strunin, L. and Hingson, R. (1987) Acquired immunodeficiency syndrome and adolescents: Knowledge, beliefs, attitudes and behaviors. *Pediatrics, 79,* 825–828.

Turner, C., Anderson, P., Fitzpatrick, R., Fowler, G. and Mayon-White, R. (1988) Sexual behaviour, contraceptive practice and knowledge of AIDS of Oxford University students. *Journal of Biosocial Science, 20,* 445–451.

Warwick, I., Aggleton, P. and Homans, H. (1988) Constructing common-sense – young people's beliefs about AIDS. *Sociology of Health and Illness, 10,* 213–233.

Watters, J.K. (1988) Meaning and context: The social facts of intravenous drug use and HIV transmission in the inner city. *Journal of Psychoactive Drugs, 20,* 173–177.

Webb, N.L. (1988) *Gallup International Survey on Attitudes towards AIDS.* London: Gallup International, UK.

Weinstein, N.D. (1987) Unrealistic optimism about susceptibility to health problems: Conclusions from a community-wide sample. *Journal of Behavioural Medicine, 10,* 481–500.

Weinstein, N.D. (1988) The precaution adoption process. *Health Psychology, 7,* 355–386.

Wellings, K. (1988) Perceptions of risk – media treatments of AIDS. In P. Aggleton and H. Homans (eds) *Social Aspects of AIDS.* London: Falmer Press.

Westley-Clark, H. and Washburn, P. (1988) Testing for Human Immunodeficiency Virus in substance abuse treatment. *Journal of Psychoactive Drugs, 20,* 203–211.

White, D.G., Phillips, K.C., Clifford, B.R., Pitts, M.K., Davies, M.M. and Elliott, J.R. (1989) AIDS and intimate relationships: Adolescents' knowledge and attitudes. *Current Psychological Research and Reviews* (in press).

White, D.G., Phillips, K.C., Pitts, M.K., Clifford, B.R., Elliott, J.R. and Davies, M.M. (1988) Adolescents' perceptions of AIDS. *Health Education Journal, 47,* 117–119.

Winkelstein, W., Samuel, M., Padian, N.S. and Wiley, J.A. (1987) The San Francisco men's health study III: Reduction in human immunodeficiency virus transmission among homosexual/bisexual men, 1982–1986. *American Journal of Public Health, 76,* 685–689.

World Health Organisation (1987) *Special Programme on AIDS: Strategies, Structure and Projected Needs.* Geneva: March, 1987.

Zuckerman, A.J. (1989) The enigma of AIDS vaccines. *Royal Society of Medicine: The AIDS Letter,* No. 10 (Dec. 88/Jan. 89), 1–3.

INDEX

ABSOLUTE SCALES 5
Achievement Place 165-6
action prototypes 40-1
activation-triggered schemas (ATSs) 35-7
Adaptive Control of Thought (ACT) theory
    107-8, 115
aesthetics 128-9
AIDS 257-74
    and behavioural control 258-9
    and drug abuse 269-71
    knowledge, attitudes and beliefs 262-5
    prevention 271-4
    and sexual behaviour 266-9
    social perceptions 260-2
    transmission and incidence 259-60
analysis
    discourse (q.v.) 76-96
    statistics (q.v.) 1-21
analysis of variance (ANOVA) 13, 19
    multivariate (MANOVA) 14
anthropology
    and knowledge representation 115-16
    and psychoanalytic theory 132-6
anxiety
    and sport performance 217-19, 225
    state vs trait 215
art, idiots savants 196-7, 203-4
artificial intelligence, and knowledge
    representation 102-4, 120
attention, and sport performance 225-6
attitude talk 82-6
attitudes 82
    to AIDS 260-3
autobiographical memory 239-40

BAR CHARTS 7
Bayesian inference 16-17
behaviour modification, and criminal offenders
    162-3
bimodality 7
bivariate measures 3, 7-8, 13
body language see non-verbal communication
British Crime Survey 150-2

CALENDAR CALCULATING 197-204
cancer, and sport 222
castration anxiety 134-5
categorization, discourse 91-5
chance, and parapsychology 241-2
chi-squared 12-13
children, as witnesses 175-91
    fantasizing 184-5

and the law 176-8
    legal reform 188-91
    lying 185-6
    memory inaccuracy 179-83
    psychological research 178-88
    suggestibility 186-8
Children and Young Persons Act (1933) 177
chunking, information 39, 99, 101
clairvoyance 232
coding and coding processes, knowledge
    representation 99-102
cognition
    idiots savants (q.v.) 204-7
    skills acquisition 40-1
    see also metacognition
cognitive maps 113, 116
cognitive psychology, and knowledge
    representation 104-8
communication 57-8
    model, parapsychology 233-4
    non-verbal (q.v.) 57-73
    see also discourse analysis
community programmes for offenders 166-7
comparisons, multiple 18-19
computers, and knowledge representation
    102-4, 120
confidence intervals 20-1
connectionism 116-17
contextual interference 214
contingency tables 3
contour plots 7
conversation see discourse analysis
coronary heart disease (CHD), and sport 222
correlation 11,13
crime 146-53
    offender surveys 148-9
    police records 147-8
    victim surveys 149-53
Criminal Justice Act (1988) 176, 188
criminological and legal psychology 146-68
    Achievement Place 165-6
    clinical criminology 161-7
    community programmes 166-7
    eyewitness memory 154-61
    measuring crime 146-53
    prisons 162-3
    special hospitals 163-4
    therapeutic communities 164
    see also children as witnesses
cross-classifications 3
cross-cultural studies, and psychoanalytic
    theory 132-6

279